E type:
End of an Era

CHRIS HARVEY

St. Martin's Press, New York

COPYRIGHT © 1977 BY OXFORD ILLUSTRATED PRESS LTD. and CHRIS HARVEY

All rights reserved. For information, write:
St. Martin's Press, Inc., 175 Fifth Ave., New York, N.Y. 10010
Printed in Great Britain
Library of Congress Catalog Card Number: 76-62775
First published in the United States of America in 1977
Reprinted 1978, 1979

Library of Congress Cataloging in Publication Data

Harvey, Chris, 1941 —
    E type: end of an era

    1. Jaguar automobile. I. Skilleter, Paul.
II. Title.
TL215.J3H35   388.34'22   76-62775
ISBN 0-312-22452-4

Contents

Colour Plates

E type: End of an Era, Birth of a Book

THERE WERE not many people involved in writing this book—it was produced at the sort of speed normally associated only with newspapers—and E types. But the contributions of these people were so much greater as a result, and I would like to offer my thanks to my wife, Margaret, who survived clouds of cigar smoke and waded through mountains of discarded scrap paper to answer the ever-ringing telephone; to my agent, Jon Zackon, for convincing me that a newspaperman who had spent his life reducing life stories to twenty words could write a book (and for buying me a meal when his horse won); to Paul Skilleter for his enthusiasm and piles of pictures; to Oxford Illustrated Press for making the book possible; to the nameless scribes of all the motoring magazines who have written on E types and whose words will not be forgotten now; to the named ones too; to Terry Moore for talking of nothing but E types for hours; to Denis Jenkinson for confirming my theories and telling me so much more; to Peter and Sally Griffiths of the Jaguar Drivers' Club for producing mounds of information at the drop of a hat; to Alan Hodge, Peter Taylor, Andrew Whyte and Craig Jenkins at British Leyland for devoting so much time to helping me when hard-pressed; to Martyn Crawford at Jaguars for absolutely invaluable research completed with great speed and efficiency; to Ron Beaty for telling me all about Jaguar engines, and other things too; to Carter and Roberta Alexander for their unfailing enthusiasm and support; to Ed and Marion Harrell for similar enthusiasm and lending me invaluable documents; to Alan Hames for telling me so much about the Series Three car that I had never heard before; to Bob Needham for keeping my car running and giving me invaluable hints; to Harvey Hingston, Tony Prins, and Les Hughes for helping me Down Under; to Dr Phillipe Renault for saying he would buy a book; to Roy Hills, Chris Colebrook and Sid Mackay for telling me so much about running E types in Canada; to Simon Watney for letting me climb over, under and through his modsports car; to Mike Cooper for not giving up hope of getting his picture back; to Jim Thompson of Guyson's, for all his help, and I owe Michael Bateman a champagne lunch for suggesting the title while we were working on the 'Look!' pages of *The Sunday Times*.

I

Tribute to the E type

THERE will never be another car like the Jaguar E type. It was so good that everything else paled before it. It was ludicrously low-priced for what it was: the last of the great racing cars that could be driven on the road, not just on the track. It was in effect the Le Mans winner that anybody could drive—even a timid learner—because it was so docile. There was nothing practical that had the same wild and wonderful performance, the same speed and beauty. There is still no other car that I know, which when you hit the accelerator hard at 100 mph, throws its nose in the air and takes off like a rocket. Only cars costing three times as much can do anything approaching these sort of tricks, and even they cannot take off in top gear, tootle along in traffic without boiling over, look as sexy, or last as long.

An E type's attraction is sexual. It spells MAN, it is the ultimate turn-on: it is a rugged, yet beautiful, beast, with one of the most distinctive profiles ever fashioned in metal. Its beauty is the epitome of the Jaguar image: every one made is a tribute to Malcolm Sayer, the aircraft designer who shaped the magnificent body, to William Heynes, who directed the engineering, to the development engineers, to the test drivers led by Norman Dewis, and to Sir William Lyons, who created it all. The E type ranks alongside the products of top coachbuilders with its classic and distinguished lines, alongside Ferrari for sheer performance, and alongside a Chevrolet truck for practicality.

The first E types were the best pure sports cars ever built: the 4.2 Series One E type was the best all-rounder, and the V12 was the last of the great sports cars that the man in the street stood a chance of buying (the last E types produced in 1974 cost only £3,700). But what made the first 3.8-litre cars the classics they were was the engine. The 3.8-litre unit was the lightest and most dependable E type engine ever. It did not matter what you did to it, within reason, it would still churn out its considerable power in a manner reminiscent of a turbine. Those first E types with the 3.8-litre engine were so far ahead of any competition that buyers could overlook the archaic, but reliable, gearbox and heart-stopping brakes. The gearbox and brakes were improved almost beyond recognition on the later Series One E types, and the 4.2-litre engine gave the same power, with even more torque, providing you did not thrash it. The first 4.2 had a sweet engine but did not have the guts of the 3.8.

Two out of every three E types made were exported, earning more than £150

Portrait of the E types that started it all: a 3.8-litre roadster in the foreground at the Jaguar Drivers' Club XK Day in 1972, with a Series One 4.2-litre car on the right and a Series Two fixed-head coupé on the left.

million in foreign currency. Most of them went to America, and it was hardly surprising that the needs of that market became the biggest influence on design and development. That is why, as the years went by, the E type was watered down and became more of a touring car than a sports car. But before British enthusiasts go wild with rage, they should remember that without the vast American market, Jaguar could never have produced the E type at all. Better an emission-controlled eunuch than no E type at all.

Some of the Nader-inspired improvements imposed on the E type were a definite advantage. The open headlights on the later series cars enabled drivers to go faster at night and were safer, even if they did take a few miles per hour off the top speed and ruined the aesthetic appeal of the beautiful bonnet. The all-synchromesh gearbox fitted to every model after the 3.8-litre, might have been made as a sop to the Americans, but it was so much better than the ancient Moss box, that it was in fact a godsend to everybody. Thanks to American complaints, as much as those of anybody else,

the brakes improved with every model.

Constant grousing from America eventually got something done about the lack of ventilation on the early models and increased the range to include the ugly duckling, the Two Plus Two; unfortunately the same grumbling also brought in the terribly light power steering on the later series cars, plus a clutter of chrome and birdcage grilles on the V12. British pressure brought in radial ply tyres and probably kept the short chassis cars in production longer than they would have been otherwise.

Such beauty of line as achieved with the first E type is quite incredible when you consider that they were essentially a collection of bits and pieces: a production version of the D type body, with the front suspension dating back to the XK120 of 1948 and the rear suspension, that did so much for the character of the car, developed partially from a one-off racing machine built before 1960; the engine and gearbox lifted from the XK150S of 1959 and a hardtop on the open roadster which bore a distinct resemblance to the rear roofline of almost every Jaguar saloon produced to that date. The E type might have been bits and pieces, but they mated well because the car went back to the basic concepts of what a sports car should be: a two-seater with performance like a racing car which can be used for everything from commuting to shopping and taking the kids to school (even if that did make the interior look like a sea of arms and legs).

The first E type was even better than the previous two great Jaguar sports cars, the SS100 before the war, and the XK120 immediately after the war. The E type unveiled at the Geneva Motor Show in March 1961 was, like the SS100 and the XK120, a true sports car with no compromise in the form of extra seats or saloon-type interior. Like its two great ancestors, it was the fastest sports car you could buy in a normal car showroom, but like the XK series, it grew fat and bulbous towards the end.

You had to be an enthusiast, with thousands of pounds to spend, to get anything similar to an E type. The E type was not just a rough-and-ready special full of sharp corners and with little padding, it was a civilised car right from the start, with superb ride, handling and comfort, to a degree far in excess of any normal car of the early 1960s. As Paul Skilleter said in his book, *Jaguar Sports Cars*, it was apparent to nearly everybody that here was another classic; a new and totally different Jaguar, and as has so often been said before, one that could never be mistaken for another make.

This is what some of the pundits had to say at the time: the US magazine, *Car and Driver*, said:

> 'The new XKE is a pleasant blending of go and slow, capable of fifteen-second quarter miles and a maximum of 150 mph. It will cruise all day with the speedometer needle stuck well in the three-figure bracket . . . it looks racy even when sitting in a dentist's parking lot. Its performance is . . . not the explosive, spine-jarring kind one experiences in an American super-stock. It has an English quality of tasteful understatement . . . it's obviously capable of going terribly fast, but it would rather not tell everybody. . . .'

The British motor racing bible, *Motor Sport*, said:

> 'What Sir William Lyons has done is to use all that was best in the race-bred and

There will always be room at the top for an E type. Here a 1969 model fixed-head coupé soars away up Shelsey Walsh.

inspired C and D type Jaguars, learn some useful lessons from the Cunningham Jaguar, evolve stylish new bodywork and combine all these ingredients in a new British grand touring Jaguar that is about as fast as they come, immensely accelerative, endowed with extremely good roadholding, handling and braking characteristics, able to be driven by grandma at 15 mph or less in top gear, of returning 20 mpg of fuel under fast-travel conditions and which sells in GT coupé form, even after the Chancellor has had his levy of well over £618, for a mere £2,196 19s 2d. Sir William Lyons has bred another winner!'

Jaguar put it well in their advertisements too:

'You don't have to be a competition driver to drive a Jaguar. You don't have to

be a celebrity. You don't have to be rich, but just slide behind that racing wheel, ease back in the butter-soft glove leather seat, turn the key, reach down and slip into first, hear that unmistakeable Jaguar roar and you'll be the fastest, most famous, richest man in the world.'

I once read of one gentleman and his numerous exotic motor cars in the 1960s: 'There was a Ferrari Two Plus Two, a car which he loved, but on which the inscrutability tended to be a bit shallow. One day he found himself passed by, and unable to catch, an E type, and that shook him. The Italian period had come to an end.'

So the E type was a great production sports car. It is a car that is always remembered with affection: by my wife, who had some of her first driving lessons in my 3.8-litre roadster; by the local policeman, who set up a roadblock for the car as it passed through a restricted zone at an unmentionable speed in the dead of night, then let me go with a caution and gave the car a pat on the bonnet as he said, 'You don't see many of those about now'; by that great motoring journalist Denis Jenkinson, who lolloped all over Europe for twelve hours at a time, year after year, in an E type, and by children everywhere, who still fight for a ride in what they consider to be a real racing car.

Racing car or not, there will never be another car like the E type Jaguar. It is the only car in which I have left London at breakfast time and arrived in Monaco for dinner feeling fresh; it is the only car I know which has always seemed underpriced; it is the only car I have ever owned for which I have never had to apologise, and there are no apologies for the intensity of the words to follow. It would not be fitting to write just for the technically-minded, just for the people who like romantic stories, just for the home mechanic, just for the bod in the bar, just for the men in the grandstand, just for the figure freaks, just for the historians or just for the American market. This book is meant to cater for everybody who ever felt a wave of emotion when he or she saw or thought about an E type.

II
The Production E types:
Part One

THIS IS WHERE the book gets technical. I make no apologies because E type enthusiasts have to be technically-minded. There are three main E type variants: Series One, Two and Three, and they come in three body styles, the roadster or drop-head coupé, fixed-head coupé, and Two Plus Two fixed-head coupé. Only the Series Three varies much from the production point of view: its massive V12 engine is dropped in from the top instead of having the whole car assembled round the engine, as is the case with the straight six power unit in the Series One and Two. The bodies of all production E types were made up of a steel monocoque with separate steel sub-frames front and rear, and the all-enveloping steel bonnet which hung on the front. The engine and gearbox help brace the front sub-frame which holds in the engine and gearbox, and supports the front wheels via torsion bar suspension. The entire back axle assembly is held together by its own sub-frame, fixed to the monocoque with rubber mountings which in the back suspension allow five degrees of movement.

All these major components are made up of many smaller pieces, of course, a large proportion of which were made by Jaguars. Outside firms were also employed extensively, such as Abbey Panels, who made the nose section and outer curved parts of the E type bodywork and Pressed Steel Fisher, who made the internal chassis sections. The parts were assembled at Jaguar's, Browns Lane factory in Coventry, along with the rest of the mechanical, electrical and trimming components, by a combination of hand labour and automation.

The XKs were assembled in much the same manner and in fact their evolution was broadly similar. The XK started as a pure two-seater, which gradually became more luxurious, and, as a result, heavier, to please the American market. Eventually the XK became a Two Plus Two and needed more power and better brakes to keep up with the original, which was exactly what happened to the E type through the three series.

Thus the 3.8-litre Series One remained the fastest of all, although the early 4.2-litre cars were nearly as quick. The slower Series Two incorporated many refinements and in many ways is today's best buy among E types, while the Series Three has the glamour of twelve cylinders, but sacrifices economy and handling, and some think, looks too. In between these distinct series came the Series One and a Half. Jaguar denied at first that this car ever existed; they said there were just a few transitional

cars between the Series One and the Series Two. Then they admitted it: there was a Series One and a Half retaining most of the original lithe coachwork of the 4.2-litre Series One, but including some of the mechanical changes that were to be standardised on the Series Two. Jaguar decided to call this car the Series IA, but the enthusiasts who first identified it still call it the Series One and a Half.

The engine of the original 3.8-litre charger needed little introduction when the E type was launched in 1961. It was the ultra-reliable 3,781 cc, twin overhead camshaft six-cylinder that had started life in that capacity in the D type racing sports car seven years before and had gained total acceptance in the XK150S production car and in a slightly different form in the Mark Two and Mark IX saloons. The standard compression ratio was 9 to 1, but there was an 8 to 1 option, chiefly for buyers who lived in countries where high-octane petrol was not readily available. The change in compression ratio simply meant different pistons. With the standard pistons the power output was initially quoted as 265 bhp at 5,500 rpm with a maximum torque of 260 lb per foot at 4,000 rpm.

The first open models weighed twenty-two hundredweight without passengers and petrol, giving a power-to-weight ratio of about 220 bhp per ton. The fixed-head coupé weighed in at an extra one hundredweight, but sometimes went slightly faster because of its better aerodynamic shape. Three two-inch SU HD8 carburetters were used, with, to the eternal thanks of Jaguar enthusiasts, a manual choke instead of the not-totally-dependable automatic choke fitted to the XK series cars and the saloons.

This is the car that made the E type a legend: the first of the 3.8-litre roadsters pictured here at speed.

The cylinder block was traditional Jaguar chromium cast iron and the cylinder head was made of light alloy to save weight. Only the handful of lightweight racing examples made by the works departed from this practice, with their alloy blocks, which proved unreliable and prone to overheating and water leaks, although the experience gained with these blocks was valuable in the development of the alloy block for the later V12 engines, which have given no such problems. The crankshaft basically was the same that drove D type racers through season after season of long distance events, running in seven lead indium bearings, with Metalastik damping. The twin overhead camshafts were driven by.Renolds Duplex chains and the petrol was pumped in by a new constant pressure unit immersed in the tank at the rear. The exhaust gas was emitted through a system which was in my opinion, more like a Heath Robinson pipe dream than anything realistic.

Transmission was by the much-criticised four-speed Moss gearbox inherited from the XK and probably designed for a pre-war truck. It was slow and cumbersome to use and lacked synchromesh on first gear. The synchromesh on the other three, particularly second, was not so good either, but the gearbox did have the virtue of being completely dependable and it certainly absorbed less power than the synchromesh gearbox which followed. It would survive almost any amount of heavy-handed crunching and is still a favourite unit for British grass track and stock car drivers. E type expert Terry Moore calls it a drivers' box; but few average drivers could handle it well. No provision was made for overdrive or automatic transmission on the 3.8-litre E type. There simply was not room and it was five years before the anguished cries of the Americans persuaded Jaguars to provide the option of an automatic box on the long wheelbase Two Plus Two E type and, one or two prototypes apart, it never got an overdrive. But then the E type could do 150 mph in fourth gear and 20 mpg was easily obtainable, so it did not really matter.

The standard gear ratios were 3.377, 1.86, 1.283 and 1 to 1, and the normal axle ratio was 3.31 to 1, although optional ratios of 2.93, 3.07 and 3.54 to 1 could be specified. In common with the XK150 and the 3.8-litre Mark Two saloon, a Powr-Lok limited slip differential was incorporated in the hypoid final drive unit.

Front suspension followed the established Jaguar practice of torsion bars and double wishbones, using ball pins around which the stub axles moved. One regrettable absence was the screw adjuster fitted to XKs to vary the ride height at the front. The E type's bottom wishbones were linked to an anti-roll bar and Girling telescopic hydraulic dampers were fitted all round, although Spax adjustable units were often fitted later by private owners, and sometimes Konis, to improve roadholding.

The rear suspension was the most notable mechanical departure from the XK and the D type. It was fully independent and gave vastly improved roadholding, although it has proved considerably more expensive to service over the years. The E type's back suspension, which took five years to develop, used the half shafts as the upper links. The bottom links were a tubular structure forming the lower support in the vertical plane, which also stopped torsional movement of the stub axle carrier. On the 3.8-litre model this was a massive and dependable unit, which was slightly weakened by reduced bearing area on later models. Fore and aft movement was controlled by a radius arm which located the wheel longitudinally, running from the lower link to a box section member of the main body structure. The half shafts were universally jointed.

Each wheel was suspended by twin coil springs, enclosing Girling telescopic dampers, although, of course, Spax or Konis could be substituted. Spax had the advantage of being adjustable while on the car; Konis lasted a bit longer, but you had to take them off to change their setting. They also cost more than either Spax or Girling. The entire sub-frame carrying the rear suspension assembly, complete with differential and inboard disc brakes, could be detached quickly by experienced

The view that most people saw if they were lucky enough to spot an E type when it was introduced in March 1961: just the tail disappearing into the distance.

mechanics. But it is a difficult and expensive unit to overhaul by those to whom Jaguars are a mystery, or those people unlucky enough to have to deal with neglected cars.

Dunlop disc brakes were fitted, operated by a controversial Kelsey-Hayes bellows type servo. This American servo, made by the Michigan Wheel Company, left a lot to be desired. It was a design that was fine in most circumstances, but had a shocking habit of allowing the boost pressure to change. This lack of consistency was sometimes disastrous when the car's long nose came close to the tail of a car in front. In fact, a person of average height cannot see the first three feet of an E type's nose from the driving seat. Nobody seemed to have a big accident directly attributable to that servo, but there were lots of little ones. Dual master cylinders provided completely independent braking front and back. The handbrake worked reasonably well when it was new, but with its tiny pads and constant need for adjustment, it soon lost its grip. The trouble was that its cable stretched so much after about eighteen months' use that it exceeded the amount of adjustment available.

Steering was by rack and pinion, with two and a half turns from lock to lock and a turning circle of no less than thirty-seven feet. The steering was terrific when you were driving, which was when it really mattered, of course, but a bit heavy for parking, and again, its poor lock, with that long nose and minimal-sized bumpers, led to lots of little dents. This was especially true in the United States where it has long been the custom to park by sound. A lot of drivers backed into E types accidentally, too, because they just could not see that long nose when they looked through their back windows or in their driving mirrors, especially with the higher construction of cars generally in use in the early 1960s. No wonder E type drivers tried to park in spaces where nobody could get in front of them—a habit which persists today!

Dunlop wire wheels, either painted grey or chromed, were standard with centre-lock hubs similar to those on the XK, but different from those on the D type or XKSS, which had peg-drive alloy wheels by the same firm. Some racing E types acquired D type wheels, but ninety-nine per cent of Series One E types were on wires, as were virtually all E types exported before 1970. For a start they were shod with Dunlop RS5 6.40 × 15 tyres all round, although R5 6.50 × 15 racing tyres could be specified with competitions in mind. Later Series One cars were fitted with Dunlop SP41 or Pirelli Cinturato radial ply tyres. The Pirellis felt better to begin with, but soon degenerated with wear and became treacherous in the wet.

The fourteen-gallon petrol tank's immersed pump was supplied by Lucas, who provided the rest of the electrical equipment, including a dynamo that could be defeated on the 3.8-litre car. If you ran everything useful at once, such as headlights, wipers and interior fan, plus perhaps a radio to while away the time in a traffic jam, you ran the battery down. The tachometer was run by its own generator on the back of the right-hand cam cover, although some racing E types were fitted with the XK's mechanical instruments for extreme accuracy and ultimate dependability.

Structurally, the E type showed a close connection with the D type and XKSS, and the 3-litre all independently sprung E2A prototype raced by Briggs Cunningham at Le Mans in 1960. The basic spot-welded and stressed monocoque was made of twenty-gauge sheet steel, braced by box section members comprising the door sills, scuttle assembly, propeller shaft tunnel, and seat and rear suspension mountings. All this, including to a lesser extent the Reynolds 541 square steel tubing front sub-frame, has proved to be prone to rust, and all this except the suspension sub-frames, was replaced by aluminium on the lightweight racers. It was a great pity that the production E types could not have been made in aluminium, but then they would have cost much more. Rust has been the chief cause of many E types ending up in the scrapyards, although in some countries such as Britain, aluminium would have suffered from salt corrosion.

The shape of both open and closed models was worked out in a wind tunnel, and the open car had a folding mohair cover when the hood was down. Taking the hood down reduced the top speed though, even if you could stand the buffeting at such a pace. Jaguar never made a tonneau cover because they say the studs needed to fix it would have been too difficult to fit to the padded top of the facia, although several small firms have supplied them. But Jaguars did make a lovely fibreglass hardtop as an optional extra. Several small manufacturers, notably Lenham's in Kent, soon started making their own hardtops, too. All E types had the characteristic fully-opening bonnet, complete with power bulge to clear the cam covers on the XK engine. The later V12 E type did not need this power bulge, but an experimental model without the bulge 'just did not look like an E type,' to development engineer Peter Taylor, and, in any case, that bulge helped keep the floppy bonnet rigid. Apart from being a bit too floppy and accident prone, this beautiful bonnet has proved to be rust prone, particularly in the box section beam which holds it all on, and in the bottom pan and the wing mountings. The very first bonnets were released by an outside key near the scuttle, although this was soon substituted by twin coachlocks inside the car. The first 3.8-litre models did not have footwells, which made them more than somewhat cramped for men over five feet eight inches tall.

On the coupé, the rear window was hinged to give access to the large luggage shelf, the floor space of which could be increased by folding down the hinged luggage retainer. The spare wheel was located beneath the boot floor on both open and closed models and the tools were carried first in the centre of the wheel in a lovely wooden toolbox, and then in a canvas tool roll. Three windscreen wipers swept a laminated screen for the first eight years and all E types, except the lightweights, had wind-up windows. The early 3.8-litre cars had a distinctive aluminium insert in the dashboard, and transmission tunnel trimming, and leather bucket seats were standard for years. To their dying day, all E types suffered from antique heating and ventilation systems that had to be lagged by sweat-soaked enthusiasts to insulate themselves from engine heat.

Apart from the lack of footwells, a few other minor points were quickly tidied up in the first year of production. Water deflector shields were added to the rear hubs, a self-adjusting handbrake was worked out and a heated rear window was offered as a rather necessary optional extra on the fixed-head coupé.

In 1962, the brake pedal angle was altered and the seats were moved back to give more legroom. Men who were five feet ten inches tall could now squeeze in with comfort. Various experiments were carried out with the brake pads and the following year, universal joint shields were added to the rear drive shafts which had been receiving a sand and water blasting in road use. Thicker discs were fitted to the rear to improve braking efficiency; racing E types nearly all used the thicker Mark IX saloon discs anyway at the front. The pad material was changed repeatedly and ended up as Mintex M 59. Many modifications were made to the troublesome exhaust system and the axle ratio, which started at 3.31 to 1 on British cars went up to 3.07 to 1 and back to 3.31. In 1964 the standard axle ratio was changed back to 3.07.

THEN it was time for a big change. In October 1964, the 3.8-litre 'Series One' was replaced by the 4.2-litre car, although the last 3.8-litre models were something of a mixture. Many of these last 3.8-litre cars were fitted with the brand new all synchromesh gearbox which was one of the vast improvements to be found on the 4.2-litre car. It was a superb gearbox, everything the old crash bang wallop Moss box was not. It was smooth and silent; a tremendous advance that even silenced American complaints. The clutch was changed to a better diaphragm type, too, although it was not quite so responsive as the earlier unit, and an alternator was fitted to take care of the discharging electrics. This meant a negative earth electrical system in place of the old positive earth employed by the dynamo. The headlights were changed to sealed-beam units for slightly better visibility in the dark, too.

The radiator was changed, a one-piece inlet manifold with water rail fitted, and the old nose-bumping braking system was replaced by divided circuit, tandem servo braking with dirt shields on the front discs. A new pre-engaged negative-earth starter motor went with the new gearbox and clutch to help Americans firing up in Arctic conditions.

The interior changed considerably, with matt black and other colours where the stylish, but highly reflective, aluminium used to be and the doors that even acquired arm rests 'borrowed' from a BMC three-ton truck. These arm rests were fitted to some of the last 3.8-litre cars, too. An oddments locker big enough to carry a few stereo cartridges was fitted as standard, although Jaguar never did get round to finding a proper place to put a stereo unit. Little covers appeared over the fixed-head's rear door hinges on every car and hidden away in the right-hand side rear wing was a brand new SU fuel pump. Under the bonnet was a different engine; you could tell that the wonderful old 3.8 litre had gone by the 4.2-litre badge on the boot and a red line on the rev counter at 5,000 rpm instead of at 5,500 rpm. You could tell the difference when you drove the car too.

The 4.2 litre was more of a saloon car engine than the 3.8 litre, pulling better in the lower ranges, but not liking to rev with the wild abandon of its predecessor. This was because it was a good deal more than a bored out 3.8 litre internally. The cylinders were repositioned, numbers two and five remaining in their original positions with numbers three and four moving together and one and six being resited towards the end of the block. This meant a new crankshaft with four balances being moved to reduce bearing loads and a new torsional damper. Water flow around the bores was modified and the bores themselves increased from 87 mm to 92.07 mm, with the stroke staying unchanged at the rather long 106 mm. All this gave a capacity of 4,235 cc, meaning that if you revved the new engine like the old one you stood a fair chance of blowing it up. Mind you, it would take a fair driver to rev it like a 3.8: the 4.2 could still do well over 140 mph in top without over-exerting itself.

Some hint of the possible—if remote—trouble with a 4.2 was seen in the *Autocar* road test of May 1965.

'Since maximum power is unchanged it is not surprising that the ultimate speed of this car is likewise virtually the same as that of the previous one at 153 mph— within a fraction of the 152.7 mph measured with the 3.8 in 1963. For our peace of mind, however, and to prevent overstressing the engine during prolonged flat-out runs, the Dunlop R S 5 tyres were changed to R 6 racing tyres during this high-speed testing. The racing tyres are slightly larger in rolling radius (27.5 mph per 1,000 rpm instead of 26.5 at 140 mph), which reduces the revs at maximum speed from 5,750 rpm to 5,650.

'From a careful calibration of the instrument using Dunlop tyre data, we discovered that after taking the performance figures that our rev counter was reading five per cent slow (this did not affect the maximum speed readings which were timed over a measured distance), causing us to over-rev the engine in third as far as 120 mph (just under 6,000 rpm, allowing for tyre growth), although normally one would not exceed 110 mph.

Perhaps the prettiest of all E types: the Series One 4.2-litre fixed-head coupé before its lines became cluttered.

Introducing the car that the Americans loved: the Series One Two Plus Two.

'During this prolonged running within the red sector on the rev counter (it starts at 5,000 rpm with a handbook warning not to hold the car above this speed for long periods), the oil pressure fell from its customary 50 lb per square inch to the minimum permitted 40. Water temperature likewise crept from the normal 70–80 degrees Centigrade to nearly 90, but no further.'

So now you know. Do not over-rev a 4.2, especially an old one, because it should be borne in mind that the *Autocar* road test car was almost certainly in peak condition.

Other points which changed on the 4.2-litre car were the D type style separate radiator header tank which acquired extra pipes to work with the water rail, and the seats. These were much more comfortable for most people, but not so good on location for the competitive types who liked to hurl the car around; they could also be tilted forwards, and were a clue to something big on the way.

Nothing much happened on the production front in 1965; the development department was too busy. There was just an improved screenwasher, better water-proofing round the distributor and factory confirmation that the new Dunlop SP41 radial ply tyres were better. After about a year the alternator was improved and in March 1966, almost five years to the day after the first E type hit the headlines, Jaguar introduced the ultimate American sports car—the Two Plus Two E type— hailed as a four-seater across the Atlantic.

The Americans loved it, and so did quite a few Englishmen. It was longer by nine inches and taller by two. It would carry four full-sized people on short journeys and two full-sized people, plus two children of preferably stunted growth, on long journeys. Engineering changes allowed the introduction of automatic transmission, for which Buddy was pleased to spare more than a dime. In fact it was the option of the Borg Warner model eight transmission which was the only real mechanical change from the 4.2-litre Series One E type, apart from obvious things like the lengthened tail shaft on the gearbox, the exhaust system, and the brake and fuel lines. Two drive ranges were provided with D1 and D2 positions on a floor quadrant. Selecting D1 meant all three forward ratios came into operation and keeping D2

What it looked like inside: a spy's eye view of a 4.2-litre fixed-head coupé's interior.

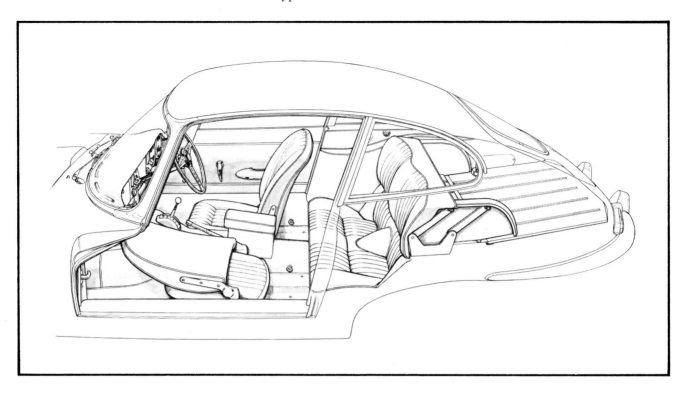

How they stretched the Series One 4.2-litre fixed-head coupé into a Two Plus Two and found room for an automatic gearbox.

meant that only the top two were used, even when kicking down. In practice, you kept in D2 for a smoother ride in town, and used D1 for maximum performance. All automatic cars got a 2.88 to 1 final drive ratio.

The extra bulk and weight meant that performance suffered, especially with the more sluggish automatic Two Plus Two. Top speed fell to nearer 130 mph than 150, but it was felt that Jaguar's many large American customers would prefer the Two Plus Two with its extra big doors, higher roofline and extra luggage accommodation. It was probably the first time that luggage accommodation had seriously influenced a Jaguar sports car design. This boost to the boot, which had previously been even smaller than that of the XK, was achieved within the longer wheelbase by using a rear seat squab divided horizontally and an upper section mounted on parallel links. This meant that it could be swung over and forward to give an extra ten inches of luggage floor space in the nine inches of extra wheelbase. The fold-forward seats gained an extra two inches of adjustment, which now meant that men or women of more than six feet could ride comfortably.

The shell was altered too: the big box section on the front of the transmission tunnel was replaced with a flat box member under the front edge of the Two Plus Two's rear seat; the front panel of the rear suspension tunnel was moved back and the whole shell was extended; the roof was moved up to give more legroom and a bigger windscreen was fitted in a more upright position. It had longer windscreen wipers, of course, but the interior remained substantially unaltered except for the extra trimming needed. Odds and ends were changed at the same time, such as screw-pattern adjusters on the facia to control the heater shutters and extra heat shielding incorporated in the engine bulkhead. The doors and their internals were different, naturally, and the weight went up by just over one hundredweight to twenty-seven hundredweight.

All fixed-head models were affected by the introduction of the Two Plus Two. They were all given new wide ratios in their gearboxes and a re-angled clutch pedal. The next year, the roadsters got the same treatment with the new gearbox being introduced at the same time as the E type changed its basic frontal shape for the first time with the new windscreen. This was in 1968 and this model was later christened the Series One and a Half, by enthusiasts such as Terry Moore, to distinguish it from the Series Two to follow it soon after. The Series One and a Half was a modified Series One primarily for the American market. The most visible difference was the loss of the headlamp covers, and a plastic hood in place of the mohair on the roadster, plus the acquisition of some of the features of the Series Two which was to follow. Removing the headlamp covers and moving the lights forward three inches to satisfy new American regulations cost quite a few miles per hour and perhaps a little extra fuel consumption. Some Series One and a Half cars were fitted with a cross-flow radiator with expansion tank and twin electric fans, which were to become standard later. The top speed attained in a *Speedworld International* road test for a Series One and a Half was 143 mph—a generally accepted figure—although the car had already done many miles when it was tested.

These changes were only the start of something big, again primarily for the American market, and everybody else had to fall in line in 1968 when the Series Two E type was introduced. In many ways the Series Two was the best E type, but as a tourer, not an all-out sports car.

III
The Production E types:
Part Two

THE TIMES they were a changin' for the E type in 1969; they started to decline. Actually the date was October 1968, but that meant that the Series Two was a 1969 model. The Series Two meant that the car which had dominated sports car classes for eight years with a virtually unchanged appearance had at last been cut down to size, in performance at least, by new American regulations. The Americans started to get really dictatorial over bumpers, lights, interior appointments, and the gas that came out of the back, so the E type had to change if it stood a chance of keeping full order books; the Series Two was a direct result of this.

To start with the small things, the helix angle of the gearbox teeth was increased to provide even more silent running, although the ratios were not changed. You would probably have noticed the ratios, but not the noise—there was so little with the old 4.2 box—but anyway the car was becoming more of a smoothie. In accordance with this policy the action of the diaphragm spring clutch was lightened, and, in keeping with everything that is right about British motor cars, the brakes were improved immensely by changing to Girling with three pistons at the front and two at the rear operating larger pad areas; the collapsible column was fitted with an energy-absorbing sleeve—not so bad—and Powr-a-Rak steering like that on the new XJ6 saloon was offered as a not very desirable option; a crossflow radiator with expansion tank was introduced and twin electric fans were fitted under the bonnet of all models.

The interior of all models changed too. All switches on the instrument panel were switched to those of the rocker type; the heating system was made more efficient, thank goodness, with recessed push-pull controls, as was the choke; the screen rail was padded and the interior mirror was mounted on the screen; the door handles were buried in the doors and the window winders were slimmed down and fitted with recessed rubber handles; the glove compartment got a lock like that on the saloons and the horn button, headlamp flasher and direction indicator switch were all incorporated in one lever. Jaguar enthusiasts also kissed their separate ignition key and starter button goodbye.

Outside, the headlamps were moved forward another one and a half inches—so soon after the Series One and a Half was introduced—and additional reflectors popped up on the front wings ahead of the wheels; the indicators got bigger; a hazard warning system was linked up to the facia; twin reversing lights sprouted in place of the neat little single unit; the bumpers were wrapped all the way round at the front and the back to meet US regulations; the rear light styling was revised, the Two Plus Two variant's great big screen was tilted back from $46\frac{1}{2}$ degrees to $53\frac{1}{2}$ degrees by moving the base of the glass forward while keeping the original crown line; two big wipers were fitted in place of the distinctive three blade set-up and they were given a more powerful motor, and the hub spinners on the wire wheels lost their ears. Pressed steel wheels were offered as an option that was surprisingly more expensive. The exhaust system took on a new turn at the back to get round American style number plates

One of the best views of a Series Two E type with its hood down, still looking very much like the Series One, except for the exposed headlamps and the loss of its eared hub spinners.

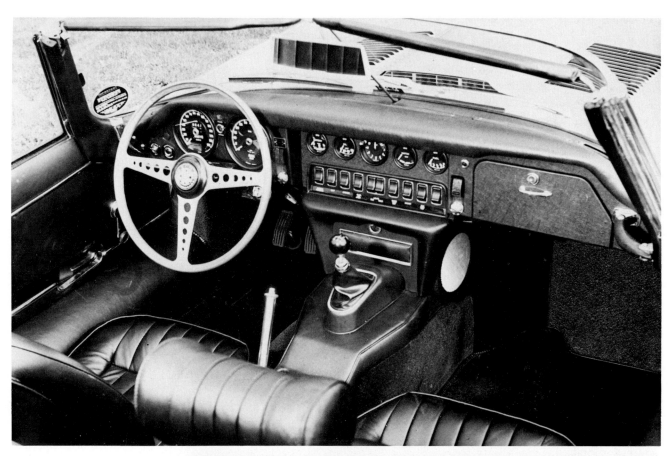

Above: Series Two or Three, the interior is virtually the same.

Right: You cannot make a Series Three screen slope much further; it is nearly touching the bonnet.

and significantly the front air intakes was increased in size by no less than sixty-eight per cent.

The new radiator and the bigger air intake were standardised on all models, but they were chiefly aimed at cooling a special emission-controlled engine fitted to US models only, which had a tendency to get very hot under the collar like many other such engines. The first models with the US engine had two carburetters with a dual induction system which developed 246 bhp against the original 265 bhp. Later six-cylinder models had a water-heated intake manifold rather than the dual induction system, dispensing with the crossover tract that took the intake mixture across the cam covers to the exhaust manifold for heating, eventually turning out only 177 bhp.

The Duplex manifold system worked rather like this; two Stromberg carburetters were combined with the two manifolds, and two throttles were used. They were connected by a linkage so that when the car was driven at part-throttle, the secondary throttle stayed closed and the intake mixture passed through the primary throttle only. The exhaust gases heated the fuel mixtures on their way to the combustion chambers. This system was used chiefly on Series One and a Half cars and early Series Two machines. On the later Series Two cars, in 1969, a water-heated conditioning chamber was used so that at part-throttle the fuel mixture went through the primary throttle, to the primary mixture pipe (by-passing the secondary). When it reached the water-heated chamber, it was warmed and returned to the intake manifold just downstream of the closed secondary throttle plate. At higher engine speeds, the by-pass allowed a full charge of non-heated mixture to enter the cylinders. This system, also used in 1970 and 1971 on six-cylinder models, ensured that the air and fuel mixture remained constant when delivered to the combustion chambers. This made it possible for a leaner mixture to be used and prevented the presence of wet fuel in the intake manifold, a major cause of exhaust emission. It also meant that the engine ran hotter, hence the larger air intake and change of radiator and fan-cooling system.

New camshafts were also fitted to the E type in 1969 and the valve gear modified to give quieter running and service intervals of 6,000 miles instead of 2,500 miles. Cold-start ballast resistor ignition was fitted; the steering lock that had been optional since 1966 became standard, the new bonnet was held up by a gas-filled stay and you could have headrests for the very first time, folks!

The distributor used on the six-cylinder cars made between 1969 and 1971 for the US had different advance curves, too, to lower those obnoxious smells. Early 1969 cars had a vacuum unit that retarded the ignition by ten degrees at the crankshaft when the throttle was closed. Later models with automatic change gearboxes (to use the proper title), were fitted with a transmission-controlled ignition retarder. Then, in 1970, Jaguar introduced more emission equipment in the form of a fuel evaporative control system. Certainly your 1970 E type should never smell of petrol. This new system controlled the release of hydrocarbon vapours from the petrol tank vents and those in the carburetters. A sealed petrol filler cap forced the petrol vapour in the tank to escape through the vent lines at the corner of the tank. These lines carried the vapour into an expansion tank and from there into the engine area, where they were passed through a charcoal canister. The charcoal filtered out the impurities before

Getting away from it all in France
with a Series Two, Two Plus Two.

the vapour reached the carburetters. Escaping fuel vapour was reduced even further by venting the float chambers to the engine side of the air cleaner.

All this must have cost a fortune to develop and it is a miracle that the price of the E type did not soar. With British Leyland's current pricing policies, this would surely have been a different tale.

But back to the fun and games. A mystifying fault can develop if one of the fuel caps intended for the no-petrol-smell cars is accidentally fitted to an earlier car: a vacuum tends to form in their tanks which would not have happened if they had kept their old-style vented caps. All it needs to cause this vacuum is a blocked tank vent, which results in fuel starvation. When the engine dies as a result of being starved of petrol, the puzzled driver switches off, gets out and looks around, then switches on and tries to start the engine. With any luck the vacuum will have disappeared and the car will start but it will keep on happening, with hours of head scratching by 'experts' and mechanics till somebody hears a bang from the back. This is merely the tank sucking air back in through the fuel lines and popping out with a bang. Then everybody realises how important a vented cap and clear tank vents are on earlier E types. All this happened to me, and the combined attention of A A and R A C men, mechanics and a party of Jaguar apprentices who stopped for hours trying to help on a freezing

cold night, did nothing to cure the trouble until I heard the bang and got the message.

All this emission controlling and shape-changing reduced the E type's performance somewhat to a relatively mundane 135 mph maximum even on the least strangled engines and more like 120 mph on the real chokers. By 1971, when the E type was really slowing down, it became increasingly obvious to Jaguars that they would have to do something to pep up the Big Cat so that it could keep pace with the exotic Italian cars which were beginning to invade their territory. The big American V8s were taking on a new turn of speed too, and the De Tomaso Pantera, with its Italian chassis and American Ford engine, was looking menacing. So they dropped the V12 engine, that had been under development for the best part of ten years, into what amounted to the old chassis to create the Series Three E type.

Many people wanted to call it the F type, including Jaguar's biggest distributors, Henlys, who said as much in an advertisement. But Jaguar's were adamant; it was still an E type. After all, with its exciting new V12 engine it was practically as fast as the glorious old Series One. The *Motor's* test car, a drophead with hardtop, managed 146 mph—slightly slower than the original E type— although in terms of power and weight, they acknowledged it as the quickest E type yet, reaching 100 mph in 15.4 seconds compared with the 17.2 of a 4.2-litre coupé they tried. And the Series Three was even more flexible than the 4.2, which could just about take off from rest in top gear if the clutch was mistreated. The V12 could do it easily.

The Series Three was a much different car from the earlier E types although Jaguar's were right to insist that it was still an E type. It was just that it was even more of a tourer— admittedly exceedingly fast—than the original sports car concept, rather like the difference between the XK120 and the XK150 of an earlier period.

The Series Two was smooth and silky, halfway towards being a saloon car. It had the Two Plus Two's long wheelbase as standard and all models had ultra-light power steering which came in for a lot of criticism from drivers who complained that they could not feel the road, a criticism you could never level at the old E types. Jaguars built one prototype V12 without power steering, but even Peter Taylor could not manage to steer it. The front suspension was changed to incorporate anti-dive geometry when the new ventilated disc brakes were applied and fatter tyres similar to those on an XJ6 saloon were fitted. At the same time, the turning circle was reduced to thirty-six feet. The wheel arches were flared to clear the new tyres and the intake grille became even bigger and less aerodynamic to cope with the greater temperatures generated by the 5.3-litre engine and its comprehensive emission equipment. Many other detail changes were made, particularly to the interior, which was much bigger, allowing the driver's seat to take in comfort, one road tester who was six feet five inches tall! The heating and ventilation were further improved, although the XJ6 style face-level vents were never introduced. A six-cylinder version of the Series Three was also listed, but apparently only two or three were made and only one was sold.

Naturally the engine was the most interesting part of the Series Three. It was much less highly tuned than the old twin cam six, even having forsaken the twin cam heads used at one stage of its development because of their weight and bulk. American pollution requirements kept a check on the tuning too and the resultant engine achieved a standard of silence and smoothness that completely changed the character

Above: The sands of time were running out for the Series Three as it parked outside the Hourglass antique shop. Only three years to go and it would become an antique itself. Below: E type motoring at its best: deserted roads and the top down on a Series Three roadster.

Above: the Series Three roadster with its optional factory hardtop in place. Below: the Series Three roadster without its top.

Above: The V-12 engine.

Right: A rare view of the only six-cylinder Series Three E type to escape from the Jaguar factory.

of the E type. The new engine was not much heavier than the old X K unit, thanks to its alloy block and the single overhead cams. No less than four horizontal Zenith constant vacuum carburetters were used to tie in with US emission laws and Lucas electronic ignition was fitted as standard to ensure smooth running. This system, called the OPUS, had no make or break points; just a revolving disc with twelve sensors which triggered off the necessary impulses for correct sparking. It did little to ensure smooth running with customers at first though, being prone to curious mis-firing at high revs.

The V12 was capable of plenty of revs—producing something in the order of 325 bhp in old terms at 6,500 rpm—although officially classed at 272 bhp on revised modern ratings. The cylinder banks were inclined at sixty degrees to each other and the face of each cylinder was flat. Each piston had a shallow depression in its crown, which together with the clearance between the head face and the piston at top dead centre, formed a combustion chamber which was relatively free of the unde-sirable 'squish.'

A bore diameter of 90 mm and a stroke of 70 mm gave a capacity of 5,343 cc which, with a compression ratio of 9 to 1 gave a gross power output of 272 bhp at 6,200 rpm and a gross torque figure of 349 lb per foot at 3,800 rpm.

The Jaguar engineers paid special attention to accessibility, with the main auxili-aries either on top of the engine or at the front, which must have been a plus factor compared with most other V12 installations. The complete unit weighed only 680 lb with all its bits and pieces other than the gearbox. The block was very heavily ribbed both internally and externally and the lower face of the block was well below the crankshaft centre line to provide the maximum support and rigidity for the seven large-diameter steel-backed lead indium bearings. The cylinder liners were free standing and the crankshaft was a fully-balanced Tuftrided steel forging. Cast iron main-bearing caps, each located by four bolts, provided the greatest rigidity for the whole assembly. Whereas the six-cylinder unit needed inclined valves because it had a relatively long stroke, the new over-square unit had room in its alloy head for really big valves in a single line and the breathing was at least as good.

Big V12s are notoriously slow to warm up, particularly in the extremely cold conditions that can be encountered in America, so the lubrication system featured a 'crescent-type' oil pump driven by the crankshaft. Oil passed from a strainer in the sump to the pump and from there to a large capacity filter in front of the sump. The oil was then circulated through the engine with a by-pass valve diverting the surplus through an oil-to-water type cooler behind the filter and then back to the pick-up side of the pump. This type of cooler provides a closer control of oil temperature than the more widely used oil-to-air unit and helps tremendously with warming up. One American Ferrari owner I know swears that his car takes nearly twenty miles to warm up in mild winter conditions against a Jaguar's two or three.

All V12 engines sent to the North American market met the emission standards by the use of air injection, using an air pump driven off the nose of the crankshaft by a belt, with the air pipes located on top of the engine. The air injector nozzles are located on the manifold side of the exhaust valves—a perfect position—for it is important to inject the air into the exhaust gas at the point of its highest temperature, to give the best burning characteristics. These provisions are backed up by heat transfer shields and hot air intakes which cut the emissions dramatically when being started in cold air.

Naturally, many changes were needed to accommodate the V12 engine in the E type chassis, although none was major from the structural point of view, partly because it had been decided not to use the twin overhead camshaft heads. The front tubular framework had to be redesigned, though, and strengthened by means of triangular plates fixed in the corners of the upper forward tubing; the bulkhead was enlarged and strengthened and a tie bar fitted under the engine to take care of the extra torque. More bitumen paint was used on the chassis, too, in the fight against the ravishes of rust. Apart from the ventilated front discs, the brakes got an air scoop—a feature of racing E types from the earliest times—to cool the rear discs and help balance the relative temperatures of front and back brakes. The entire floor area of the car was also brought down to the level of the previous footwells and, now that it had power steering as standard, a smaller fifteen-inch steering wheel replaced the old sixteen-inch woodrim wheel to give more interior space, and an extra nine inches was put on the wheelbase for the same reason. It was reputed that you could actually wear a bowler hat inside an E type now. The longer wheelbase also allowed the Borg Warner model twelve automatic transmission to be offered as an option both on the roadster and fixed-head in place of the old model eight. The gearbox did not alter in the manual cars, but the clutch grew from $9\frac{1}{2}$ inches to $10\frac{1}{2}$ inches.

The development from 1961 had increased weight by some 5 cwt to 28 cwt and brought down the fuel consumption to around 13 mpg from 20, and that is what helped to kill the E type. At any rate the E type continued in its Series Three guise, with progressively less power as emission control regulations carried on with their policy of strangulation, until 1974, when the last fifty were produced and took a few months to sell. Now two years later, they are being snapped up at much more than their original price; it is always the same. As soon as a great car goes out of production everybody wants it, even those people who would not have considered buying it when it was still in production and cost a lot less.

IV
Contemporary Road Testers' Reports

ROAD TESTERS have generally waxed lyrical over the E type, particularly those fortunate enough to have conducted their tests in the first 3.8-litre models. This is hardly surprising when you consider the rest of the mundane transport they were using at the time. It was all Hillman Husky estates and Austin A40s in 1961, and, in the E type's last year (1974), Honda Civics and the like. So you have only to read John Bolster in *Autosport* on 17 March 1961, to realise what the E type meant to him, and also to remember that John of Bloody Mary sprint car fame, was certainly used to driving hairy machinery. This is what he had to say about his fixed-head E type test car (registered 9600 HP): 'It is one of the quietest and most flexible cars on the market, capable of whispering along in top gear at 10 mph or leaping into its 150 mph stride on the brief depression of a pedal. A practical touring car, this, with its wide doors and capacious luggage space' (well, I suppose it was after Bloody Mary), 'yet it has a sheer beauty of line which easily beats the Italians at their own particular game. . . .' Praise indeed from a man well acquainted with Ferrari as well as Austin A40s, even if he was prone to travel light. Luggage space in an E type has always been restricted.

Bolster was quick to spot the advantages of the new independent rear suspension over that of the D type and X K150 S and to comment on sound insulation, which he said was a breakthrough. He was not particularly enamoured with the gearbox, however, saying that the synchromesh was 'not very potent,' but adding in a flash, that you hardly needed to use it anyway. The speedometer amazed him, actually reading slow on his car. He found it best to change up at 5,500 rpm, and managed 145 mph 'from time to time during ordinary road motoring.' Shades of Bloody Mary. . . .

Bolster was quite happy to call the E type a genuine 150 mph car, because a strong side wind was blowing during the timed tests, when 9600 HP hit a mere 148.1 mph. His other performance figures were 107 mph in third gear; 71 in second and 38 in first; the standing-start quarter mile was covered in 14.8 seconds in the dry and 15.1 in the wet: 'a tribute to the independent rear suspension and a feat previously only equalled by racing cars,' said Bolster. From a standing start, he hit 30 mph in 2.6 seconds; 50 in 5.6; 60 in 6.8; 80 in 10.8; 100 in 15.8; and 120 in 23.2 seconds. All this driving averaged out at 18–20 mpg, and the man with the mighty moustache was happy to report that 'quite appreciable curves may be rounded at 110 mph and full throttle may be held without any tendency to lose it.' You have to hand it to Bolster, he certainly knew how to drive cars; you have always had to use power-on cornering techniques with an E type because of its basic design, but not everybody could round 'appreciable curves' at 110 mph. At any rate the rapid scribe from *Autosport* wound up by emphasising that the E type was not only Britain's best sports car, but one of her quietest and most comfortable touring cars, too. Historic words about 9600 HP, which is believed to be the same car which popped up in 1974 under the registration number 480 HYT, having received a new floor, wheel bearings, suspension joints and brakes after mouldering in a garage for a while.

The *Autocar* was rather more staid in its description, but no less lavish with its praise the following week of the same car. It said that the new Jaguar sports model was a major advance and represented a breakthrough in the design of high performance vehicles for sale to the public. In the *Autocar*'s opinion, it was vastly superior to its predecessors and to competitors sold within £1,000 of its list £2,256 15s, which included purchase tax and the optional chrome wire wheels which were fitted to most E types in those days.

Autocar said the E type offered 'what drivers have so long asked for, namely, sports-racing-car performance and handling, combined with docility, gentle suspension and the appointments of a town car.' Then their testers wound it up to their best-ever performance figures, which were much the same as those recorded by Bolster, with the exception of that top speed. *Autocar* broke the magical 150 mph maximum with an average of 150.4 mph on two runs in opposite directions. It has since been pointed out that not many private owners achieved this, but one or two who had asked the factory to do £200 or £300 worth of tuning managed it easily. That aside, *Autocar* found the acceleration between 50 mph and 130 mph to be 'quite breathtaking' and discovered that it was possible to hit 78 mph in second gear 'while leaving heavy traffic.' That E type must have really blasted off the A40s, leaving them in a haze of blue smoke if I know anything about old 3.8s. Like Bolster, *Autocar* found the synchromesh 'rather feeble' and commented favourably on the new rear suspension 'which provided all a driver could hope for in such a car.' They explained that the test car had done a great deal of bench and road running, which, no doubt accounted for its abnormally high oil consumption of 650 mpg, having found that similar engines did not normally consume more than one third of that amount. Yes, we all know that the 3.8 was an oil burner, but these comments confirm that the test car was well and truly run in which might account for the exceptionally good performance figures. Three-point-eight E types do not really start to go until they have had 20,000 miles good hard road driving.

Autocar's testers loved the handling, saying that at 140 mph 'the car seems in one sense to be clinging to the road, so stable is its progress, yet in another sense it feels to be flying over it.' Flying or not, they certainly appeared to have confidence in the car, explaining that the steering wheel 'could be released momentarily' at 150 mph. Confidence? They must have been in a state of euphoria.

The same third week in March 1961, *The Motor* tried a drop-head, registered 77 RW, and managed a mean time of 149.1 mph for a flying-start quarter mile, with broadly similar acceleration times to those attained by *Autosport* and *Autocar*. Their road testers were rather proud of getting the first E type roadster, by waiting up all

Facing page: You can drive an E type virtually anywhere—even through a blizzard—it is so tractable. Here is one of the road test cars being put through its paces in extreme conditions.

The most photographed E type of all: the 3.8-litre 77 R W heads for the wide open spaces on its *Motor* road test.

night for it. And once they got the car—which later became what must be the most photographed E type ever—they went rather further afield for their 2,859-mile test than the other two magazines, using Italian petrol in their maximum speed runs and commenting on the way the 220 bhp per ton was 'no embarrassment at all on the packed snow and ice of Swiss mountain passes, using ordinary racing tyres.' Descending those mountains must have been like the Cresta Run, but then British road testers have always had stiff upper lips!

The Motor's intrepid investigators emphasised that the E type's acceleration was twice as fast as that of an average family saloon, yet it could climb the one-in-six Birdlip hill in top gear! Their roadster used oil at the rate of 1,300 mpg—obviously it was not so loose as 9600 HP—and had a tendency to soot its plugs slightly in London rush hour traffic. Like the fixed-head coupés' drivers, they did not think much of the synchromesh, saying it was impossible to make silent changes at high revs (what's that one about a rolling Moss gathering no stones? Clearly the gearbox was just about as vague as the joke). They also thought that the car, on its standard 3.31-to-1 final drive, was undergeared for maximum speed and said they considered that racing tyres were highly advisable at that rate of progress. Like *Autosport* and *Autocar*, *The Motor* were most impressed with the rear suspension and the tremendous feeling of security while driving the car.

Their men at the wheel were constantly amazed at the amount of power that they could pile on while cornering and found that it seemed quite natural to throw the car about in a manner usually reserved for smaller and lighter sports cars. They were also impressed with the low build especially when they saw a small foreign G T car towering over their E type. Perhaps the most significant tribute paid to the E type by road testers that year was their comparison of its roadholding and handling with that of other cars of the day. They said that the only car which could match it was the Lotus Elite, which like the E type, was race bred.

In *The Motor*'s opinion though, the roadster needed some development before it could be considered a really good long-distance grand-touring car, particularly with its limited luggage space and imperfectly-fitting hood. The seats did not really suit the testers either, who had to sit in them for between 400 and 500 miles every day for six days. They said: 'The squabs are effectively concave where they should be convex to support the small of the back and the cushions are rather hard and flat, so that one tends to slide forward . . . and seat adjustment is not adequate for most taller (than five foot ten inch) people and neither is the headroom with the rather upright sitting position.' Thus spoke two men who did nearly 3,000 miles in a footwell-less roadster in less than a week. They were the first to criticise the ventilation in print, finding that the inside of the car could 'become rather hot in sunny weather, even if the very quiet two-speed fan is used.' They also felt that the Le Mans-type headlights were not really adequate for the performance, although they concluded by saying: 'The sheer elegance of line which Jaguar seem able to produce by total disregard for fashion trends is allied to a combination of performance, handling and refinement that has never been equalled at the price, very seldom surpassed at any price.'

Six months later *Road and Track* in America went mad over their roadster. 'Sensational is the word for this Coventry cat,' said the men from Newport Beach, and added: 'If a new car ever created greater excitement around our office than the new Jaguar X K E, we can't remember it. The car comes up to, and exceeds, all our expectations.' So spoke America, although the unfortunate testers had only a much shorter time to try out the car than their British equivalents. All the same, they reckoned that they could have got 180 mph out of it on the optional 2.88-to-1 axle ratio. I should think that they would have had to have popped over to Utah in July for that.

Road and Track found that a stock showroom Chevrolet Corvette could just about 'nip' an E type on acceleration, but was left behind on top speed and the only thing, apart from seating space, that they had to complain about was vulnerability. 'Sheet metal protection front and rear is minimal for American parking conditions: the front parking lights, in particular, look vulnerable and the rear bumper is located very high, exactly six inches higher than that at the front in fact. This exposes the twin mufflers and tail pipes. The headlight covers are also vulnerable,' but they did not really mind. They thought the car was just great, especially the appearance, and said that they had not heard anybody say anything against it.

Bill Boddy, on *Motor Sport*, saved his go in an early E type until May 1962, when he took the opportunity of going across the Channel in a Carvair car-transporting plane to Basle, then driving over the Alps to report on the Monaco Grand Prix. Deep in rally country between Gap and Sisteron, he opened up a small crack in the sump,

Hammering away through France, 77 R W shows signs of having a hard time: mud-splashed sides, back down, cornering under power.

but this was repaired in Monaco by the local B M C dealer, who also supplied a replacement universal joint to New Zealander Bruce McLaren for his personal E type. Bruce took an hour or so off between the last practice and winning the Grand Prix to fit his new universal joint. Boddy had fixed himself up with a drop-head E type, hoping for blazing sunshine, but sadly for him, he got only pouring rain. As it happened, his car did not leak a drop of water into the interior, although it had lost a lot of oil from the cracked sump and it needed exhaust repairs, too, as it leaked fumes after the ravishes of the mountain roads. Otherwise, his only trouble was one which was to become characteristic of open E types. The boot lid kept popping open and there was an occasional smell of petrol; small price to pay for the wonderful experience of blasting an E type through the Alps on the roughest of roads.

Later, on Whit Monday, the car was wound up to 153 mph and averaged 104 mph for the full length of the M1 motorway, passing no less than 900 cars while doing this. All but one kept to their lanes, the E type's driver reported happily. Boddy moaned about the tank holding only 14 gallons of petrol, and about the gearbox, but he loved the performance:

'Experiments on wet twisty roads showed that the rear end is extremely reluctant to break away, even when the power and torque were turned on hard in second gear, such is the grip of the Dunlop R S 5 tyres . . . The suspension of the E type is soft enough to give an excellent ride over rough roads, yet is fully in keeping with the car's phenomenal performance, for there is very little roll. It is

possible to dodge obstructions with alacrity, and, apart from a trace of tail happiness, there are no vices whatsoever . . . we have always advocated properly-designed independent rear suspension and the Jaguar E type and Mark Ten saloon endorse our views!'

At the end of the test, Boddy made one of his characteristic attacks on bureaucracy, no doubt feeling inspired by his 2,800 mile trip in an E type:

'One matter baffles us,' he said. 'Insurance brokers cannot be unintelligent, for it takes intelligence, allied perhaps to a certain low cunning, to make oodles of money and the insurance business makes it all right—just look at the marble halls from which they issue policies and the liveried commissionaires who guard their portals. How then, as intelligent beings, can they demand high premiums to insure that "dangerous" car, the Jaguar E type? I can only conclude that they have never seriously driven one, for no car could be safer, more docile, instil greater confidence, than this stupendously clever 150 mph Jaguar, that is priced so modestly.'

It is words like this that have gained *Motor Sport* its dedicated readership and I can but say that I agree with them absolutely, adding only that it is possible to find reasonably priced insurance for an E type, but you need a good broker.

During 1962, *Motor Sport* carried out several surveys of readers' opinions of their cars, and they came out very favourably in respect of the owners of Jaguar saloons who had almost identical engines to those fitted to the E type, which was then obviously too new for long-term evaluation. There were some complaints of engine and gearbox faults, but very few: they seemed to be confined to timing chain tensioner failure, high oil consumption and carburetter troubles, with clutch judder and weak synchromesh too. It was these faults, of course, that were encountered sometimes by E type owners. Later in 1962 E type designer, Bill Heynes, replied to the criticisms.

On the engine, he said the timing chain tensioner failures were usually due to fracture of the tensioner bracket (which was strengthened later), or because the engine oil had become very dirty. This sometimes affected the tensioner, despite the fitting of an oil filter. Engine oil leaks had also been a problem from time to time, and improvements had been made to oil seals. The sump gasket material was also changed. Complaints about oil consumption invariably occurred during the early life of the car, and this was because piston rings had not had time to bed in. Judging by the oil consumption of 3.8-litre cars generally, the piston rings must have taken an incredible length of time to bed in.

Mr Heynes went on to say that carburetter problems were usually due to incorrect balancing and clutch trouble often emanated from the owner who used it to supplement his brakes, but he admitted that the synchromesh was 'not powerful' by current standards, although he emphasised the reliability. It is a pity that manufacturers' replies are not seen more often with road tests and reader surveys in the motoring press. A useful dialogue might result.

Two years after *Motor Sport*'s intense look at the E type, *Road and Track* had another crack at a 3.8-litre car, this time a fixed head. They echoed their previous good comments, then opined that the car had become established as the greatest crumpet collector known to man. But they also emphasised the desire of many Americans for a new engine to replace the fifteen-year-old XK unit and said that the transmission was totally archaic. 'In 1964, one can expect synchromesh on first in a $6,000 car, and furthermore, one can expect synchromesh that really synchronises with the other three, but in the case of the Jaguar, this is not so.'

They liked the interior improvements over the earlier 3.8-litre cars, although, as average Americans, they still found it hard to get in and out. They also offered some sage advice: 'The Jaguar is a complex automobile, and therefore difficult and expensive to service, and the prospective purchaser would be well advised to bear this in mind before putting his money down. The factory is well aware of the service problem confronting it in the American market . . . however, one feels that Jaguar has itself on occasions compounded the problem by launching a new model on the market before it has been thoroughly tested under American conditions.

Road and Track went on to comment on the number of letters it had had from Jaguar owners with service problems, and said: 'At $6,000, the E type is within the reach of a surprising number of people, but, because of the complex nature of the car, potential owners should make sure there is still some money left after making their monthly payments to pay for routine servicing and repairs.'

Apart from that, the Californian magazine loved the car, as did the redoubtable Mr Bolster, when, in October 1964, he again led the field with a road test of the 4.2-litre E type fixed-head coupé for *Autosport*. 'Let me say, straight away, that it is a superb car, a veritable magic carpet, which can make haste unobtrusively and automatically achieves fantastic averages,' he said after a quick blip across France. It seems there was some urgency in the journey, and the E type did not let him down. His vivid description read like this: 'I had a most dramatic drive to catch a boat when an aircraft was grounded by fog, and I was able to motor disgracefully fast in congested areas without exciting the fury of gendarmes or the populace.' The way Bolster drove they probably could not catch him. He thought that the 4.2-litre engine seemed smoother than previous Jaguar units and found that it was delightful to have a fully-synchronised gearbox which permitted really rapid changes. He said the brakes were much better than those of previous E types and he found the seats more comfortable than the old ones, although he still thought there could be more room for a tall driver.

Then that other doyen of the motoring world popped up with one of the first comparative tests. Bill Boddy compared his road test 4.2-litre coupé with a 3.8 version being run by his assistant editor as a staff car. *Motor Sport* reported that the 4.2-litre engine was quieter without a doubt than the 3.8, and that it seemed less fussy than the 3.8 at the red line on the rev counter; acceleration seemed much the same and the carburetters on both were rather lumpy and erratic. The new starter motor was noisier, according to *Motor Sport*, and, like Bolster, they said the 4.2 gearbox was much better. First gear could be selected at 40 mph with no drama, and this particular gear could also be selected when at rest 'nine times out of ten.' Such sophistication and such praise, when you consider that they added 'which is more than can be said for the box on the 3.8 version.' Boddy and colleagues must have helical teeth. Handling was reported as being much the same (which was hardly surprising, as it was the same chassis), and the brakes were better. Like Bolster, *Motor Sport* also found the seats to their liking.

Battling Bill then proceeded to blaze round every available British motorway at speeds of up to 140 mph, being overtaken only once, by a Lotus Elan on trade plates. He repassed it immediately, and 'may I say emphatically, that there were no incidents of any kind, nor did we see any evidence that any one of the hundreds of cars overtaken was in any way inconvenienced.' Both Boddy and his passenger 'were happily married men with children and no desire to be snuffed out and, apart from one van which pulled across suddenly in front of us on the M6, there was never the most momentary suggestion that we should. If this account proves that England has at least some motorways which expedite fast travel in this very congested island, our expedition will have served its purpose.' Sad to say, a panic-stricken Government committee imposed the blanket 70 mph limit soon afterwards, following a series of motorway pile-ups in the fog. Boddy promptly organised a mighty petition, which was duly ignored by the non-driving transport minister, Barbara Castle, in much the same way as many E type drivers have ignored the 70 mph limit without having an accident since. An E type doing 100 mph is infinitely more safe than many hotted-up saloons travelling at the same speed.

Pristine and sparkling: the first of the 4.2-litre fixed-head coupés wings along an English country road.

'Grace, pace—and now, more space' was the best description of the first Two Plus Two, seen here heading for the continent on one of its English road tests.

Autocar's 4.2 fixed-head coupé test, which followed a little later, gave a clue to how the new engine could heat up if run consistently in the red sector of the rev counter. Their 4.2-litre managed an average of 153 mph over two runs, with 156 mph in one of the directions, to become the fastest car they had ever tested. Their drivers all liked the new improvements and said that the bigger engine was much more relaxing for driver and passenger alike. 'In fact, driving a car of this calibre sets one a higher standard and one feels almost duty-bound to treat the machine with as much care and respect as the engineers have used in creating it,' said *Autocar*. The Jaguar men must have loved reading that, and their chief, Sir William Lyons, must have liked the comments of *The Motor* on their 4.2 as well.

It was 'a combination of performance, handling, looks and refinement . . . still unequalled at the price,' said *The Motor*. And the price, in days before inflation, was still almost exactly the same as that of the first E type four years before, despite all those improvements. *The Motor*'s 4.2 litre became the fastest car they had ever tested at more than 150 mph. Like everybody else, they loved the gearbox and other changes. They noted a dramatic improvement in oil consumption to around 400 miles per pint, because of new oil control rings and warned of the consequences of not keeping the brake fluid in good condition. This was realised after they saw their brake discs glow bright red during a severe Alpine descent, and needless to say, they were thankful that their fluid was not old and gummy.

The new seats were well treated too, with one driver completing a trip back from Italy to Britain in one day without any aches or pains. He must have had a deadline to meet, but then E types are like that. *The Motor* men added that the E type 'belongs to the (happily) growing ranks of modern sports and GT cars in which outstanding handling has been combined with the ride of a comfortable saloon....' Happy, indeed, but a sign that others were catching up with Jaguar, although not with the price.

Bolster was slow off the mark for once with the first road test of the Two Plus Two. *The Motor* did theirs in April 1966, *Autocar* in June, and *Autosport* not until August, although that in *Road and Track* in October 1966 is the most significant, because it was at the American market that the Two Plus Two was chiefly aimed. 'Grace, space—and now, more space,' said *Road and Track* happily as they digested their Two Plus Two and remembered Jaguar's saloon car slogan of the 1950s: Grace, Space and Pace. 'We made a perfect demonstration of the car's utility as a Two Plus Two after the Pebble Beach concours when we transported a pair of stranded golf widows back to their hotel in Monterey,' said the men from *Road and Track*. 'They were admittedly a bit derisive about the lack of knee room, but if we had been driving one of the original X K E coupés, they would still be stranded at Del Monte Lodge. So the Two Plus Two was an even bigger crumpet collector than their 1964 coupé. The testers, who had emphasised earlier that, if there were any mistakes in basic body design, the E type was still undoubtedly one of the sexiest shapes ever to catch a lady's eye.

Golf widows apart, *Road and Track* managed to pack 2,500 miles into ten days— 'we don't often get to drive a road test car this much'—and said, with some surprise, that nothing went wrong, except for an indicator which needed an occasional tap to get it going at the proper rate. You do not need an indicator to see which way the wind blows. And even the clock kept time, said the amazed Americans. The E type had really arrived over there. They were thankful that there was no polished walnut to worry about and would have been thankful for the automatic transmission if they had been the type, like many Americans, who were weary of 'shifting and clutching' through heavy day-to-day traffic. *Road and Track* did not mind the standing-start quarter mile time being up to 16.7 seconds and the two-way top speed being down to 128 mph. They were a bit worried though that the engine seemed to run rather hot at 80–100 degrees Centigrade!

'It is not easy for us to assign the Jaguar its proper place in the automotive scheme of things,' said *Road and Track*, 'we expect a lot from it and we get a lot. Yet there are curious little disappointments such as louvres that are not quite perfect . . . and the test car was so full of rattles and squeaks that it almost made us laugh.' On the other hand, it was obvious that they expected too much, said the magazine. 'Because of its beautiful lines, its handsome engine, its luxurious interior, its good road manners, its excellent brakes and all its other virtues, we tend to class it with cars costing far more, and thus demand the same sort of perfection that we have a right to expect from a $10,000 Iso, a $14,000 Ferrari or a $15,000 Aston Martin.... This may be unfortunate but it also demonstrates just how great a value the Jaguar really is.'

Back in Britain, *The Motor* liked the Two Plus Two automatic because it was the first E type they had tried that was suitable for six-footers and family men who wanted to extend their ownership for another seven years or more. It was also acceptable if you had passengers who did not mind travelling transversely in the back. The automatic change was not perfect in their opinion, though. They considered that the Borg Warner box was not so smooth as the Americans might expect and not so versatile as the English enthusiasts might want. It fell between two stools, and their opinions were later proved to be true, in Britain, at least.

Using the D2 drive range, *The Motor*'s car reached 60 mph in a 'leisurely' 12.3 seconds, reduced to 9.1 seconds by the use of the D1 range, against a manual coupé's seven seconds or so. However, with that sort of acceleration and 136 mph, it was still quicker than any other automatic car they had tested. Funny how it went so much faster than *Road and Track*'s car. Fuel consumption at eighteen to twenty miles per gallon was, surprisingly, much the same as that of previous E types. *The Motor* found that handling was affected by the automatic gearbox and gave some wise advice to readers on how to corner a cat with a mind of its own:

> 'Without the drive line rigidity, it is impossible to vary the attitude of the car on the throttle in the way that you can on the manual car; stability is considerably enhanced by the use of SP41HR tyres, which further limit slip angles until final rear end breakaway, now rather more sudden, but at very high cornering forces.
>
> 'Up to this point the handling remains neutral and the car goes just as fast wherever you aim it, but if you prefer a more obvious final oversteer and want to corner fast, you can brake sufficiently deep into a corner to provoke the tail and use the extreme sensitivity of the steering to warn you that this is about to happen; when it does you can release the brakes, put on the power and balance the car on the throttle. This is smoother if you use left foot braking so that releasing the brakes and starting to accelerate appears to be one continuous movement.'

Now read that again and imagine trying to do that with the hopelessly light power steering fitted to later E types.

Autocar screwed 141 mph out of a manual Two Plus Two—were all the road test cars exactly the same?—although they admitted that the needle veered into the red section of the rev counter as it had been prone to do on their previous tests. They also managed a standing-start quarter mile in 15.4 seconds and reached sixty miles per hour from rest in 7.4 seconds. Handling techniques were far more conventional than those deployed by *The Motor* with their automatic Two Plus Two. *Autocar* suggested that you simply kept your foot steady on the accelerator when cornering, and also made the observation that the E type had one of the flattest steady speed fuel graphs of any car. It bettered 20 miles per gallon at 100 miles per hour.

Bolster was thrilled with the automatic Two Plus Two when he eventually tried it for a full-length test involving London traffic, although he found parking a bit of a chore with the considerable length of the car and its poor steering lock. He commented, too, that the Borg Warner model eight gearbox was not so smooth as some of the more sophisticated American equivalents. He thought the lighting arrangements at the front were pitiful, and asked for the summary dismissal of the person who designed the prop which held up the back door. Apparently the door fell on him twice while he was manoeuvring his two large dogs out of the back of the car. The dogs liked the Two Plus Two, though, said Bolster, who, no doubt, was protected by his famous deerstalker.

Next year, the *Autocar* tested one of the Series One and a Half drop-heads and commented on the new open headlights, which they said were hardly any better than before and cost two to three miles per hour in top speed. They said that the new heater was better, but the ventilation with the hood up was just as bad. The handling was still superb, although the test car went soggy at the back after one thousand miles of hammering. The brakes also went soft during the 3,000 mile test, but they were relieved that the E type had an efficient handbrake. Fuel consumption, despite 'very spirited' motoring abroad and a 140 mph maximum speed run, averaged 22 mpg. The flat-out run was achieved with the hood up, and a similar maximum speed run with the hood down was recorded at 130 mph, probably the first time such comparative figures on an E type had been seen in print.

The car, which had done 19,000 miles at the end of the test, seemed rather well used. Various electrical connections had fallen off and the hood came unstuck in parts. But all the same, *Autocar* concluded: 'The E type's performance, ex-works price, steering, roadholding, tractability, economy, comfort and good looks may be matched by other sports or GT cars, but no one of them has the lot.'

Douglas Armstrong of *Speedworld International* also had one of the rare road tests in a Series One and a Half roadster, regretting only the passing of Jaguar's old separate starter button, the poor ventilation (testers were using Ford's through-flow Cortina ventilation as a standard then) limited luggage accommodation and headlights not in keeping with the car's performance. However, he liked the actual performance, the price, the low fuel consumption, the quiet engine, 'fantastic brakes' and undiminished eye-appeal. Yes, you guessed it, he had the same car the month before *Autocar*. Now, who did not change the brake pads and back shockers between tests?

Road and Track were less lyrical than of late when they tried out a Series Two fixed-head coupé in August 1969. Their headlines said soberly that safety and emission control regulations had resulted in some changes to a long-time favourite.

After detailing all the awful changes to the engine, they went on to say, that exciting as the E type was when it was introduced in 1961, time had made it rather dated inside and out. 'The interior,' said *Road and Track*, 'though retaining that wonderful smell of leather and the aura of a cockpit with a million dials and controls, lacks the spaciousness and ergonomics of more recently designed cars.' They did not like the lack of numbers on the heater controls or temperature gauge, either, suspecting that Jaguar did not want people to know just how hot their engine got or care how hot the occupants became. Acceleration figures on the Series Two were much the same as earlier cars up to 119 mph—then, what with air conditioning and anti-smog, their Series Two would go no faster. It did not matter much though, said *Road and Track*, because top speed, by then, had become pretty academic anyway in the States. The gearbox, for once, came in for good comment, shifting beautifully with infallible synchromesh in the hands of its American testers. Chevrolet and Porsche had overtaken it on cornering power although *Road and Track* felt that Jaguar could do better.

They had to wait two years for Jaguars to do better with Series Two cars going slower and slower, until the Series Three was unveiled. Everybody in the professional

The Series Three: its character softened.

motoring world and a lot of non-professionals knew something new was on the way. *The Motor* found the V12 nearly as quick as their original 3.8-litre car, but a good deal thirstier, at 14.5 mpg. However, it did 146 mph and left long lines of black rubber again by reaching 50 mph from rest in 4.7 seconds. What was really impressive though, was the massive increase in torque, which *The Motor* thought made even the manual E type now seem like an automatic. But the appeal of the E type had changed, said the road testers; its character had softened. The new power steering was too light, in their opinion, and the brakes seemed at their limit. They appreciated being able to use their six foot five inch tall road tester in the car, and liked the improved heating and ventilation, although they wished it had been improved further.

Bolster was as enthusiastic as ever in *Autosport*, when referring to the engine. It gave a standard of silence, smoothness, and flexibility which was largely without equal and though these things may not be of ultimate importance in a sporting car, he said, one can imagine how they will be valued when this power unit becomes available in more luxurious Jaguars, and 'it is hoped' the Daimler limousine. (We never thought we would live to hear old blood and thunder talking about E types and limousines seriously in the same breath!)

He said the sheer ease of running was now uncanny, but he disliked the V12's steering, especially on slippery roads; surely though it could have been possible to offer an alternative setting for this side of the Atlantic, with less power assistance and more feel?

Autocar was getting distinctly nostalgic though when they tested a V12 roadster late in 1973. They commented on its considerable improvement in stowage space, superbly smooth and tractable engine, excellent braking, roadholding and ride, poor minor controls and ventilation. They then remembered its remarkable value for money at £3,378.38 on the road, and said:

> 'There is a very distinct paucity of open sports cars on the market at this time. With the disappearance from this market of Ferrari, Maserati and Aston Martin, the choice has narrowed considerably. The American Federal regulations may well banish fully open sports cars forever, but in the meantime, it is still very pleasant to be able to appreciate the joys of open-air motoring in considerable luxury in the E type.'

The E type had come full circle, from the rorty-torty 3.8s that took the world by storm in 1961 with more than a suspicion of hotting up for the road testers, to the great lolloping near-limousine of a V12 that could still ruffle your hair. Within a year of that *Autocar* test, the last E type had been built. The classic age had ended.

V

The Racing E types

RACING E TYPES split neatly into three categories: virtually standard production cars, lightweights, and modsport freaks. In tribute to the E type it should be remembered that its racing career started with standard cars in 1961, that it continued with some success with the lightweight racers, went on to dominate in modsport classes for the best part of a decade, and that it finally wound up back where it started with standard V12 cars winning all the production sports car championships that mattered on both sides of the Atlantic.

The late lamented Graham Hill scored the first racing win for an E type in April 1961. He led home fellow Grand Prix star Innes Ireland in an Aston Martin DB4GT that cost twice as much as the E type, with Roy Salvadori third in another E type. The E types were virtually showroom models, complete even to cigar lighters, which was more than you could say for the highly-developed ultra-lightweight Aston. Scores of early successes followed for the E types, culminating in Salvadori finishing fourth at Le Mans in 1962 with the great American Jaguar lover, Briggs Cunningham.

The tale of 63 CJU, a grey-green fixed-head coupé, is typical of the early racing E types. It is believed to be the car that rolled off the production line in the autumn of 1961, to be registered CUT 7 by one Elmer Richard (Dick) Protheroe. Its chassis number was 860004, the fourth fixed head to be produced, and it would seem that Protheroe, who had campaigned an old XK in club racing for years, was held in high regard by the Works. He was one of the first private customers to get an E type.

He took delivery of CUT 7 with a 'production' D type head and cams, triple 45DCOE Weber carburetters and competition wide rim wire wheels. Somebody at Jaguar's must have known what the garage proprietor from Husbands Bosworth, Leicestershire, was going to do with his gleaming new coupé. They obviously considered that the well-proven D type head was a better boost for power than modified versions of the ultimately more efficient straight port head used on standard E types. It should be noted that the production D type head (as distinct from the wide-angled Le Mans head), used an ordinary C type casting of the sort that was an optional extra on the XK140. The only difference is large inlet valves measuring 1.875 ins and whatever gas flowing the customer fancied. When set up with D type cams and triple Webers, plus perhaps a six-branch bunch-of-bananas exhaust manifold, the result is a very pleasant engine giving around 30 bhp more than the standard unit, which, of course, uses triple two-inch SU carburetters and a more mundane cast exhaust manifold. You get more low-speed torque with the alternative head, too.

Protheroe made a few other modifications as well. In the light of his experience with the XK, he whipped off the front discs and bolted on thicker ones intended for a Mark IX saloon; he got rid of the awful Kelsey-Hayes servo, substituting a normal vacuum unit, and changed the electric oil pressure and water temperature gauges for the mechanical units from his XK. Finally he added an oil temperature gauge for the engine's safety; all very sensible and acceptable modifications. Dick was also lucky in that CUT 7 left the factory with a close-ratio gearbox—eminently suitable for racing—and worth getting hold of, if possible.

With these changes, CUT 7 sallied forth to meet the mighty racing Astons and Ferraris and did very well. It ended the season as winner of the over 3,000 cc class in the *Autosport* championship at very little cost to its owner; in fact, a really successful weekend racer. It was becoming obvious, though, that the standard-steel E types, which weighed in at the best part of $1\frac{1}{4}$ tons, were going to be outclassed by the titanium and aluminium Italian aristocrats such as the Ferrari 250 GTO. So men like Protheroe turned their attention to lightweight E types and he sold his coupé to Roger Mac. Roger won several races with it in 1963 and made his reputation in production sports car racing. Protheroe kept his number, CUT 7, so the coupé was re-registered—probably 636 CJU— and some time after doing sterling service for young Mr Mac, the car disappeared onto the roads of Britain. In the next ten years it

Code-named E 2 A, this immediate predecessor of the E type, was raced by Briggs Cunningham at the Le Mans race in 1960. Although setting the fastest lap in practice, the car did not finish. It was later given a 3.8-litre engine instead of its 3-litre unit used at Le Mans and it was raced with some success in America. Today it is back in England, in the Guy Griffiths collection.

The first E type to win a race, pictured in the hands of Graham Hill. This car is now in the Robert Danny collection.

acquired a radio and sunshine roof and popped up again, very cheap, at £750 in the classified advertisement section of *Exchange and Mart*, under a Henley telephone number. Eventually a Jaguarophile named Ted Walker bought it and after some attention to the brakes, he put 636 CJU back on the track and enjoyed a moderate amount of success in historic races. To see it now, it looks very much as Protheroe left it. The paintwork is the same colour and the absence of bumpers reminds you of its D type ancestry and the marque racing of the 1950s and 1960s.

The lightweight E types were conceived when the manufacturers' championship was changed from sports cars to Grand Turismo cars in 1963. This let in cars such as the 250 GTO, which took full advantage of the loosely-worded regulations. All a manufacturer had to do in 1963 was to produce evidence that 100 identical units had been made, or were scheduled to be made, in twelve months and they could enter. The word identical applied only to the engine, chassis and running gear and evidence presented was, naturally, rather scanty. Also, you could do what you liked with the bodywork, and believe me, Ferrari did. The old master took the lightweight Pininfarina coachwork from the 1960 Superfast and the engine from the racing Testa Rossa. After all, the mechanical side was similar to around 100 Ferrari 250 GTs produced since 1958. Sad to say, Jaguar had not built a pure racing car for years, but they felt that they ought to do something to help the faithful, like Protheroe, and perhaps get some useful publicity. They had been giving John Coombs, of Guildford, a hand with his racing E type, and felt that this was the way to go. They also realised that they might learn something from the development of such cars. By the end of 1962, the Coombs E type had many special parts including a thinner-than-usual steel

monocoque. As it worked out, of the dozen or so lightweight E types made, none was exactly the same.

Nearly all began life as right-hand drive open two seaters with aluminium hard tops, rather than the floppy fibreglass top that was acceptable on the standard-steel machines. Light alloy was used wherever possible, except for parts vital to strength, like the suspension sub-frames. Suspension geometry was varied, stiffer torsion bars and springs were used, Spax or Koni shock absorbers were substituted and anti-roll bars uprated.

Mark IX front brake discs were fitted and Girling came up with some alloy calipers. The back suspension acquired bits and pieces from the heavier Mark Ten saloon, to give it more strength, and sometimes a ZF differential was fitted in place of the cast iron Powr-Lok unit. Peg-drive D type wheels were fitted in most cases and the whole body was made in alloy, a tribute to the rivetting skills of Jaguar craftsmen. Engines varied enormously, but they were all well above the 300 bhp mark, and one, which must be the wildest six ever, churned out 344 bhp with the aid of its Lucas fuel injection and special long-exhaust system. Four-and-a-half litre XK racing units are only just starting to approach these power outputs more than twelve years later. But those alloy-block engines had a weak point: the block. It was prone to overheating, oil leaks and all sorts of trouble.

Apparently the alloy blocks needed gentle treatment until they had thoroughly

Great rivals: Roy Salvadori leads Innes Ireland in an Aston Martin DB4GT at Snetterton in September 1961. Note the number on Salvadori's car, BUY I. This now appears on many cars entered by John Coombs.

Side by side, two of the lightweights
battle it out in the Guards Trophy
race at Brands Hatch in August 1964.

warmed up all over. If they were used at full pitch as soon as the flag fell in a short
race they were likely to blow up, partly because the massive ZF gearbox was more
rigid than the alloy cylinder block. In fact, the extra weight of the gearbox virtually
made up for the weight saved by the alloy block and some of the lightweights have now
been converted to cast iron blocks and Jaguar gearboxes.

Wider wheels were tried on the lightweights, with other modifications, but after
a while they were not enough to keep the cars up with their Ferrari and AC Cobra
opposition, so in 1965 the lightweights were retired to club racing and finally to today's
historic races, which they lap up.

One of the most famous lightweights was called Rosie. This red car was first
registered on 12 July 1963, in the name of Peter Sutcliffe, a well-known Jaguar racer
of the time. It won several races in 1963 and 1964 and went to South Africa in 1965,
where it finished, never lower than third, in all eight races entered. Sutcliffe sold the
car to Red Rose Motors, of Chester, via Richard Bond, and in 1966 it was sold to
Richard Vincent, who kept it another year before selling it to Bob Jennings, who sold

Side by side, two of the lightweights battle it out in the Guards Trophy race at Brands Hatch in August 1964.

it to Mike MacDowel, the then British hill climb champion. MacDowel won numerous hill climbs with Rosie, before eventually selling it to Jaguar collector Brian Corser in 1968. He converted it into a road car with very little work, and today its finish is such that it can easily win a concours.

Brian fitted a standard E type exhaust system, changed the sprint axle to a 3.31 to 1 road ratio, refitted the original aluminium wheels in place of the racing magnesium wear, and fitted road shock absorbers and petrol tank. He also popped in carpets and headlining, bits and pieces of trim and fitted more powerful headlights. And that's all it took to turn Rosie into the super road car which she still is. The fuel injection gives no trouble and it gives 17 mpg; the same as a normal road-going E type. I doubt whether there has been another racing car built since that would take so little modification to make it into a smooth-running, comfortable, civilised road car.

All in all, the lightweights were the last really serious Jaguar racing sports cars. They won a variety of races against the Astons and Ferraris, and the E type was weighed in at a fraction over 2,000 lb; 100 lb lighter than the Ferraris and 500 lb lighter than the standard-steel E types. They proved to be competitive on speed, but not on reliability, and lacked factory development, which was being directed towards the mid-engined V12 racer, project X J13. The V12 engine first ran in 1962, eventually producing more than 500 bhp in twin-overhead cam form at 8,000 rpm in 1967.

Meanwhile, the private owners soldiered on in the modified sports car classes with some considerable success, winning hundreds of races, well into the 1970s. Many purists consider the modsport classes of club racing to be a joke. But the drivers who take part are real enthusiasts who are totally committed to their car.

Two of the first front runners were John Quick and Warren Pearce, followed by men such as John Burbidge, Brian Murphy and Bob Scantelbury, who still race E types. John Quick bought his car, WOO 11, second-hand for £1,200 in 1964. Within a month, he was driving the fixed-head coupé in Holland's Tulip Rally with nothing more than a good service and a couple of big spotlights as preparation. The brakes faded badly and the exhaust pipes fell off and had to be tied on with wire, but he

One of the famous Briggs Cunningham lightweight twins that are still mopping up the historic races.

One of the greatest of the early mod-sports cars: John Quick's coupé pictured at the Jaguar Drivers' Club meeting at Silverstone in 1970.

finished fourth in his class! As soon as he returned to England, John had the brakes beefed up, Koni shock absorbers fitted and the engine rebuilt with balanced crank and gas-flowed head. The suspension was lowered, and thicker anti-roll bars and stiffer springs were fitted. The axle ratio was changed to 3.77 to 1, wider wheels were fitted and the bill for £500 was paid. Then it was back to the Continent and second place in its class in another Dutch rally, with the brakes under fire again. So it was back to Britain for cooling vents to be cut in the front wings and air scoops and breathers fitted for the rear discs. A fiery D type exhaust system sprouted from under the passenger door, racing tyres were fitted, and the bill for £600 paid.

To quote John and his unflappable co-driver in the *Motor Sport* of January 1967: 'We entered the car for the Alpine Rally in August 1965, and the best we can say

about that was that it turned out to be a fine social junket, starting in Marseille and ending in Monte Carlo. The journey down was not without its moments, as when it got dark we realised that long flames came out of the exhaust pipes on overrun. After a substantial meal in Tournon, on the N7, we cleared five pavement tables of diners with two quick bursts on the throttle. . . .'

During that year the faithful second-hand E type covered 33,000 miles on the road, in rallies, races and sprints and suffered only a broken valve guide at the end of a season which had seen such violent motoring that the brakes were faded going uphill in one mountain rally and the sump was holed after leaving the road in another.

That winter woo 11 came in for a certain amount of attention. It turned into a track car. The head was modified by the legendary Harry Weslake whose works at Rye in Sussex were still being visited by such celebrities as Dan Gurney for his Grand Prix cars and Bill Heynes for Jaguar development work. The engine was bored out to 3.9-litres, a 4.2 clutch and gearbox was fitted, everything readily removable from the body was thrown out and a flimsy fibreglass bonnet was clipped on. The doors and bootlid were made from the same material and track wheels and tyres were

Prolific winner John Burbidge collects yet another garland by courtesy of his Thruxton Racing Services' fixed-head coupé.

fitted. After initial testing of 100 laps of Brands Hatch at 5,000 revs, John decided to have the steering solid mounted: that is without the rubber bushes which reduce road shock. This needs an exceptional amount of precision in setting up and takes a couple of days of skilled work, but makes the car more responsive.

Win after win followed and after one victory at Castle Coombe, which included a class record lap of the Wiltshire circuit, John recorded in his diary that while doing his lap of honour, waving his trophy out of the window and steering with his knees, his ultra-responsive machine nearly went into a ditch. In two year's racing, WOO 11 won forty-eight awards, at an average of one per weekend during the season, and ended up as one of the fastest Jaguars in the world, alongside another legendary E type, the Warren Pearce modsports car.

Warren's E type roadster won seventeen outright victories from thirty-five starts in 1966. It started its life as a badly-repaired 1962 roadster that had been in a big shunt. Warren saw it as the cheapest car he could buy with all independent suspension, disc brakes all round, a robust and powerful engine like the one in his old racing XK 150, and the same infallible, if slow, gearbox. With no special preparation other than fitting racing tyres, it could lap Brands Hatch in sixty-five seconds; only six seconds slower than the fastest modsports racers of the day. The substitution of a 3.54 axle ratio for its original 2.9 and the fitting of Koni dampers all round reduced the lap time to sixty-three seconds, and then the handling had to be improved. Six-inch rims were fitted at the front and 6½ inch rims were fitted at the back. The rear suspension was lowered, longer wishbones fitted and the shims were removed from the drive-shafts. Mark IX brake discs, alloy calipers, a Lockheed servo, a 3.9-litre engine, D type cams, and triple Webers speeded things up too. Brands Hatch lap times came down to the sixty second mark, but as he needed still more speed the gearbox was swopped for a close ratio job and he had Minilite centre-lock wheels fitted. The axle ratio was changed to 3.77 to 1 and Warren produced what he claimed was the best 'bunch of bananas ever'; he says the exhaust system alone took two seconds off his Silverstone lap time. The car, despite weighing 2,550 lb, also proved itself faster round Mallory Park than the record set by a Le Mans winning Ferrari 250 LM.

Somebody once remarked to me that the story of 7 CXW was also typical of racing Jaguars. It was bought by Ken Baker in 1961 and was raced with considerable success for the next couple of years or so. Notable wins for 7 CXW, before it was written off by Ken in the BOAC 1,000 kilometre race, included a runaway victory at Brands Hatch on Boxing Day 1962, where it was racing against such opposition as Zagato Aston Martins. Nothing more was heard of 7 CXW (despite that registration number it was never a road car), until it reappeared, repaired with the aid of Lenham's fibreglass effects, in the hands of Rob Schroeder; he proceeded to break many club lap records in 1965, 1966 and 1967, during duels with Warren Pearce and John Quick.

It was in this period that the car became best known to the public with its Post Office red and white livery (which inspired the colour scheme of the author's E type.) It survived several major crashes which needed near total rebuilds, before entering another dark period, after which it was bought by Alan Minshaw, who did little except write it off again at Oulton Park. But 7 CXW returned once more to the fray in 1971, when it appeared wearing the green and yellow livery of Forward Engineering.

It won nine modsport races that year with fourteen second places, plus a class record at Oulton Park.

The *Jaguar Driver* magazine said: 'It is likely, if an accurate record could be traced, that this car has won more awards during its history in private hands than any other Jaguar; although it should be said that WOO 11 has probably won more awards for one owner against the several owners of 7 CXW.

'The technical development of 7 CXW, which started its life as an ex-factory standard model, has, of course, been extensive. It is true to say that probably the only part of the car which came out of the factory in 1961 is the chassis plate measuring $1\frac{1}{2}$ ins by $1\frac{1}{2}$ ins, bearing the number of the chassis, Z166.' That's a typical top modsports car?

Current modsport E types split up into two categories: the grand old warhorses

The E type on the right is that famous old warhorse, 7 CXW, pictured in the hands of its first owner, Ken Baker at the Crystal Palace in September 1963, with John Miles in a Turner-Ford coupé being overtaken, and Roger Mac in Dick Protheroe's first fixed-head coupé in hot pursuit. Note the battered bonnet of 7 CXW; just the start of a hard life.

such as 7 CXW, which in its last phase was prepared by Ron Beaty, and cars of
mysterious origin like the 3.8 fixed-head coupé raced by Simon Watney from Berk-
shire, plus, of course, the only competitive fuel injection V12 modsports Jaguar, raced
by Guy Beddington. Strictly speaking, Guy's car, which went tremendously fast for
short periods, should never have been raced in modsports, where fuel injection was
banned, but nobody seemed to mind. Maybe they thought Guy would not keep his
car on the track till the end of a race. Cars such as 7 CXW and later E types prepared
by Beaty are now becoming very expensive, with highly-developed 4.5-litre engines,
breathing through big Weber carburetters on Mangoletsi manifolds. This all makes
them go very fast and they are brought to a halt rather quickly by Girling's twin
servo Can Am brakes operated by a balance bar installation through Aeroquip lines.
There is no rubber in the steering mounts or on the sub-frames, to ensure extra sensi-
tivity, and fourteen-inch wheels keep the monsters on the track, with the aid of
spoilers on the front and back of the fibreglass body. It was one of these cars which
was the first to break one minute for a modsports car around Silverstone's short
circuit, Beaty proudly reports.

   Out in the backwoods, cars like Simon Watney's are still winning races. Simon
bought his 3.8-litre fixed-head coupé from a dealer called Fred Cliffe, who was
advertising it as the cheapest modsports E type ever at £1,000. That is only about
one-fifth of the cost of a really hot 4.5-litre engine alone. What Simon got was a
basically hill climb car of uncertain age. It is believed to be one of the earlier models
because of its aluminium insert dashboard, although it has no chassis or engine
numbers to confirm this. Apart from a fibreglass bonnet and plastic windows, the
shell is substantially standard, being strengthened along the sills, and fitted with a
massive roll-over bar.

   It had been fitted with ten inch, eleven inch and twelve inch Minilite or J A

The last of the really competitive six-
cylinder E type racers: the Forward
Engineering car built from the remains of 7 CXW which became the
most successful E type ever.

Pearce wheels for its selection of slicks and wet tyres, and it has brakes from a Series
Two E type with a master cylinder from an XJ6. Simon had the rear suspension
lowered by Albert Betts of AWB Motors in Clapham, South London. He underslung
the dampers on the wishbones, fitted better-looking rounded wheel arches and carried
out various engine modifications, such as fitting an XJ6 oil filter and twin oil coolers
with oversize hoses. Simon also had the head modified by Weslakes to include Isky-
pattern cams and says 'it looked too beautiful to bolt on to the car when I got it back
from them. They had made such a good job of it with its special cams and 1.91 ins
inlet valves. I could have had the biggest inlet valves—1.97 ins—but they are a bit
risky being in such close proximity to the exhaust valves.' The fuel pump was also
replaced by a dual unit from an XJ6 and after steeling himself to fit the beautiful £250
head, Simon started lapping the Silverstone short circuit in sixty-seven seconds.

Sideways, as he so often was, Guy
Beddington corners his fuel injection
V12 fixed-head coupé.

Jaguar development engineer, Peter Taylor, spins the wheels off the line at Brands Hatch; the scene of the V12's first competitive appearance and Taylor's first race. He finished fourth.

There was more to come though, and after lengthy discussions with Radbourne's Weber garage in West London, he changed the 45DCOE's jets and knocked a couple of seconds off his lap times. Eventually, in 1976, he won a race at Castle Combe, but in that moment of triumph, disaster struck.

He had fitted a spoiler like those on the super E types—and this spoiler, which Simon says did not make much difference to his speed—caused the engine to overheat and the crank to break. As this book goes to press, Simon is busy rebuilding his engine and looking forward to more races against the cars run so successfully by firms such as Forward Engineering, which have dominated British club racing for a decade.

But what about the production E type in racing? It took the 5.3-litre V12 to

make up for the handicap of emission control and the like on the 4.2-litre, and by the mid-1970s, modified sports cars with the exception of those such as Watney's had lost much of their affinity with the road cars from which they had developed. With this in mind, and the sheer cost of the top modsports cars, the current British production sports car formula was inaugurated in 1973, using price classes.

In 1974, the price classes were up to £1,200; up to £1,750; up to £4,500 and over £4,500. It was thus made possible that the production sports car champion-to-be could be driving a car from other than the most expensive class, and this is exactly what happened. The car that won from the start was a Series Three E type owned and prepared by Jaguar development engineer Peter Taylor, racing in the up to £4,500 class. Within the regulations of production sports car racing there are close limits on what is allowed, but stiffer dampers, the softer of two types of standard anti-roll bar (.75 in against .82 in), a different torsion bar in the power steering, a racing seat, an oil cooler, and experiments with the car's Michelin XWX tyre pressures was all that Peter needed. Obviously, he built the engine to the most exacting standards possible, but he says the most important point was getting the rear damper rate right so that the heavy Series Three could be prevented from pitching under braking. When this happens too much weight is taken off the rear wheels so that the rear brakes lock and send you off the tarmac. The most critical item in the car was the brake fluid, of which every kind except Duckhams boiled. Ferodo DS11 pads were fitted for better race braking, although Peter emphasises that these must not be used on the road, because they only become effective when the brake discs are glowing red hot.

His car started life as a Series Two Plus Two with a 4.2-litre engine, and was then converted to twelve cylinders as a Jaguar prototype. It became the first Series Three and was eventually converted to full production specification with the exception of the rear panel under the bumper, which stayed as it was on the Series Two. Peter bought the car from Jaguar in 1972 and after preparation wiped up the production sports car championship in no uncertain manner, having no trouble at all with the engine, and, boiling brake fluid apart, little trouble with anything else except a burst tyre, which fortunately stayed on the rim. Meanwhile Bob Tullius, was getting similar ideas about the Series Three E type in America.

Tullius persuaded British Leyland that racing the V12 would give a fillip to its flagging sales in much the same way that Merle Brennan's racing E type had when it won thirty-nine out of forty-two Sports Car Club of America production races between 1964 and 1966. British Leyland liked the idea and Tullius's Group 44, based in Virginia, and Huffacker Engineering of San Rafael, California, who had raced the Brennan car, launched a joint campaign on their respective coasts. Using data from Coventry supplied by men like Taylor, the SCCA cars needed only six months to bring up to winning form and promptly wiped up their championship, beating the E type's old rival, the Sting Ray, and other sports cars including the Ferrari 365 GTB Daytona, Porsche 911 SC, Shelby 289 Cobra, Shelby 350 GT, Alfa Romeo Montreal and AMX sports coupé, often with a ten-year-old 4.2-litre E type driven by Ed Bighouse, hot on their heels.

It would be easy to list the hundreds of successes and stories of racing E types, but there would not be room in any one book and there would always be new stories

Above: The British Leyland Quaker State E type run by Group 44.

On the left, Bob Tullius, Group 44's E type Jaguar driver in the States and on the right, his opposite number on the west coast, Lee Mueller, driver of the Huffaker Engineering, Series Three E type.

and results to come. Today, the lightweight E type, especially a dynamic duo once
owned by Briggs Cunningham and still in the blue and white colours of America, are
a force to be reckoned with in the crowd-pulling historic racing, while E types derived
from the production steel cars remain highly competitive in modified sports car
racing. The E type's production run might have ended, but the racing cars run on.

The Huffaker E type in action.

VI
Strengths and Weaknesses: Part One

THE magnificent XK six-cylinder engine is the great strength of the early E types, whereas the independent rear suspension is the Achilles heel of all E types: six-cylinder Jaguar engines rarely give trouble, but all Jaguar independent rear suspension is prone to wear and needs careful maintenance. No wonder, with all that power going through it, and it is a fact that if the rear suspension is allowed to degenerate it can be positively dangerous. But if the E type had had the old easy-to-maintain, absolutely dependable, XK or perhaps D type rear suspension, the car would have been suitable only for a smooth surface, so in many respects, the independent rear suspension is well worth all the trouble and must be considered to be one of the E type's strengths. It is also the reason why a good E type can outrun a D type. It is easier and more practical to drive and again it does not cost the fortune you have to pay for a D type.

The E type's body construction is very strong, but sadly rust prone. Rust is the pitfall with all E types. They simply rot away from the inside, although the Series Three models are reputed to be slightly better in this respect with their extra internal paint. Unfortunately, condensation accumulates inside the massive box sections that make up the monocoque of all E types, and the bonnet internals, too. The rust corrodes the metal until a pimple appears on the surface and your sparkling E type starts to crumble. But modern anti-rust treatment helps tremendously and the old cure of a pint of oil poured into the sills helps immensely. Otherwise, all E types are likely to need attention from the welder after as little as four years unless they have been exceptionally well looked after.

You should always start by checking the heart of a suspect patient: in the case of an old E type, it is the easiest part to check, and often the easiest to repair. The very first thing to do is to make sure that the car has the proper engine. Most six-cylinder XK engines are interchangeable, and, sadly, many old E types have acquired engines from the Mark Two saloon over the years, or perhaps, the Mark Ten, which needed only a sump change to slot in. The engines may look alike if they have triple SU carburetters fitted, but their giveaway number is stamped on the right-hand side of the block above the oil filter and on the front of the cylinder head. Compare these numbers with the one stamped on the chassis plate under the petrol filter, and if they are different, ring up Jaguar and make sure that the replacement engine is that for an E type.

Normally, the engine should run quietly and smoothly, with an even tick-over. An uneven tick-over is often caused by incorrect synchronisation of the carburetters or worn spindles in the carburetters themselves. Carburetter repairs and synchronisation are not simple and should be left to the experts to avoid frustration. If there is any clattering, it may simply be a timing chain, and can often be cured by adjusting the chain at the top. Even if the clatter comes from the bottom chain, it is not too serious. If, however, the clatter comes from the valve gear, then it may be three days' solid work for a specialist, which can be rather expensive. Oil pressure is vital, of course, and if the gauge shows less than 40 lb per square inch at 3,000 rpm, or more than 60 lb per sq in when cold, get it checked on a mechanical gauge. Less than 40 lb can be a faulty oil pressure sensor, which costs about £5, and will show up with the mechanical check, or it could be a worn oil pump, loose oil pipes, faulty pressure relief valve or split O-ring, all of which are not difficult to replace. Or it could, of course, mean that a major bottom end overhaul is needed, which, as we all know, costs a lot. The wonderful old 3.8-litre engine used to be an oil burner, so do not worry too much at a clean blue haze on acceleration, but do worry about a smoke-screen, and that applies to all Jaguar engines, although the later XK engines and the V12 unit are not bad on oil. Piston trouble can mean a new engine, but is not frequently encountered on E types, which tend to be driven harder than the other Jaguars, and as a result keep their engines cleaner inside. They do sometimes suffer from head gasket trouble

A specially-made 3.8-litre rolling chassis, showing most of the points where the trouble starts.

though, and this shows itself particularly when it blows out a pint or so of water after a run of a few miles at 3,000 rpm or so. With a V12 engine, carry out all these sort of checks, and be especially wary of misfiring, especially on early models. This can mean a whole new transistorised ignition.

Gearboxes are virtually indestructible, although the early Moss box on the 3.8-litre models rarely has any synchromesh left. With odd exceptions, it is slow to change and is best substituted with the close ratio 4.2 box from the late 1964, 1965, 1966, or early 1967 roadster. Fixed-head coupés in late 1964, 1965, and early 1966 had this box too, and in my opinion, it is the best unit fitted to any of the six-cylinder models. The earlier box had a pronounced whine in first gear as standard, and made a noise in second and third too, but should have been quiet in top. Reverse is usually raucous. On the 4.2-litre box, first gear is frequently a bit noisy, second quieter and third and top silent. Reverse should be reasonably sweet. A good test of the synchromesh on the 4.2-litre box is changing into first gear at speed, although, of course, you must not engage the clutch when you are doing this. If the stick slips into first without any fuss, the box is good. If not, do not worry too much: they are not very expensive, although you must remove the engine to change the gearbox. Beware of any signs of the job having been done without removing the engine, such as weld marks around the gearbox tunnel. You have to hack away an awful lot of metal to change a gearbox without taking out the engine.

Then you come to the Achilles heel, the rear suspension. Axle ratios are usually 3.07, or 3.31. although some cars have 2.93, 3.54, 3.77 or 4.09; but even with the highest ratio, acceleration should be around the seven second mark for 0 to 60 mph in a manual car. The most obvious sign of trouble is a leaking differential, which can smother the inboard rear discs with oil. This can be caused by heat from the brake discs, by distortion, due to overheating if the oil level is too low, or by pumping out oil because of a blocked breather or overfilling (the latter can occur when topping up the differential with the rear end only jacked up). Oil around the rear discs can come from the inboard rear brakes, too, but more about those later.

After the differential, the next most likely parts to be worn are the Metalastik bushes between the subframe and the body, bottom pivot bearings of the rear stub axle carriers, the inner needle roller bearings at the inboard end of the wishbones and the anti-roll bar mountings. After a visual inspection, the best way to check the rear end is on the road. Drive backwards and forwards quickly, listening for clunks and clicks, which can mean worn universal joints, stub axle splines or bottom pivots. Then try a long fast corner, and if there is any directional instability or wallowing, it is probably the Metalastik mountings. Bottoming on a rough road is usually caused by weak shock absorbers and, or, springs, which can also be checked by bouncing the car when it is stationary. But as you slow down after your long fast corner, pick a smooth surface and listen for any axle whine. It should be silent, or, at the worst, making very little noise. Then, when you stop, jack up the car and see if the wheel bearings have much float—a little is acceptable—then with the handbrake applied or the car in gear, see if there is any play in the universal joints. If there is any, it must be attended to at once.

The front suspension is less complicated. Just listen for clunks and clicks and

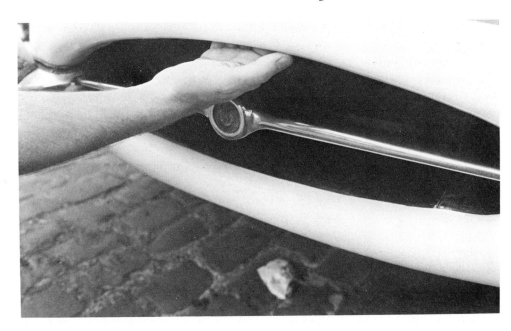

Don't just give your E type a pat on the nose—feel inside for rust.

check the steering play. There should be no wasted movement at all in the steering, apart from a little movement on the rack rubber mountings. If there is play anywhere else, start at the top. The universal joints in the steering column are prone to wear, and so are the rubber rack mountings. Like all Jaguar racks, there can be play there too; then check the top and bottom ball joints and the track-rod ends. These can be checked by levering the suspension sideways. None of these joints is too expensive, and rarely are they all worn out. It is usually a case of replacing one or the other.

Make sure to check anything rubber with great care: everything made of this material is surprisingly expensive. The rubber mountings holding the sub-frame to the body and the anti-roll bar and radius arm rubbers are particularly important from the safety and handling point of view. The rubber gaiters on the steering rack and swivels must be in good condition, too, or else these components will soon wear out and obvious items like radiator hoses need careful attention. Replacements are expensive, as are the door seals, which are prone to let in water at the best of times.

This only leaves the clutch and the brakes to check of the major running gear. With the brakes, look for pads rusted in their carriers, glazed, scored or juddering discs, leaking brake and master cylinders, worn brake lines and any obvious visual faults. Beware of broken hand-brake cables and leaking rear brake cylinder seals: they both take many hours to replace in most cases and cost far more than on most other cars. With the rear brake seals, it is best to remove the entire back suspension assembly and overhaul everything while you have it out of the car. Handbrakes are rarely efficient and usually it is a case of adjusting them to pass the Department of the Environment test and then accepting that their efficiency will deteriorate rapidly.

Check the air scoop to the rear brakes on a Series Three car, too. The scoop has minimal ground clearance and damage frequently ensues when the car is driven onto a garage hydraulic lift. If you can make the clutch slip or the pedal only works the clutch near the end of its travel, it has not much life left and is best changed immediately. They last around 30,000 miles in normal circumstances. Do not try to change the clutch without removing the engine. It is not worth botching a job like that.

Of the major components, that leaves only the body, and that is the real trouble spot with all E types. Rust attacks it everywhere. Beginning at the front, look along the joints between the wings and the bonnet. Pimples here, or at right angles to the joint near the headlights, mean new wings soon and maybe a whole new bonnet. This costs a fortune and nearly as much again to fit. Then open the bonnet and check the bonnet hinge mounting beam. There is often considerable corrosion here, but it can be patched up quite cheaply if it is caught in time, although the proper repair is quite expensive. But these patched up jobs do not show when the bonnet is shut, so, in my opinion, they are acceptable. While the bonnet is up, check the front sub-frame for corrosion or stress cracks, especially near the bulkhead, and see if the bulkhead has any dents in it. Do not touch the car if it has: it means that it has been in a major shunt and is worth nothing more than the value of its parts. Shut the bonnet again and feel inside the air intake. If you can feel loose scale it means that the nose is on the way out, and like all replacement panels on an E type, they are expensive. Then examine the bonnet again with a magnet to see how much filler has been used in repairing it. If there is no filler, your car is probably unique. But remember, the bonnet is not a stressed component and can be replaced at a price, which is more than you can say for the monocoque.

It used to be possible to get an exchange monocoque and it is still possible to fit a new floor, but the eventual cost is considerable and if this sort of repair is contemplated, do not bother about buying a smart car. It is worth remembering that the parts for a new floor cost only £50 or so from Terry Moore. But you still have to fit them and you might as well start with a scrapyard special and begin building your E type from scratch. The first point to check on the main body shell is the sills. Give them the magnet test if they appear sound, and do not worry too much if you find filler. Just make sure that it has been used only for filling in dents, not holes. If there is any fault with the sills, inside or out, get them replaced or repaired immediately. They are essential for strength and safety. The same goes for the floor and especially the radius arm mountings at the back of that area. Then check the whole rear end of the body. It is often corroded above the rear wheels round the wheel arches, the number plate or the luggage boot floor. But it is not very important, except for appearance. You can patch it up almost endlessly and the car remains safe, providing there is enough metal to support the rear suspension. But do check the points where the two main bulkheads meet the outer skin. These are important. Check the header tank and the petrol tank, too. They are prone to rust at the corners and in the case of the petrol tank, are expensive to replace. Patching up properly probably costs more in the long run than a complete rebuild.

The condition of the interior and electrics is easy to see, but remember that interior parts are expensive and difficult to obtain except from specialists. Do not worry too much about electrics, except from the safety point of view. The wiring is reasonably easy to repair and not expensive, although the cost of the other electrical

Facing page, above: Look inside the front wings for signs of corrosion; start with the top joint between the wing, the centre section of the bonnet and the bonnet bulkhead.

Facing page, below left: The end of the line for an E type which has been scrapped because of extensive rust, particularly around the sills and floor as shown here.

Facing page, below right: The same once-proud E type showing what is left of its wheel arches.

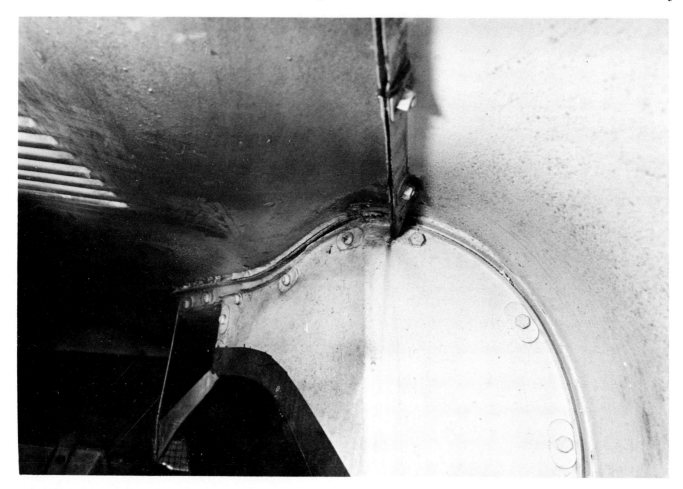

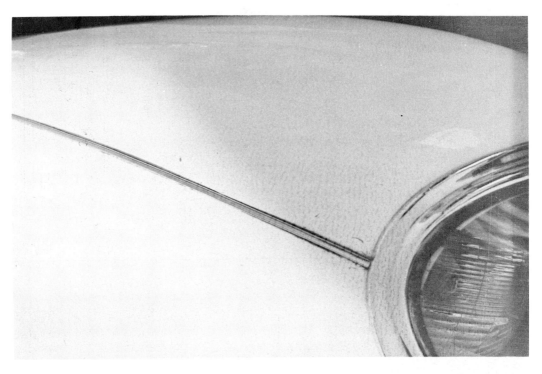

Above: Rust strikes all along the beading. Below: Flying mud and spray from the back wheels eats into the rear wheel arches; the first sign of trouble is under the bumper.

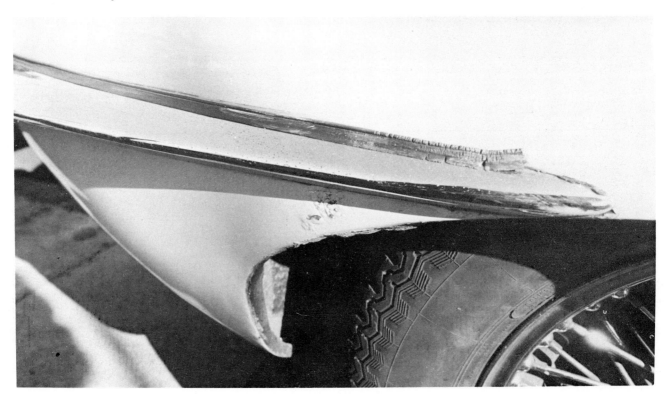

Above: A sore spot on the Series One cars was the header tank which corroded easily. Below: Rust strikes everywhere, particularly on the lips of folded metal on the doors.

components matches that of any other car.

Door and boot lids are expensive and very rust prone, although the cheaper door skins are available now. Do not dream about fibreglass doors. Fibreglass bonnets are practical, in some cases, but the doors are not and neither are the boot lids; they fly open when you go over bumps, even if you can get them to fit in the first place. They may be all right on a racer, with everything held in place with great big ugly catches, but impractical and dangerous on the road. For the best results it is probably wise to avoid fibreglass parts altogether.

Exhaust systems are prone to corrosion, too, and rarely last more than a couple of years. The stainless steel ones are better, but they tend to be brittle in some cases, especially around the flexible connections and silencer welds. Do not bother about replacing the rear mufflers unless you are worried about a slightly higher noise level, or originality. They are not worth the bother and it is easy to get a pair of straight-through pipes made up.

One last point: check the wheels, especially if they are wires. Do this by running a spanner round the spokes, rather like a piano tuner. Any loose spokes will soon show up, although they can often be spotted by the ring of rust at the rim or hub ends which forms if they are loose. The chrome spokes look lovely, but they are more brittle than the stove-enamelled ones; neither are so good as the lovely Minilite or Pearce knock on conversions. If you want these wire wheels in bolt-on versions, simply swop the hubs for those of a late E type.

VII
Strengths and Weaknesses: Part Two

E TYPE owners probably fall into two categories: those who like driving them, and those who like looking at them. The needs of the people who want to keep the cars purely as museum pieces are simple. They just have to make sure that they are kept dry and lubricated. The people who like most to drive them have to keep their cars dry and lubricated, too, and they will find that the E type is an extremely rugged and reliable machine providing they keep up with the minor routine jobs; if they let them slide, the Big Cat will deteriorate in a big way. No great skill is needed to run an E type on a shoestring, just careful attention and one or two tricks.

The first priority is, of course, that of servicing to the schedules laid down, plus one trick: changing the brake fluid every 20,000 miles. The **brakes** get very hot on an E type and the fluid can boil with disastrous results. Old fluid does not lubricate the rubber parts in the braking system very well either and can lead to premature replacement of these seals; an expensive and needless task. Also, if you have the car off the road for more than a week or two, pump the brake pedal once or twice to get some fluid moving. The same goes for the engine and gearbox: start the engine once or twice a month and let it warm up with the gearbox lever in neutral. Make sure the clutch is used every now and then, too, because some unfortunate owners have had them seize up when the car has been out of action for a long time.

My next trick applies only to the 3.8-litre models. Make sure you check the free play on the **clutch** actuating lever every 3,000 miles. If the clearance is taken up by normal clutch plate wear and you overlook this adjustment ritual, you are quite likely to have a burned-out clutch before long because of the slip caused by constant slight release pressure. Clutches, generally speaking, should last between 30,000 and 40,000 miles of average motoring, although their effective life can be prolonged considerably if you are willing to put up with a sharper action. All you have to do is saw a quarter of an inch off the end of the clutch actuating rod and the slipping clutch will go on for a lot longer. This trick is useful if you are a thousand miles from home and nearly as far from the nearest Jaguar dealer, but it does endanger the health of the flywheel. It is essential though that you either have the flywheel refaced or replaced when you change an old clutch plate. Changing a clutch plate alone is a waste of time and money if you do not attend to the flywheel at the same time. New clutches on old flywheels rarely last more than a few thousand miles.

Clutch judder can be mystifying; the unit is often perfectly all right, and yet it still judders. If this happens the rubber bushes on the top engine stabiliser have probably deteriorated, or somebody before you might have lightened the flywheel too much.

The **gearbox** on a Jaguar is a really tough item, although the old Moss box on the 3.8-litre E type had synchromesh which worked slowly and wore quickly. It was also very noisy, particularly in first and reverse; there is no need to worry about the noise, but there is if you get a sizzle from the gearlever. When the lever starts to do that you can come unstuck, and the best thing to do is replace the gearbox. Gearboxes, like the differential, are difficult to work on. And the differential, like the gearbox, is very strong.

Just test the **differential** every now and then, by accelerating on full lock. If you listen carefully, you should be able to hear a clicking and feel the limited slip working. E type specialist Terry Moore blames non-working limited-slip differentials for several mystery crashes he has investigated on winding slippery surfaces.

Another vital part to check regularly, from the safety point of view, are the Hardy Spicer joints on the **drive shafts**. They are best checked by trying to twist the drive shaft against the hub. Imagine you are wringing a chicken's neck and if you can move them, think of your own neck, because breakage means a suspension collapse that can be fatal. Much the same goes for the suspension bushes, which often suffer from lack of attention. Brake cylinders are a problem to keep in good order too, although changing the fluid is a great help. The main thing to remember other than fluid changing is to keep everything on the braking system clean, and when reassembling to smear all the cylinders, seals, threads, joints and so on with Girling rubber grease where appropriate.

It does not do any harm to smear the bushes and rubber suspension mountings with this grease either. If there is any deterioration in these rubber parts, the car starts to wander under acceleration, and, of course, bad rubbers can be spotted during a close visual inspection. It is no good economising on rubber parts for an E type.

The expensive **steering** rack can wear too, if the rubber gaiters on the end are neglected or the rack over-lubricated. While on the subject of rack lubrication, try heavy gear oil in the steering box, it often works better than the recommended grease. But, generally speaking, stick to the recommended lubricants and change them regularly.

Oil leaks out of an E type frequently and some leaks you have to worry about and some you can learn to live with. Three-point-eight litre engines, especially of earlier vintage, always burn oil and the underside of the car often looks like an oil bath, but there is no need to worry about it providing the exhaust smoke stays thin and blue. Surprisingly, the driveshaft oil seals on the differential often start leaking. Unless the oil reaches the rear brake discs, there is little to worry about. Just top up the differential fairly frequently, although you must not overfill it, and remember that the leaking oil is probably doing a much better job of lubricating the oil seal now than before. It was probably lack of lubrication combined with the heat of the brakes (which have been known to glow red), which caused the seal to start leaking in the first place. But do worry about leaky caliper seals. Escaping fluid reduces braking power dramatically and needs instant attention, especially as the E type has always been a car on the limit of its braking power. It is worth looking under the back of an E type once a week to see if oil is coming out, and to identify which sort it is and where it is coming from.

Oil comes out of the gearbox on occasions, too, but it is easily kept topped up from inside the car, so there is rarely any need for further attention until the engine has to come out for some reason, which is the only way you can get at the gearbox for major work. But if the engine's oil consumption rises rapidly without clouds of evil smoke from the exhaust, check the sump gasket. Oil leaking from here really comes out in a big way and can lead to bearing failure in what is normally a well-nigh indestructible bottom end. The sump will come off with the engine in place and if you have low oil pressure, check the oil pump first. They seem to wear quicker than the big ends.

Should you need to attend to the bottom end, the clutch or the gearbox, the whole unit has to come out, and naturally this is a lengthy job, like that of dropping the rear suspension to change the caliper rubbers. So why not check, or replace for a precaution, the universal joints in the propeller shaft? Either the engine and transmission, or the back axle, has to come out to change these joints, and with all that power on tap, they take a hammering. It would be a pity to have to take the engine or back axle out just to change those little joints.

One of the points not mentioned on the factory service schedules is **tappet** and **timing chain** adjustment intervals. The latter needs adjustment only when you can hear it and the former need adjustment particularly when you cannot hear them. Silent tappets mean that the gaps have closed dangerously. Tappet setting is a complicated carry-on in which you set up one camshaft by putting shims under the cam followers, then remove the shaft to avoid valve clashing and do the same the other side. A good trick here is to set the tappets at 0.008 in and 0.010 in instead of the recommended settings. The sound level is not much higher and you have more tolerance for overheating and closing up of the gaps. If you cannot find any Jaguar tappet shims, remember that the twenty-four supplied for a Lotus Cortina will fit.

Stick to the workshop manual on everything else mechanical or electrical and you will not go far wrong. But the workshop manual does not tell you how to look after the **bodywork** of an old and, maybe, neglected car. Neither does it tell you what you have to replace immediately and what you can get away with for years. The golden rule to running an E type on a shoestring is to cut out any corrosion on a stress-bearing part immediately and patch up the rest for as long as possible.

Keep a close eye on the sills and have them replated when any minor rust starts to appear. If you just paint them and leave them for a bit, you will find that the metal is so thin that you will have to replace them immediately because there is nothing left to weld to. The same goes for the floor and bonnet beam. Replate as soon as you spot rust and you will be able to avoid expensive repairs for a considerable time. Keep a close eye too on the front sub-frame. Rust can get into the tubes, and the brazed joints with the end plates can crack. Immediate formal attention is needed for either of these ailments.

The same goes for the floor area around the radius arm mountings, and any part of this general area on the roadsters. They can break in half at this point if there is enough corrosion. But do not worry too much about rust in the front wings, under bonnet, or rear bodywork. Just patch it up as best you can if you cannot afford to replace the panels immediately. The same goes for the doors and boot lids, which are prone to corrosion and likely to crack from slamming. As long as they will stay shut there is not much to worry about from the safety point of view.

There is plenty to worry about however when you **jack up** an E type. Never use the standard jack for anything other than changing a wheel in an emergency and then use only the recommended jacking point under either sill but carefully for these have been known to collapse even when nearly new. Small bottle jacks are far better for lifting an E type, especially if you suspect that your sills or jacking points might be deteriorating. When using a bottle jack, take advantage of the alternative jacking points. The best possible one is at the back between the exhaust pipes under the differential. Use a block of wood at this point to insulate the car from the jack. At the front, the best point is under either of the wishbone inner pivots or, again using a block of wood, under the front sub-frame centre tube. While changing a wheel, always keep the spare wheel for as long as possible under the sill of the side which is raised. If an E type slips off its jack and you survive, it can still present a terribly difficult task to lift.

Towing is best done via the inner wishbone pivot, and take a tip: use a low breaking strain rope, or one that is just plain weak, to use shoestring language. It is better for a rope to break than something on the car. If you suspect transmission trouble with either manual or automatic cars, remove the driveshaft before moving the vehicle.

If it is an automatic car, try to avoid having it towed at all, or if it must be towed, add two or three pints of transmission fluid to the gearbox before towing—which must be no more than thirty miles and at a slow speed—and remember to drain off the excess fluid after towing. In the case of brake failure, and if it is absolutely necessary to tow the car, don't just rely on the handbrake. Put the car in first gear and drive it with the clutch pedal depressed. Obviously extreme caution must be taken when driving a brakeless car, but at low speeds suddenly taking your foot off the clutch pedal can slow the car dramatically, providing the ignition is not switched on, of course.

All E types benefit from **rust-proofing**, and there are several commercial ventures in this field, but both a full rust-proofing session or the buying of all the compounds needed to do it yourself can be expensive. Terry Moore is developing a new system of pre-determined quantities of rust-proofing fluid for E type box sections though, which could be useful. The best way of doing it on the cheap comes from Terry Moore again, who spent a lot of time turning out what he considered to be the smartest E type ever. And naturally he spent a lot of time working out the best way to protect his investment.

It is evident from what you have read about the E type's rust problems that nobody thought much about making provision for water and condensation drainage in the large hollow sections that make up the monocoque and bonnet. The main rust areas which show up, even on concours cars, are the joints between the wings and the bonnet top; the joint between the wings and the underbonnet; the wired edges to the wings; the bonnet mounting beam; the headlight area and the internal wheel arches.

Terry's way to prevent corrosion in the wing and bonnet joint, is to remove the chromium joint beading on top of the wing by straightening the tails of the brass clips on the underside of the joint. He then eases out the chromium strip carefully and equally carefully opens the underside of the joint flanges to a regular gap of about one eighth of an inch. Then, without unfastening the flange bolts, he cleans out any rust and debris and makes sure that everything is thoroughly dry and free from loose scale. The next stage involves a builder's mastic gun which you can get from almost any builder's suppliers. Once you've got your gun, attack the joint from the top. Force in Evomastic Gunk of the natural grade until it shows uniformly through the bottom of the flanges. If you cannot get hold of any of this solution, try a little of whatever you think is the equivalent, but try it first on a piece of the car's paint which is normally hidden from sight. This will make sure that there will be no disfiguring reaction between the Gunk and the paintwork.

The next thing is to close the underside of the flange edges carefully with a pair of big flat pliers. Press the chromium joint beading back into position and secure it as before. The surplus mastic or Gunk should be taken off with a stiff card or something similar—and again—if you are not using Evomastic, check that the Gunk is not the sort that sets too fast. Good mastic will never set completely, and does not mark paint.

Those lovely headlamp covers on the Series One cars are a problem when it comes to corrosion. Terry Moore's suggestion for preventing this is to remove the chrome rims and glasses, taking care not to damage the rubber seal under the rim, and then if any watermarks are showing, to smear all the rubber jointing places with Evomastic or its equivalent, which will make sure that the components will part easily if you need to remove them later. This, of course, can be necessary from time to time for maintenance, such as changing the headlamp units or bulbs. Grease the threads of the fixing screws, too, which is not a bad principle for virtually any other screw on an E type. Then put everything back together again.

On the later, open-headlight E types, remove the chromium motif and aperture fasteners and replace them solidly on mastic, wiping off the surplus in the same manner as that on the wing beadings. Much the same applies to the bumpers, fore and aft. Remove them and force Evomastic into all the joints and clear off the surplus. Do not forget the bumper mounting plates and body holes while you are doing this. Another concours man, Alan Hames, has a good way of dealing with yet another disfiguring rust trap on an E type. His particular patch was the circular support welded under the rear valance below the spare wheel. 'This is always badly painted and a particularly bad rust trap,' says Alan. 'The best thing to do is to remove the plate by drilling out the spot welds and then to weld up the holes in the plate and valance. Both can be thoroughly cleaned back, de-rusted and repainted. The plate can then be replaced using 2BA nuts and bolts, so ensuring easy removal should the rust re-establish itself.' Welding may sound expensive, but the amount needed here is small and worthwhile to deal with this rust spot.

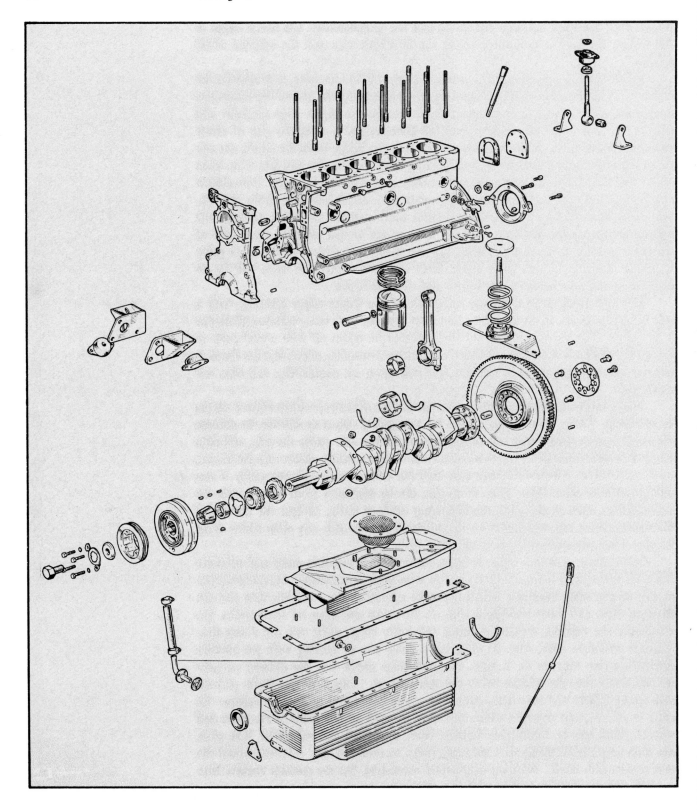

Left: Exploded view of the six-cylinder XK engine.

Above: Exploded view of the twelve-cylinder engine.

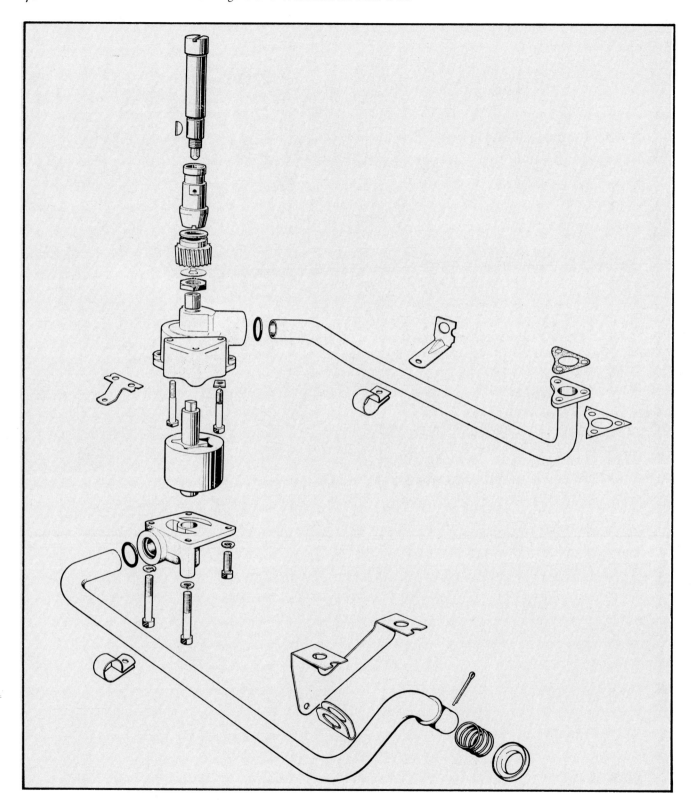

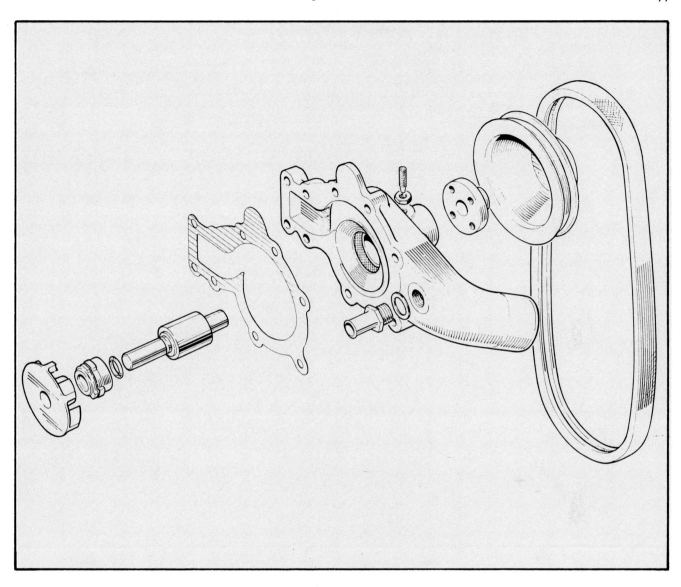

Left: Exploded view of the oil pump on the six-cylinder engine.

Above: Exploded view of the water pump on the six-cylinder engine.

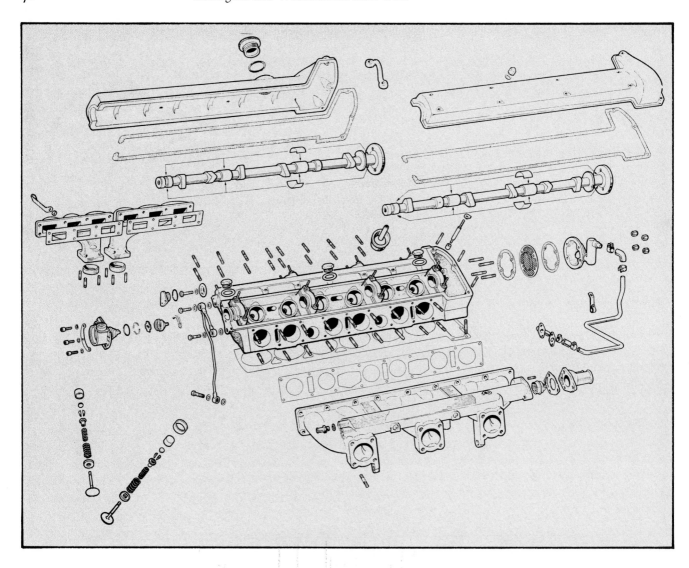

Exploded view of the cylinder head on the six-cylinder engine.

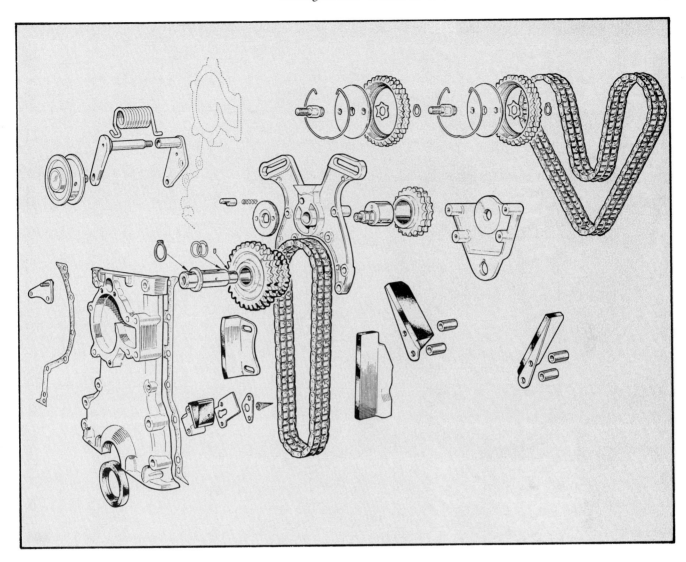

Exploded view of the timing gear on the six-cylinder engine.

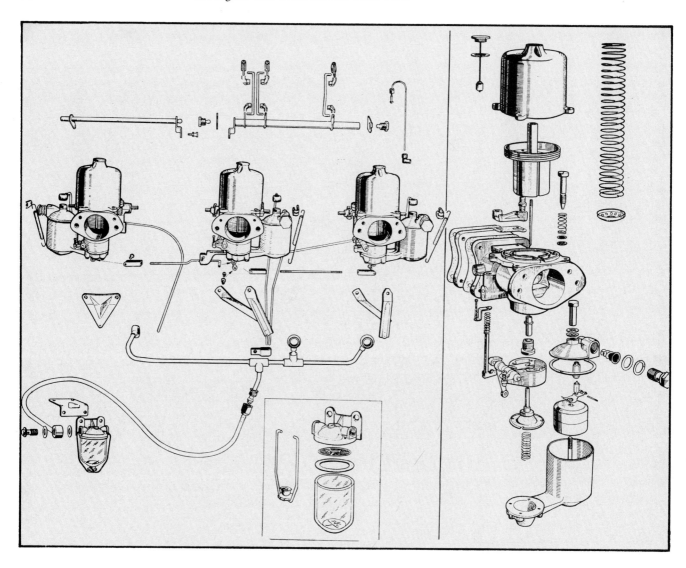

Exploded views of the carburetters and petrol filter on the six-cylinder engine.

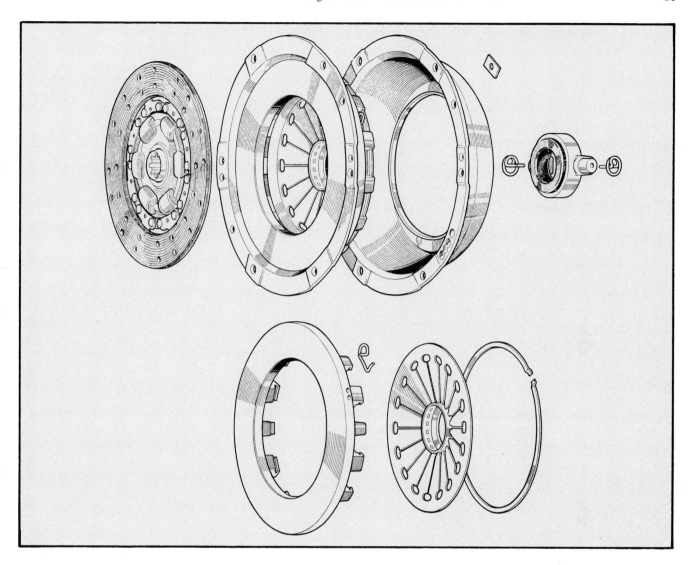

Exploded view of the clutch for a 4.2-litre engine.

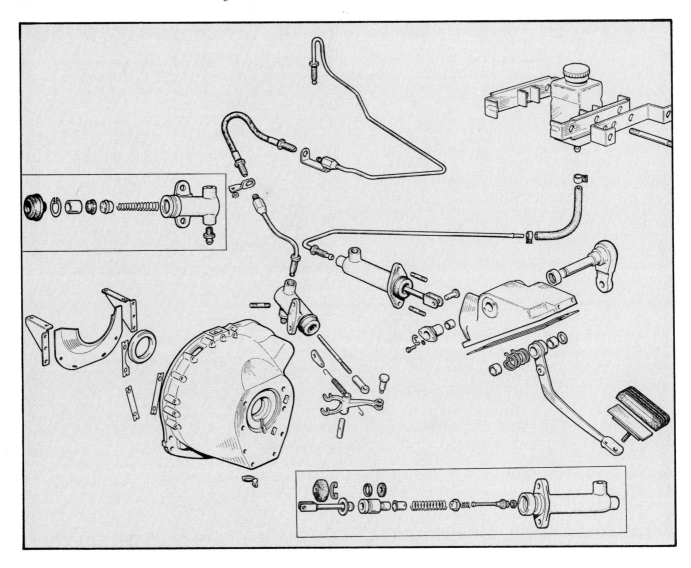

Exploded view of the clutch controls from a 4.2-litre car.

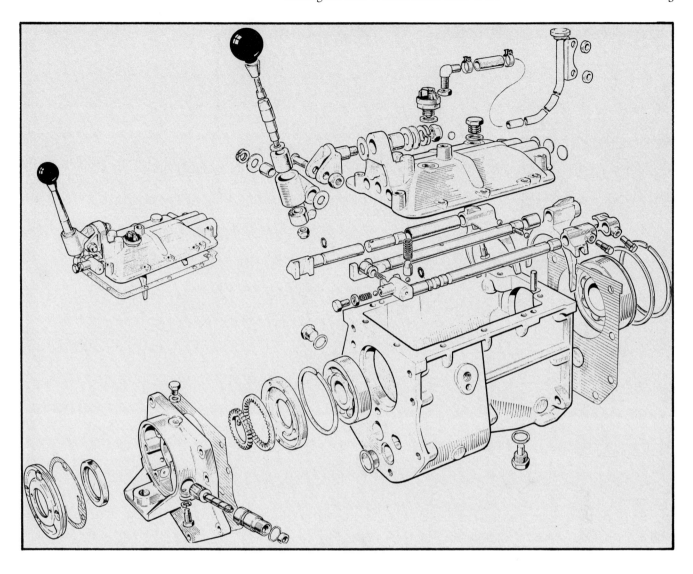

Exploded view of the all-synchromesh gearbox.

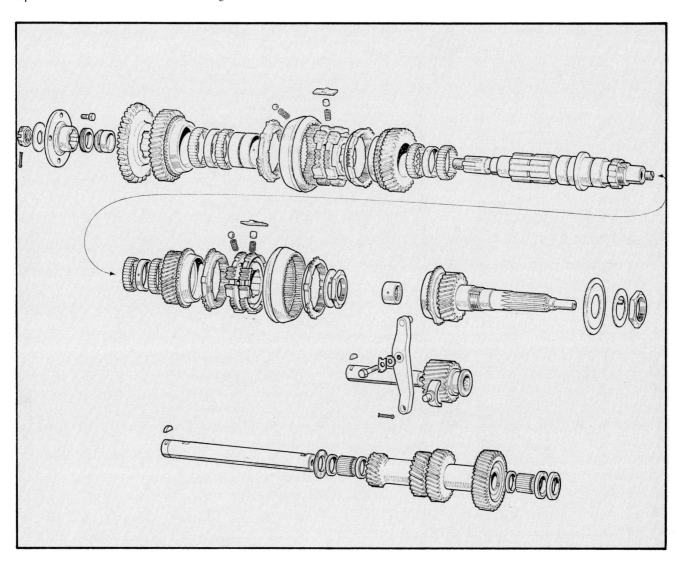

Above: Exploded view of the all-synchromesh gear clusters.

Right: Exploded view of the propeller shaft.

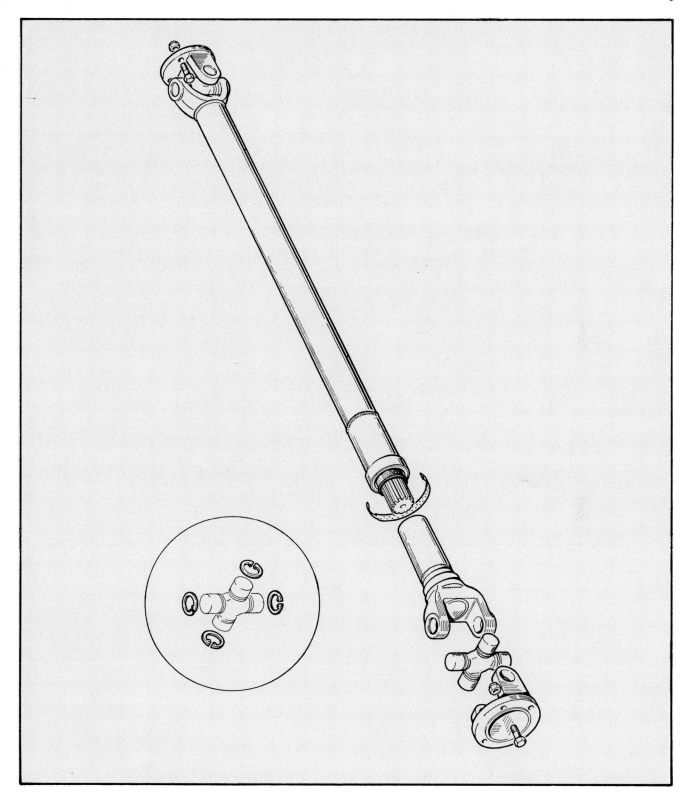

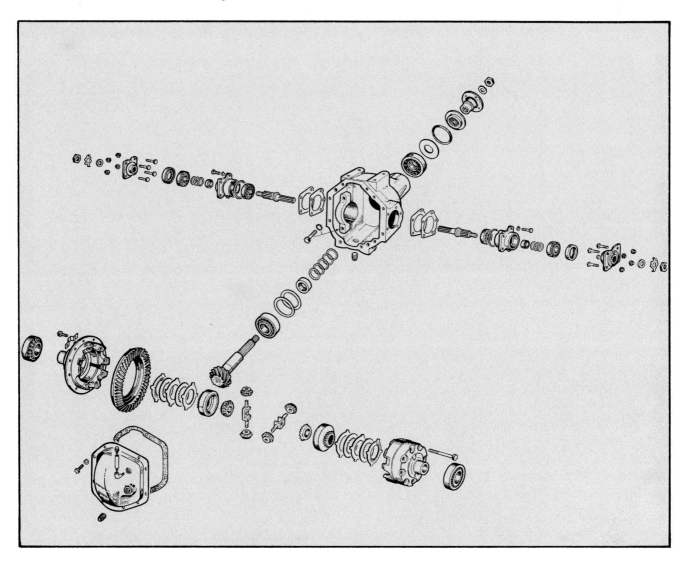

Exploded view of the final drive unit.

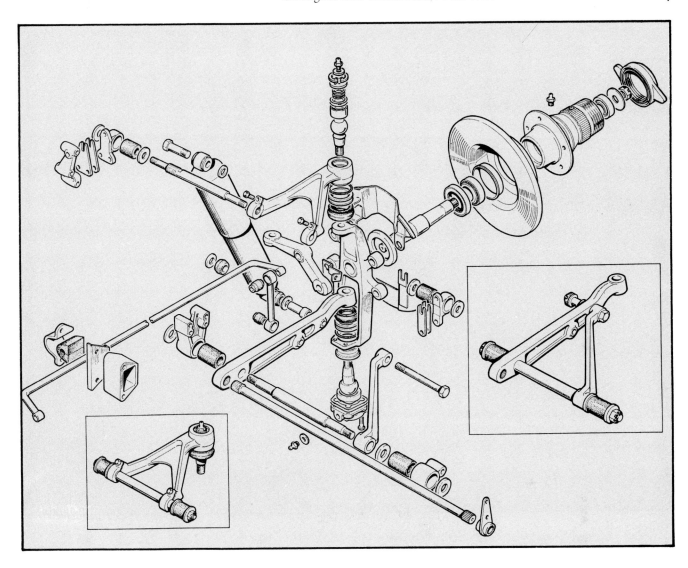

Exploded view of the front suspension.

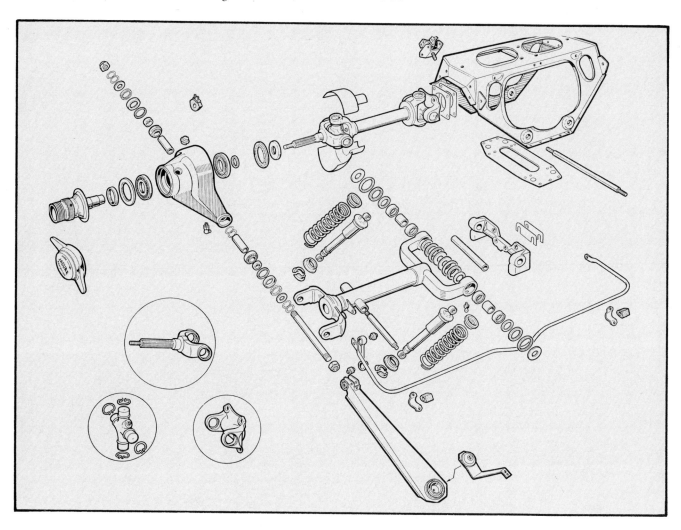

Exploded view of the rear suspension.

The rear suspension assembled.

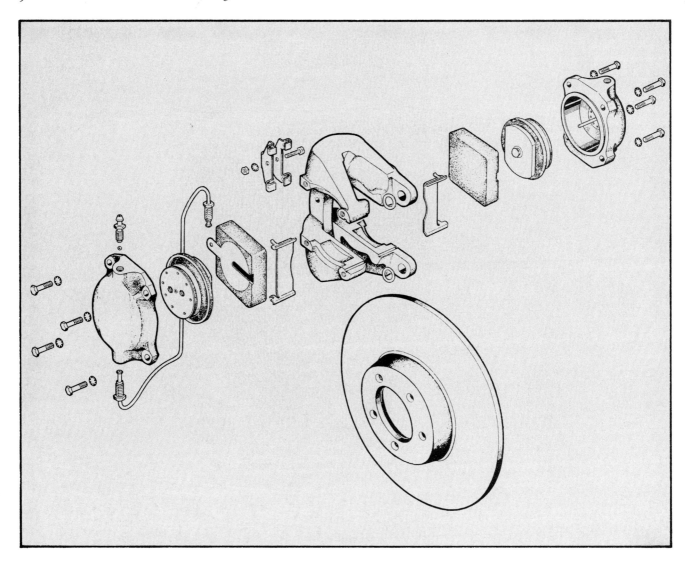

Above: Exploded view of the front brakes on the 4.2-litre Series One.

Right: Exploded view of the rear brakes on the 4.2-litre Series One.

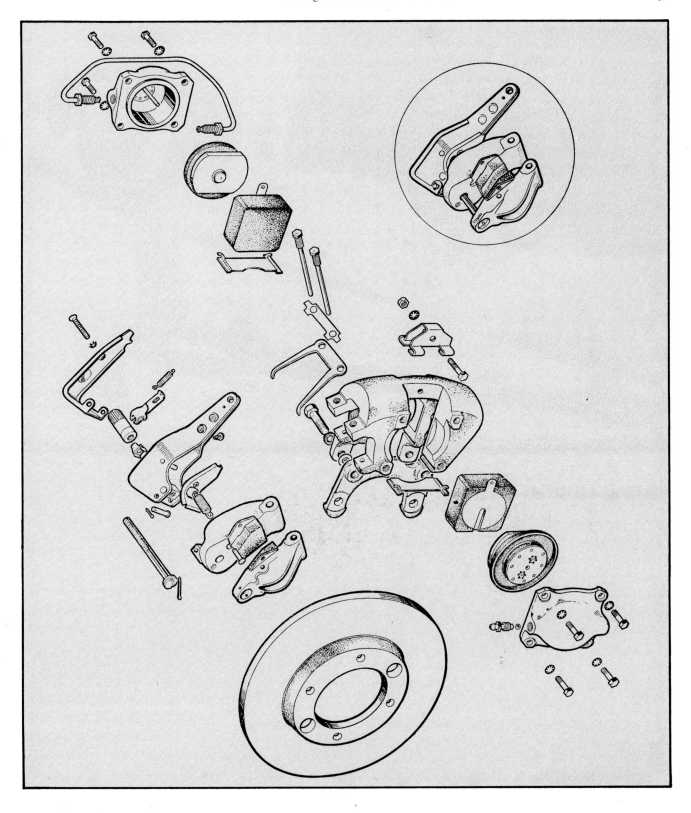

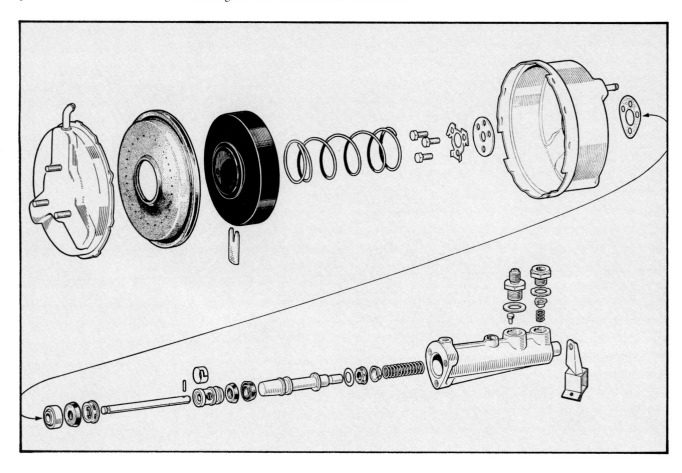

Exploded view of the brake servo on the 4.2 litre.

Bird's eye view of the brake servo on the 3.8 litre.

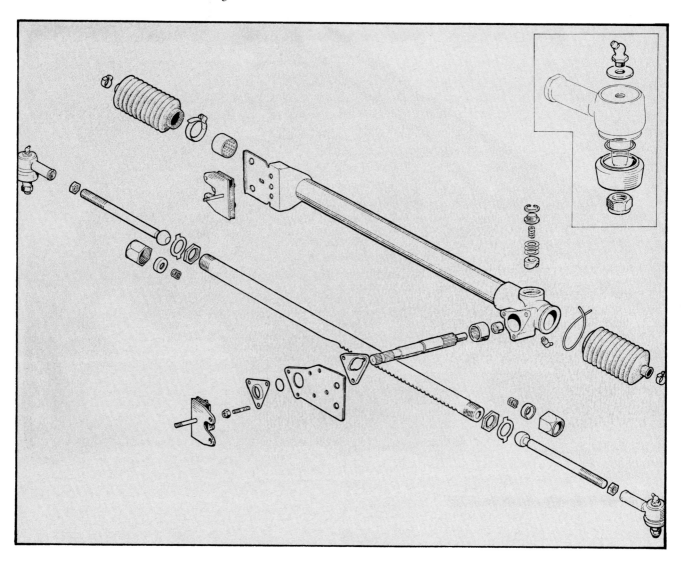

Exploded view of the non-power assisted rack and pinion.

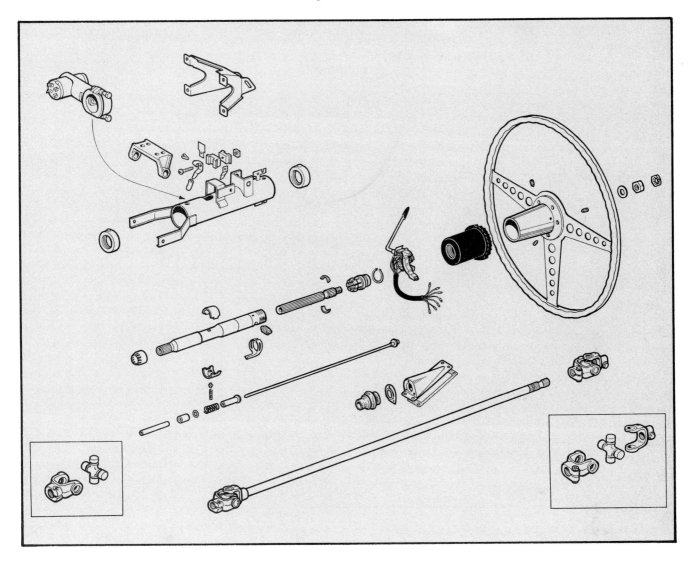

Exploded view of the steering column.

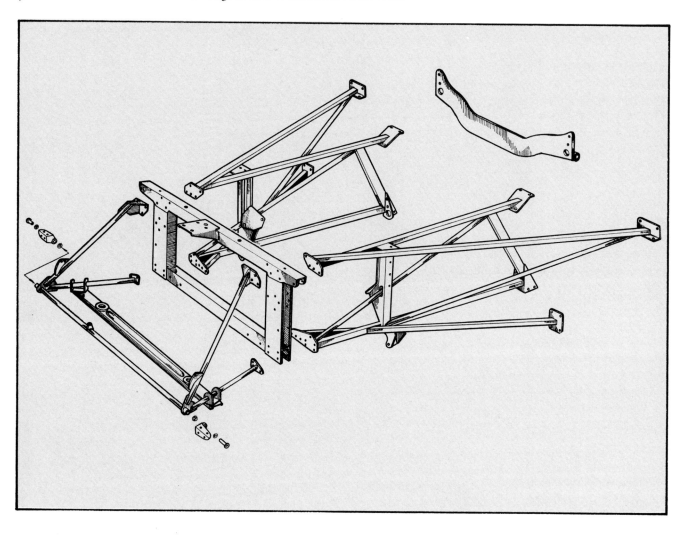

Exploded view of the front subframe on the Series One and Two.

The front sub-frame assembled on a Series One shell.

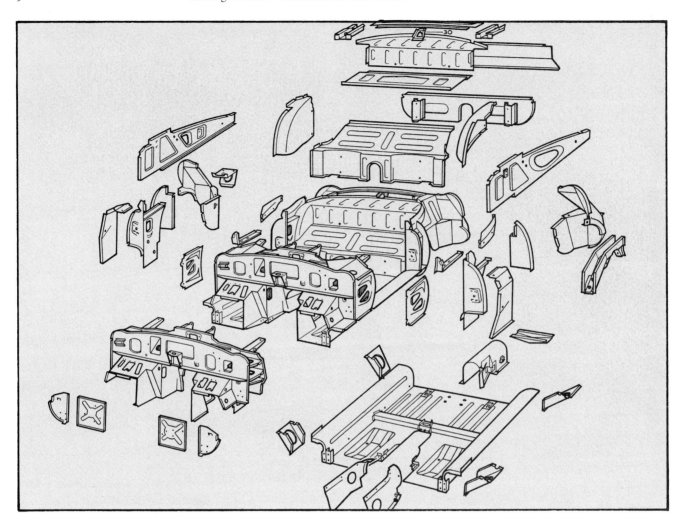

The body underframe and panels on a short chassis E type.

Assembling the monocoque of a Series One car for the benefit of Prince Philip (in the background).

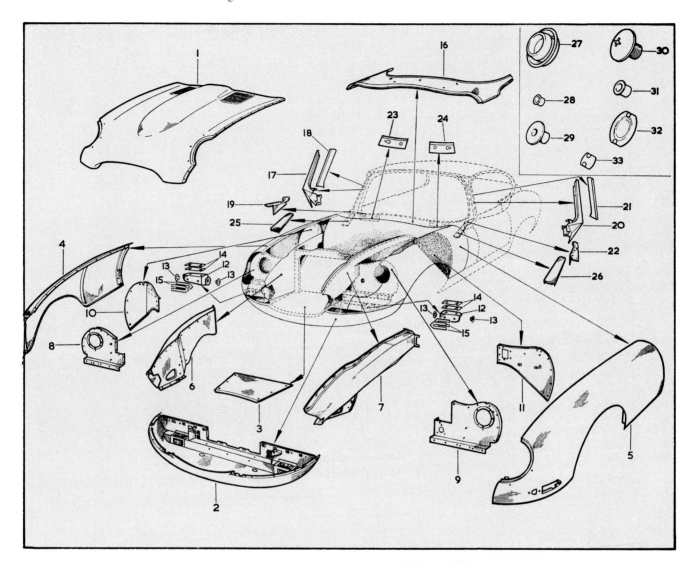

All the bits and pieces that make up the fixed-head coupé (short chassis).

Body fittings for the Series One.

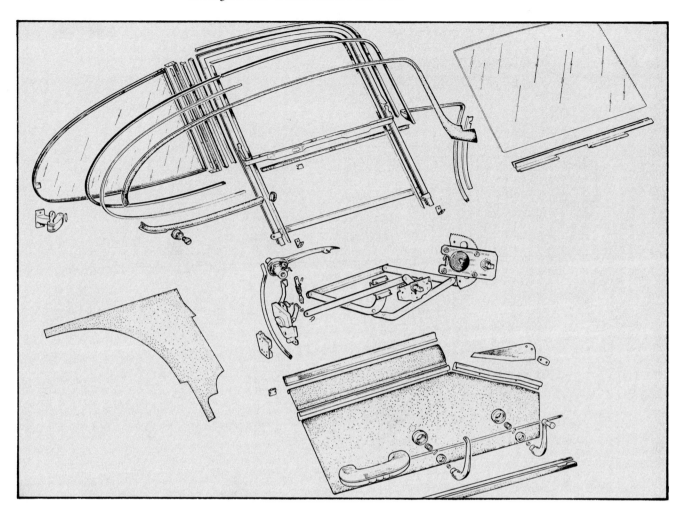

Body fittings for the fixed-head coupé (short chassis).

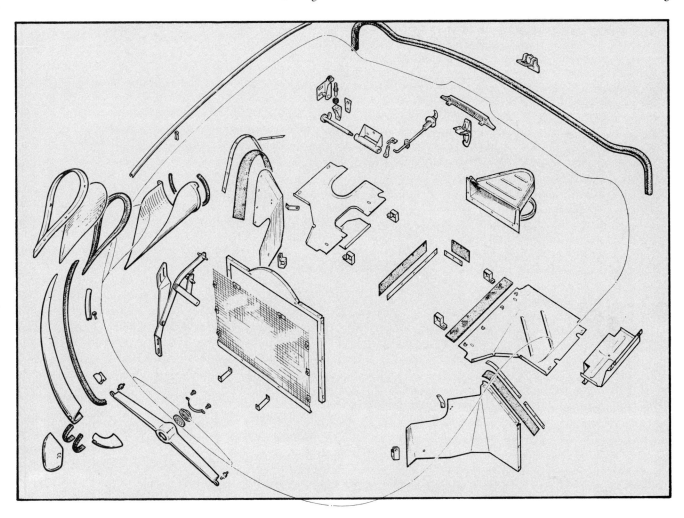

All the pieces of rubber in the bonnet (Series One).

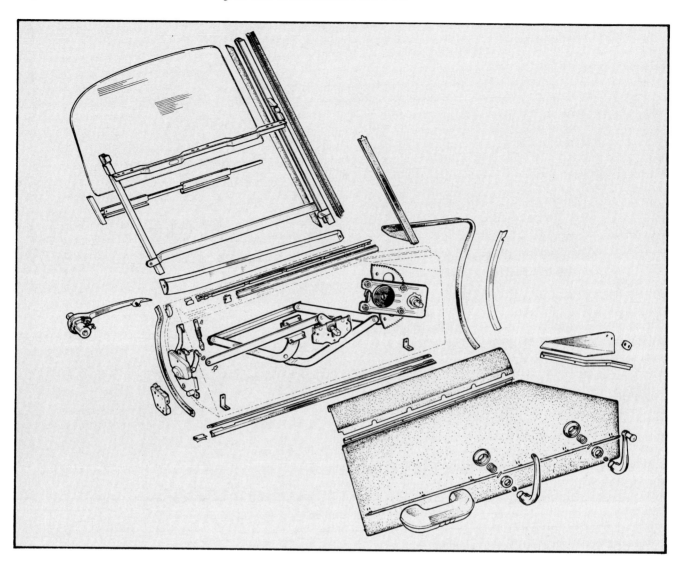

Door trim (Series One fixed head).

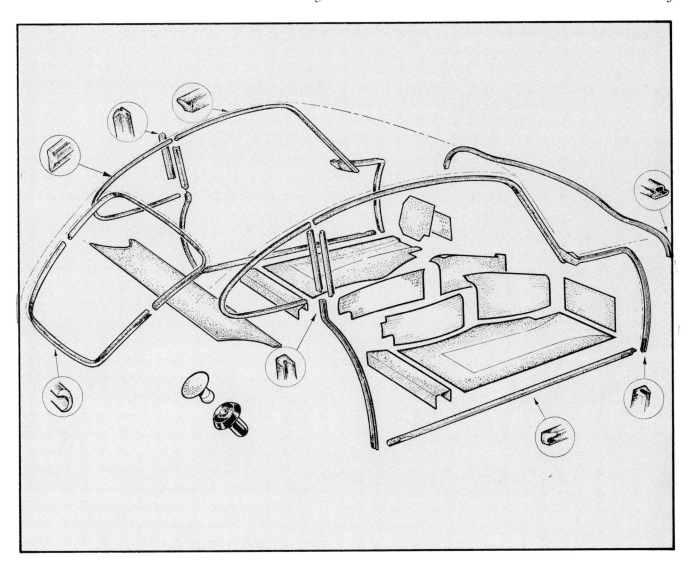

The interior carpets (Series One roadster).

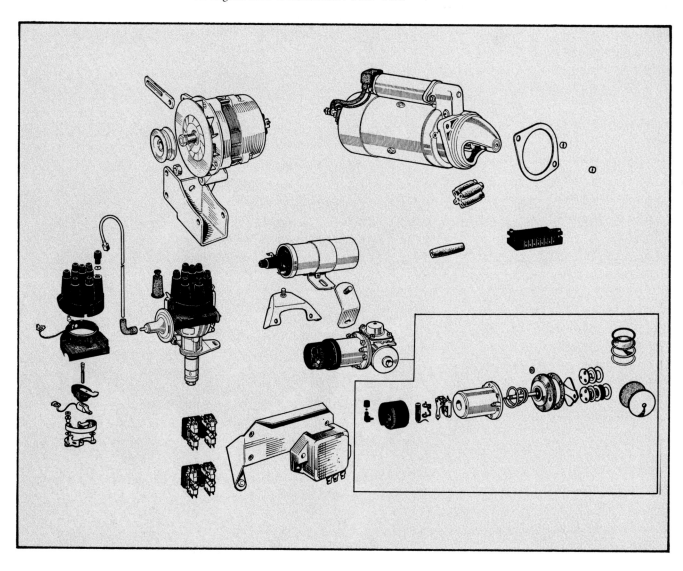

Starter, alternator, distributor, coil, fuel pump and other electrical equipment from a Series One 4.2-litre E type.

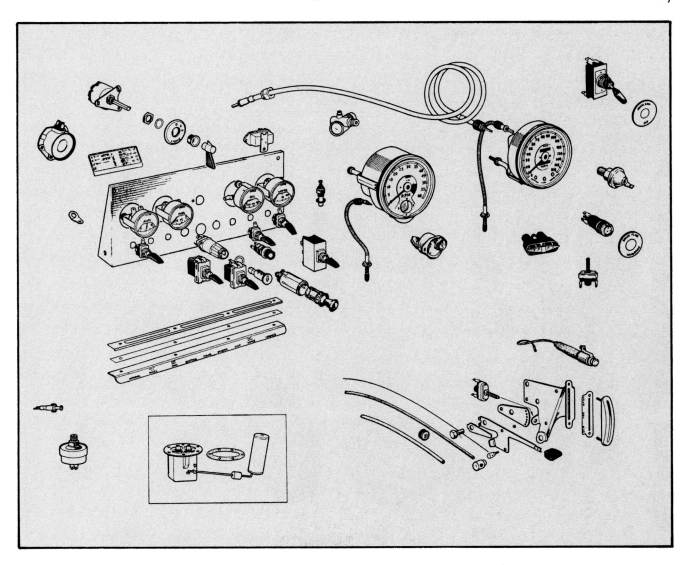

The Series One instruments.

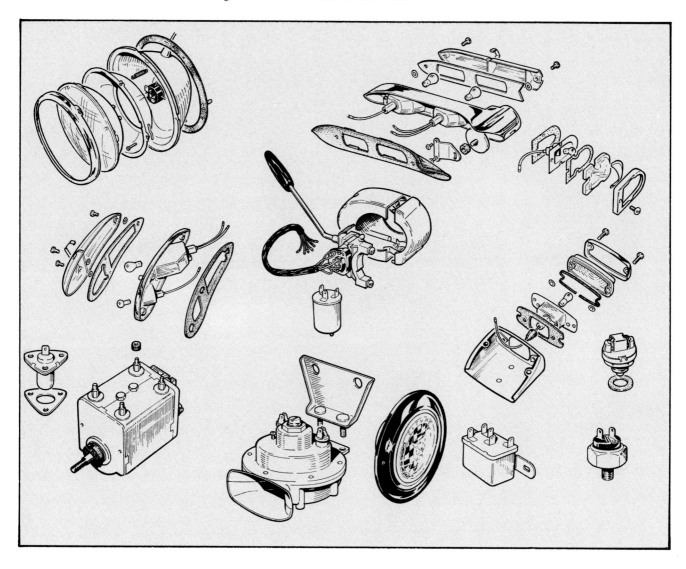

The Series One lighting equipment, wiper gear and horn.

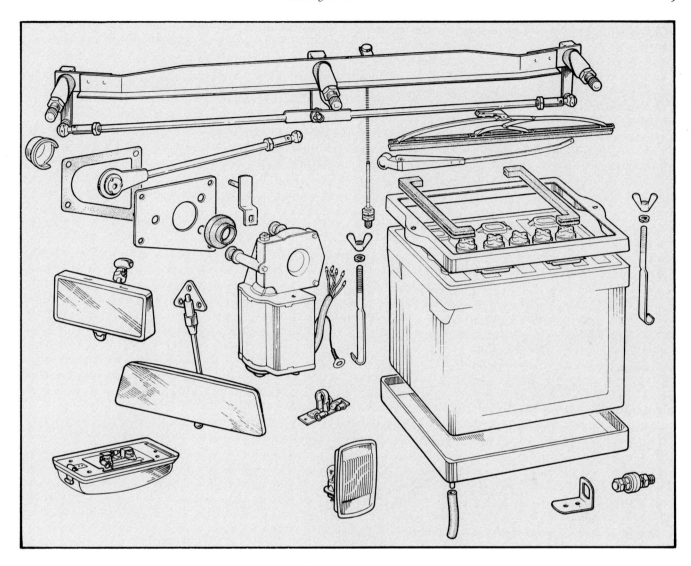

Wiper gear, battery box and fittings from a Series One E type.

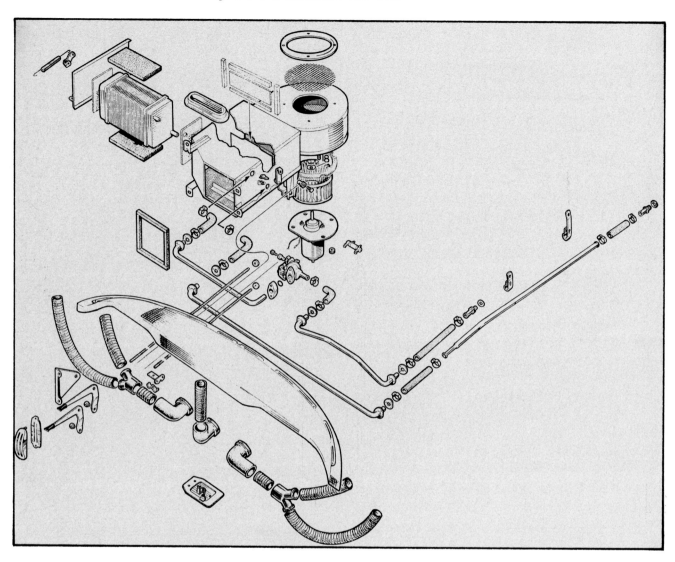

Above: Exploded view of the Series One E type's heating equipment.

Right: Windscreen washers from the Series One E type.

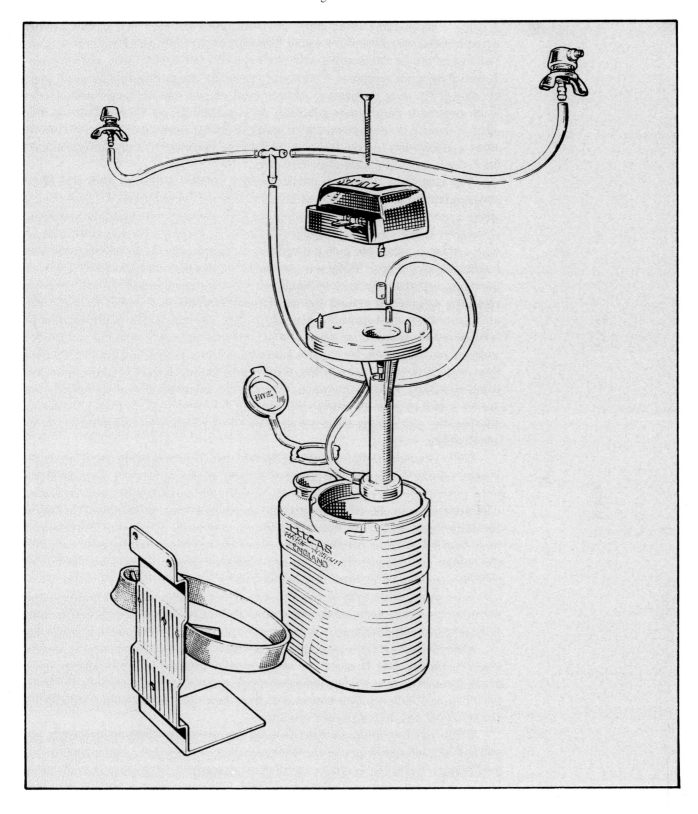

But back to Terry's rust cures. You will need a different type of Gunk to deal with the rolled wire edge of the wings. The wires are actually rolled in the wing edges, running round the wheel arches and along the sills to the bulkheads, and they are a favourite point for corrosion. You have to clean out the part where the metal meets the side of the wing thoroughly, using a small screwdriver and wire brush, mix up some twin-pack epoxy resin adhesive, such as Araldite or Plastic Padding, then smear the crack between the metal turnover lip and the wing interior quite liberally, using a small brush. As the material starts to set, point it off vertically so that it deflects water down and away from this joint.

The next thing to do is to attack the tight internal radius on each side of the underpart of the bonnet top and wing joint where the flange is formed. Clean this out with a wire brush and do the same up to the bulkhead at the front and the inner wing at the rear. When it is all completely clean and dry, apply some epoxy resin adhesive with a brush to about one inch each side of the radius, and fill the radius up to form a concave rounded face. While you are buried in the wheel arch, thoroughly clean off the metal, including the front bulkheads and all the inner wings. Fill in all the holes, cover the screwheads around the wing-to-bulkhead joints, the wing-to-inner wing joints, and all the other joints that become evident. The exploded body diagrams in this book will help you spot these joints. Use a bitumastic gun grade semi-hardening filler, such as Evomastic black, for this job. Leave it until an initial surface has been formed, then apply at least two coats of Bitumastic paint to the whole of the inner wing and wheel arch areas. Before application, warm up the paint to a thin consistency, but do not let it boil or give off fumes; just warm it up enough not to burn your hands. Incidentally, you can get other colours than black if you want to brighten up your wheel arches.

Terry has more tricks to apply to bonnets too. He removes the motif bar in the bonnet mouth; this pretty little piece of chrome trimming is easily detachable and often missing from E types. He then removes the plate in the bottom of the bonnet, which is held on by six self-tapping screws on top and three at the back of the bonnet mounting beam. Be patient, they will come out eventually. Clean out all the rust and loose material as far as possible, in fact down to the bare metal, by getting in from the bottom and through the top via the headlamps on the Series One. Series One reflectors are held on by three tiny screws on the back of the bulkhead plates. Reach up the air intake holes as far as you can, too. At the bottom, where the underbonnet meets the mounting beam, clean and scrape all along its length, then brush in epoxy resin adhesive, building it up to prevent moisture getting into this spot-welded joint.

Using Waxoyl or some such anti-rust solution, and a suitable spray gun, do your knuckle-scraping best to cover the whole interior and inside the headlamp voids. Spray the underside of the bottom access plate and replace it, then seal everything— including on the Series One bonnet, the joint between the headlamp reflectors and the bonnet front—with natural Evomastic.

When you have been messing about on the underside of the underbonnet, you will have noticed two large circular holes near the mounting beam, that were intended for drainage. Terry has no doubt that they let in more harmful substances than they let out and has an ingenious solution to all this. He cuts two squares pieces of rubber about three-eighths of an inch thick of at least half an inch larger diameter than the hole. Put these over the holes and, using reinforcing washers, Pop Rivet them on to the front of the holes, so as to let water out and stop water and road salt getting in. On E types after Series One, you will have to cut additional holes to accommodate the headlamp bucket drain tubes. Make sure of course, that these tubes have not routed themselves somewhere else. The rubber drainage flaps are a good idea for E types that leak; which is most of them. Cut two half-inch holes in the lowest part of the floor and the luggage boot to let the water out that accumulates there in the same way.

The headlamp buckets on après Series One models have a typical Jaguar body device: the drainage tube which does not really work. Poke around under the head-lamp bucket with one hand (you develop tough knuckles with an E type), until you find a short metal drain tube which should have a little piece of rubber hose fixed to it. The idea of this was to direct water, which is forced down the tube by the car's slipstream, into the underbonnet, and theoretically out of the big holes at the bottom. Well, you can throw that piece of rubber away and replace it with a much longer piece of hose, and route that through the drain holes and your rubber covers if you have decided to fit them, leaving about one inch projecting to stop the hose curling back into the bonnet. Remember, when you are sliding your new hose on to the metal tube, use adhesive to seal the joint and contain the force of the water flow. Check out the drainage tubes on the luggage boot lip in the same way.

Proofing the sills never seems to be really successful, except perhaps by the commercial pressure injection of anti-rust solutions at frequent intervals, but the best shoestring method of stopping the rot there, in my opinion, is simply to remove the interior covering of the sills and get rid of as much of the scale and debris as possible, bung up the drainage holes and then fill the sills as far as possible with old gooey sump oil. Then with the interior mats removed, slop the sticky oil about as much as possible by driving the car vigorously—that's always a pleasure—and when you have slithered to a stop, remove the drainage bungs and let the old oil pour out; somewhere people do not mind the slops of course. It is worth doing this as the oil seems to get everywhere inside the sills, all round the little bulkheads and the seams where the metal is welded; it is also worth repeating once in a while. Providing you keep the drainage holes clear during normal motoring, this sloppy business can delay the rot for ages.

You can carry out the Terry Moore treatment on the front and rear cockpit bulkheads, too, and it is worth using the Araldite treatment on the joint of the luggage boot lip and the door outer and inner skins and in the big lip at the back of the body where the luggage boot lock is housed. All E types tend to rust at these points, but it can easily be prevented. Undersealing is really worthwhile when you have done internal jobs and the way to stop door rot is not laborious.

Use the Warren Pearce method. Dismantle the whole door and clean out the internals. Then paint everything necessary and loosely reassemble the window frames, hinges and so on. Mark their position and underseal every surface. Then, when the underseal has set—make sure it is the old-fashioned setting sort—reassemble the whole door. Maintenance after that can be confined to keeping the door drainage holes free.

All of this, is only really effective though, if the car is in really good condition, but it is worthwhile either as a preservative or as prevention.

Then, of course, there is the **interior** of an E type, which seems to wear out at an incredible rate. The leather seats benefit from proper cleaning and attention in the same way as leather seats in any car, but the rest of the interior is rather special. It is mainly made of plastic and hardboard and replacement panels can still be obtained. It is quite feasible to make them yourself, providing you have the old worn-out panel to copy and any metal part that might be attached to it, such as the chromium strips on the door interiors.

All you have to do is take the panel to a specialist trimming centre such as Roy Creech's in South London—they do mail order as well—or in the case of difficult rubber pieces such as the big seal on top of the door-to-scuttle joint, to Edgware Motor Accessories, to get the replacement materials. Creech's can supply everything from complete hides for seats, to a variety of carpets, adhesives, vinyls, piping, window felt and rubbers, canvas, beading, hood materials, fasteners and grommets, screws and so on, plus free advice on how to use them. Advice is one of the most valuable things you can get when it comes to running an E type on a shoestring.

VIII

Common Problems

THERE'S nothing more infuriating than not knowing what causes mystery clunks and clicks in a complex car like an E type, so I have compiled the following fault-finding analysis. It can often be more expensive to have to pay a garage to find out what is wrong with your car than simply to commission them to rectify the fault if you know what it is to start with. Here then is what to watch out for and to listen for on your E type. If the engine will not start, first check that the ignition is working, then the fuel pump, assuming, of course, that the starter will turn it over. If there is a big click from the ignition or the bowels of the bonnet, check the battery terminals: they are notoriously prone to work loose or corrode on an E type; make sure the engine is not damp or flooded; and make sure that the petrol tank vent is not blocked: the easiest way to check this is to remove the filler cap and see if this makes any difference. If the engine stalls or idles badly, check the plugs first: E type engines do not run well on badly set or defective plugs, and if this is the case they sometimes misfire when revved hard. If the plugs are working, check the ignition, then the carburetter settings, making sure, of course, that there is enough oil in the dashpots if SUs are fitted.

Obviously, all this is conditional on not having worn piston rings, valve stems, guides or weak valve springs. Wear in the valve gear shows up in smoke in any case, as does piston ring trouble. Piston and valve problems will show up on a compression check, too. Much the same procedure applies if the engine is down on power, except that it can be also caused by a blown head gasket, the carburetter pistons sticking or the automatic timing advance not working. The best thing to do with a blown head gasket is first to check the cylinder head bolts with a torque wrench, then pour in a couple of cans of Bar's leaks fluid; it often works. Non-advancing or retarding of timing is often caused by the small elbow joints on the advance pipe either perishing or falling off. Engines often get coked up from 40,000 miles upwards and sometimes suffer from worn camshafts at this time, although 100,000 miles or more without an overhaul is common on XK engines, and V12 units are reputed to be at least as strong now that minor initial faults in them have been ironed out. The OPUS ignition on the V12 engines sometimes causes mystery misfires too, even today after most of the original units have been replaced.

All early XK engines tend to use a lot of oil, particularly the 3.8 litre, but really excessive oil consumption can be caused not only by general wear, but by an over-high oil level. Make sure you check your car on level ground when the warm oil has had time to drain down to the sump and that the car has the correct dipstick fitted. The engine will gobble oil too if the sump gasket goes, which has happened a few times on hard-driven E types.

Generally speaking, the XK engine will continue to run on extremely low oil pressure if treated reasonably, although it is obviously wise to do something about it if the oil pressure falls below 35 lb per sq inch at 3,000 rpm when the engine is hot. Check that the sensor is working properly before you go any further though, as these instrument-operating devices are notoriously prone to give false readings. The gauges should always be checked against a manual gauge from time to time in any case. A weak oil pressure relief valve spring or choked oil filter can also cause a low oil pressure reading. Mystery knocks in the engine should be treated seriously. They are usually caused by worn bearings, pistons or badly-adjusted tappets, although only worry about the tappets if they are really silent. Worn valve guides are noisy, and in fact all these things are common on E types. This is because there are so many examples on the road that have received little attention because of the sheer strength of the engine. If the car pinks on petrol of more than ninety-nine octane make sure the ignition is not too far advanced or that the top end does not need an overhaul.

Overheating is a common problem on E types, and in hot climates the under-shields around the engine compartment should be removed to allow as much hot air as possible to escape. The intake of air into an E type bonnet is rarely a problem, particularly if the car is travelling at the speed of which it is capable, but the exit of hot air is another matter. The lightweight racing examples, for instance, had extra louvres on their bonnet tops, but you have to be careful if you intend to have more cut in the bonnet: the angle and quantity can be critical to your prospects of keeping the bonnet shut when the car is travelling fast. With overheating, after checking the obvious things like water leaks, thermostat and loose fan belt, make sure that the fan motor itself is working properly. This can be done by short-circuiting the thermostat wires. If the engine is running well from the ignition and carburation point of view, suspect the head gasket, particularly with the 4.2-litre engine, which is prone to blow if the car is hammered. Blocked radiator cores sometimes cause overheating too, and this must always be attended to as soon as it occurs, because overheating itself can cause expensive engine trouble. Carburetters are best left to the experts, although, with practice, they can be sorted out at home. Many owners think they can maintain their own carburetters but not many have had enough experience. Dirty fuel (check the filters), eccentric fuel pumps and general leaks can cause some mystifying carburetter troubles too. Check the contacts in the fuel pump from time to time: it is surprising how many people forget that this unit has its own points. Ignition trouble can sometimes be caused, too, by mould forming inside the distributor cap in damp weather, and in one case on my own car, by the distributor earth wire working loose.

One of the most common complaints with E types is **clutch** slip, but as soon as this unit goes—usually at intervals of about 40,000 miles or less if there has been a lot of violent use or traffic driving—do something about it. Clutches on E types go very quickly once they start to slip. Check the hydraulic system before you do anything else, though, because this sometimes causes drag, spin or slip. Clunks and clicks from the clutch are usually a worn release bearing and judder is often caused by oil or grease on the driven plate or by faulty engine mountings.

Do not worry too much about the noise from the **gearbox** of a 3.8-litre car, and a little noise from the later gearboxes, providing they have sufficient oil. But if the gearlever jumps out of its slot, first check that it has not broken the spring behind the striking rod's locating ball. Other than that, the gearbox is likely to be worn badly. Automatic boxes, of course, are far more finicky and complicated and best left to the experts if they do not function properly, although a lot of clunking can be caused by the breather pipe being blocked, which is simple to cure. Cleanliness and oil level are critical with these gearboxes, too.

Then there is the **suspension**. Anything untoward in the back axle must be seen to at once as this is an expensive unit to overhaul, and can be quite dangerous in use if it becomes badly worn. Bad vibrations are caused by the propeller shaft being out of balance, worn or wrongly assembled universal joints. Rattles are usually bad rubbers on the radius arms or anti-roll bar, and a hang-dog look to the car can be caused by worn or damaged springs. Trouble with the springs or sub-frame mounting rubbers should be evident by the general precarious feeling of the car on the road. Keep the wheels in balance, too, and get the track and camber checked front and back from time to time, because anything out of line costs a fortune in tyre wear. Wheel wobble can be caused by worn hub bearings or suspension linkages. Or worse, it can be a wire wheel loose on its splines, although the cure for this is simple.

Watch out for rust at either end of a spoke too, because this can mean that it is about to snap. Rocking and rolling can be caused by a broken anti-roll bar or loose mountings and general clunks are often the result of worn or loose bushes in the dampers. Bear in mind that almost every rubber part in the suspension deteriorates every year.

Steering trouble in the non-power assisted cases usually manifests itself in obvious slackness, but stiffness can often be lack of lubrication in either the rack or steering joints, particularly if the car has not been used for some time. Lost motion on the steering wheel can also be caused by worn splines or universal joints in the column or simply by a loose steering wheel. Some wheels have the disconcerting habit of suddenly releasing themselves to the full extent of their adjustment; the best thing to do here is check the tightness of the lock-ring frequently. If the car has power steering, listening for rumbling noises on full lock; this means a defective pump, low oil level or a loose power belt, all or any of which should be attended to immediately. Hissing is simply the overload valve working. Power rack trouble can cause wander, inconsistencies in the feel of the steering, general lightness or heaviness. A generally sloppy or unsafe feeling at the front of the car is most frequently caused by worn joints in the suspension.

Needless to say, the **brakes** are of the utmost importance on the E type. A spongy pedal can be caused by hydraulic leaks, worn operating cylinders, leaking seals or air in the system; too much pedal movement can mean excessive pad wear or a fluid level not far above the low warning light mark; pulling to one side or the other, or wheel wobble under braking, can be caused by a damaged disc, oil-soaked pads or trouble with the calipers, particularly on the earlier models fitted with Dunlop brakes, which were prone to stick when they received little use.

Electrical troubles on an E type could almost fill a book themselves if described in detail, but briefly, they are: if the battery is flat, suspect loose or dirty terminals, if there is a short circuit somewhere, the dynamo or alternator might not be charging, the voltage regulator might have gone haywire, something might have gone wrong with the battery itself, or it might be a loose dynamo or alternator belt. If the battery goes flat very quickly there may be a low electrolyte level, battery plate trouble, electrolyte leakage, or ineffective plate separators. If the dynamo output is inadequate or there is no output, suspect a loose belt; bad wiring, a crazy voltage regulator, a diode failure in the rectifier pack, badly worn bushes or dirty slip rings. If the starter motor is down on power or will not turn over the engine, check its connections after you have made sure that the starter switch and battery are working.

The small starter button on the pre-1968 E types was prone to wear flat on the contact behind the button and often a starter can be made to function by simply twisting the button round a fraction with the thumb. This is a surprisingly common complaint on old E types, although you must remember that most of these starter buttons are about ten years old now.

But back to the starter motor: it is sadly affected by pinion assembly damage or getting jammed in mesh, solenoid troubles, faulty brush gear, worn or dirty commutator, defective armature or fields coils. If the starter spins, but does not turn the engine over it means that the pinion engaging gear has failed to engage, there are broken teeth on the pinion or flywheel gears, or, on the 4.2 model, the roller clutch assembly has failed. Sometimes the pinion drops off the end of the starter motor, right into the bell housing. Do not panic if this happens. You do not have to remove the engine and gearbox to get at it if you are lucky: you either fish out the offending item with a long piece of wire after removing the starter motor, or you open the hole in the bottom of the bell housing and remove the pinion. If the starter motor is rough or noisy, the mounting bolts might be loose or it might have a weak or broken return spring, apart from the obvious damaged pinion or flywheel.

Lights go out sometimes on E types or even frequently, depending on your luck. This is most often caused by a blown fuse (always find out why, fuses do not blow for nothing) or a bad earth or a faulty lighting switch, which is quite common, especially on later models. The wipers go wrong sometimes, too; the adjustment is affected either because of a dirty or short-circuited commutator or faulty armature, or incredibly enough, because of scuttle shake. This shaking also accounts for the occasional habit of the wipers starting themselves, or at the rear on the roadster, for the boot lid flying open. Both can be cured by careful adjustment to compensate for the flexing.

Any of these faults can assail an E type owner on the road. I know from bitter experience!

IX

The American E Men

AMERICAN E type owners are different to those in the rest of the world. They like the Two Plus Two, and they like wide wheels even if they do not do good things for the roadholding. They do not have a rust problem unless they drive on the salt-infested roads of New York State, and they consider the 4.2-litre car much better than its 3.8-litre equivalent. They worry about dents in their bonnets and they spend a lot of time polishing their seats. As it happened, they also bought two out of every three E types made and were responsible, one way or another, for changing the shape and character of the car.

Computer executive Ed Harrell is one of America's greatest E type fans. He used to drive one of the most popular sports cars in the States—the Triumph TR4—back in 1964.

'That is till I saw Merle Brennan clean up B production in the SCCA championships,' [says Ed]. 'Then I decided that I just had to have an E type. It was the best-looking sports car I had ever seen . . . and boy, didn't it go. I thought about it for a year, and then they brought out the Two Plus Two. I ordered one right away and flew all the way from the West Coast to little ol' England to collect mine on November the First, Nineteen Hundred and Sixty Six. I headed straight for the Continent at a steady 2,500 rpm, bearing in mind Jaguar's warning on the windshield: "Important: We are equally as anxious as yourself that you should obtain the best performance and the most satisfaction from this car. We hope therefore that you will carefully observe the following recommendations: During the first 1,000 miles, do not exceed 2,500 rpm. Do not overstress the engine. Use the gears so that the engine runs lightly with minimum of throttle opening. After 1,000 miles and up to 2,000 miles, do not exceed 3,000 rpm, and continue to drive without overstressing the engine. Only if the above recommendations are observed will the high performance of which this car is capable be obtained."

'How could anybody fail to observe such beautifully-worded running-in instructions? I just stuck to that 2,500 rpm limit, then the 3,000 limit, as I cruised round the Continent with other cars wondering why an E type was going so slow. . .

'Then, when the 2,000 miles came on a motorway near Paris, I just put my foot down, the nose came up, and didn't that Big Cat go. She leapt forward just like a real Jaguar . . . and she still does. Every so often I look back to that warning on the windshield and remember that moment. Yes, the warning is still there after 186,000 miles . . . and the same wonderful performance is still there, too.

'My car cost me $5,360, plus $185 to ship it back to the States, and $165 in duty as a second-hand car because I had had it for more than three months before I took it back. It would have cost $6,800 if I had bought it new in the States, so I had a holiday on the car for a start. Mind you, I had to leave the car for ninety days in Paris after my month's holiday, before eventually getting it shipped back home in March 1967.

'Some time after that I quit my job in San Francisco, sold the family Oldsmobile, put the furniture in store, packed the wife and two children into the Two Plus Two, piled everything on a roofrack and headed for Europe again. We hadn't gone more than 100 miles from Frisco when she started overheating. The Monterey Jaguar dealer said the head had not been torqued right and he said it would be fixed free of charge. So I sent the family over to my wife's parents in Colorado and the head was fixed next day.

'She was going really well as I ran for Colorado. As I crossed the Utah-Nevada border doing sixty-five, there was nothing in sight for miles, and no speed limit any more. So I just put her in the middle of that four-lane highway and let her go. She soared up to 140 mph and I took my hands off the wheel—she was that steady. But after I had been rolling along like that for a while the red light came on, steam came out of the bonnet vents and smoke out of the back. Yes, you guessed it, the fan belt had gone.

'I called up the breakdown truck and he took one long look and said to me: "You'll have to sign an indemnity form before I'll tow that car." It's always the problem with the E type in the States. There's no obvious place underneath to fix the tow line. But he got me to his place and I rang the Jaguar dealer in Salt Lake City. He said they were short on fan belts, but he had one he could send over on a bus. Well, the bus came, without the fan belt, and when I rang back he said the taxi he had sent to take the fan belt to the bus didn't make it on time, so he would take another fan belt off one of his cars in the showroom. He sent that over on the bus, and, of course, the other fan belt was there beside it when the bus arrived. But there was no charge, and I set off again for Colorado.

'I picked up the wife and kids and drove all the way to my parents' home in Birmingham, Alabama. That's 2,400 miles and I was still worried about the temperature that car was running at. So I checked into the local dealer and he said to me: "Didn't you get a letter? All the E types made around that time had suspect clutches." I said mine was fine, but he wouldn't have it and he fitted another clutch . . . no charge. He had plenty of clutches, but no fan belts. That's the way Jaguar service is in the States. Since then I have had fan belt trouble twice a year and more trouble trying to get a fan belt.

'Then I decided I'd go get a job in Europe, and shipped the car over. And, you know, the new clutch didn't cure the overheating. So I went on up to Henlys

Plate 1 Opposite page: Just reflect . . . if ever a car crossed every gulf, it was the E type.

in Piccadilly and they sent me on up to Coventry. It was 11 pm when I hit that town, so I just booked into a bed and breakfast and asked what time did the works open? They said seven am, so I was there at the front gate at that time and they said I would have to see a Mr Bell, who didn't arrive till nine. So I went away and had some coffee and came back at nine am. Sure enough, Mr Bell was there then and he said he was sorry, he would see what they could do. Could I come back after dinner?

'Well I went back there at two pm, and Mr Bell said they just could not figure out what was wrong with that motor car, would I like a tour round the factory while they made some more checks? So I took the plant trip and at 3 pm he said the fault was still a mystery. Did I mind if they took an engine and transmission off the assembly line and put it straight into mine? I said sure, go ahead, and he said: "Where are you staying?" I told him at the bed and breakfast, and he sighed and stroked his forehead and said: "Let us look after you, sir," Up rolled Sir William Lyons's limousine—looked like some special kind of Mark Ten Jaguar to me—and took me off down to the bed and breakfast. The chauffeur told me to stay in the car and came out of that bed and breakfast with my luggage in his hand. He then took me to the best hotel in town and next morning I had eaten and slept well, and had a new engine and transmission . . . no charge.

'All that happened at 26,000 miles and that old E type has rolled on with the same engine ever since, although I did have to rebuild it at 86,000 miles when a rear oil seal went.

'With Jaguar's good wishes ringing in my ears and that old warning on the windshield, I headed home by a round about route. In fact I stayed in Belgium for a year and one time when I drove over to Paris I left the car in the St Germaine area. There were a lot of good-looking girls around, and one slipped her boyfriend's arm and swooned right in front of my car. She said: "Oh, you beautiful Jaguar," and kissed it right on the bonnet. It's then that I made up my mind never to trade that car. . .

'The 1970s were coming up when I went back to LA, and one day when I parked the car at a shopping centre, gas started coming out of the back. The bottom of the tank was like a cullender, but I fixed it up with solder and it stayed like that till I changed the tank in 1975. Apart from that, I have not had much trouble with that car, just the odd universal joint or so, three header tanks, three fan motors, countless fuel pumps, and a lot of fan belts. But since I came over to England to work for a while, I have been buying up all the spares I can lay my hands on. Right now I have almost everything mechanical and electrical duplicated for that car, and when I go back to the States I'll just swop the parts around and rebuild them as needed on my car and maybe keep it running for another thirty or forty years. Body parts are not too much of a problem on the West Coast because you don't get rust there, although the bonnets get knocked about by bad parkers. There's a whole lot of E types over there that are just worn out mechanically and boy, the bodies are just great.

'In the States, most E type drivers take off the undershields behind the front wheels to help the cooling. They have always had a heating up problem over there. And most of us have fitted wide wheels—just for appearance. I had mine made up using Cobra rims on Jaguar hubs and boy, they look good. But when I get back to the States I reckon I am going to take my spare rear axle with its bolt-on hubs and put magnesium wheels on my E type and put those wide chrome wires on the X J 6 which I have over there. And wouldn't they look swell, standing there together?'

A Briggs Cunningham prototype of the E type on parade in Britain.

Apart from widening the wheel arches to take the Cobra rims, Ed has carried out few modifications to his car. He has a smaller steering wheel, American exhaust with four-inch diameter tailpipes, and he has swopped the instruments around on the centre panel so that they read, from the left, ammeter, oil pressure, water temperature, then fuel. This is chiefly because his hand masks the ammeter gauge. He has also substituted a copper header tank for the standard Series One rusting unit.

The E type's principal competitor in the United States was the home-brewed Corvette Sting Ray and the German Porsche 911, and the Jaguar's principal handicap was considered to be its service arrangements. Jaguar enthusiasts allege that at one time it was taking six months to get an oil filter, and even longer to get a more unusual part. Engine rebuilds cost around $1,000 if you can find somebody to do it for you.

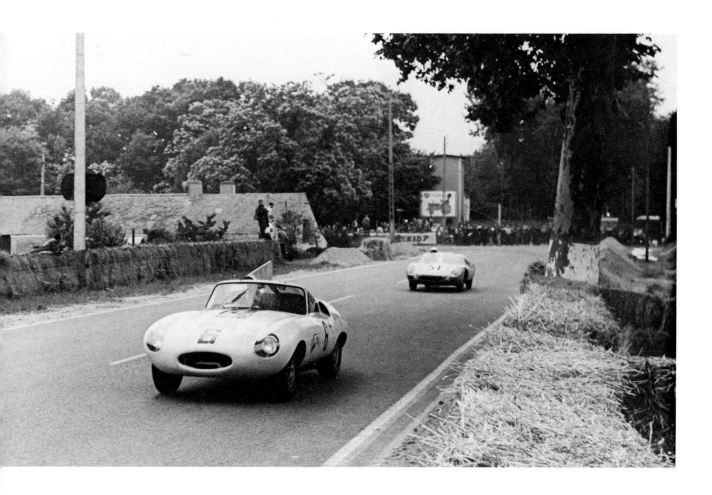

Plate 2 The E type that was in many ways the best tourer of all: the Series Two fixed-head coupé.

Plate 3 The E type that the Americans loved first, the Series One Two Plus Two.

Plate 4 Opposite page: Jaguar's last three roadsters: from the back, in order of seniority, an XK150S; in the middle, a six-cylinder Series One; and in the foreground, the very last E type made, the 12-cylinder Series Three, HDU 555N.

This might not sound unreasonable in the Falkland Islands or Outer Mongolia, but in the United States, where 8,000,000 cars are sold every year, they expect real service. If your Chevvy heats up, you just drive it round to the neighbourhood garage first thing next day and one, two, or twenty of the mechanics who may number up to 1,500 will fix it straight away. There's no question of 'Come back tomorrow,' or 'We can't touch anything for three weeks,' or 'Sorry, you'll have to wait till next year for a fan belt or oil filter.'

So why did the Americans buy E types in such great quantity? Because there was just nothing else like it. They liked the absence of chrome. They liked the shape. They liked the sound and the fury of an E type accelerating. They liked the feel of a real sports car. And they liked it because it was British. When the Datsun 240Z came out it was considered to be a copy of the E type fixed-head coupé, and although it cost half as much as a Jaguar, it was still just a cheap Japanese copy and there is no prestige attached to driving cheap Japanese copies.

Big Healeys, which might have been expected to compete in the same class as the E type in the United States never caught on, mainly because they were too spartan. They did not really want hulking sports cars in the Sixties. If they were going to buy an exotic car they wanted something which was sleek and comfortable besides being wild and exciting.

In fact they nearly did not buy the 3.8-litre E type because of that awfully slow, crunchy, non-syncromesh first gear. It took all of the E type's other qualities to get over that. But when the 4.2-litre car came along, Jaguars were really made. The gear change was silky, the low-range acceleration was good and the brakes were much better than anything else the States had experienced. 'And boy, when you could pack your wife *and* kids into the Two Plus Two, that was really something. And if you didn't have the kids, you could get your golf clubs in,' says Ed Harrell. 'The only people who really bought the roadster were the smart young chicks. They looked great with their hair streaming in the wind, but I guess they couldn't have handled a Ferrari or a Maserati.'

Well, if Jaguar were largely indifferent to luggage space in the roadster, they were not indifferent to Ralph Nader. The E type's changing face throughout the years, detailed earlier, was almost entirely due to American safety regulations. After the introduction of the 4.2-litre engine (chiefly to keep the Americans happy), everything else that was changed was almost purely for this market. That is why Jaguar eventually standardised the Two Plus Two wheelbase; that was the reason for the automatic E type; that was the reason for the open headlights and the de-toxed engines; that was the reason for the use of the twelve-cylinder petrol-gobbling engine to get back the performance and glamour lost by the de-toxing, and that no doubt, was the reason for the wide wheels and the over-light power steering on the Series Three. It was impossible to steer it without power assistance, but there were two other racks available with less power. But despite all the enforced modifications, the E type remained the fastest and most economical proposition in the world. With its easy application of power out of corners, its firm grip on the road, its hands-off at 140 mph stability, and its classic shape, it was offering something different to the American pony cars.

Facing page above: Sebring 1963 and Cunningham's second lightweight holds off the Le Mans Ferrari of Willy Mairesse.

Facing page, below: Sebring 1963 and the lightweight E type of Briggs Cunningham and John Fitch blasts past number 54, a Sunbeam Alpine driven by Jerry Titus, Jim Adams and Dave Jordan. *Picture courtesy Alice Bixter.*

Plate 5 A car for all seasons: four Series One-and-a-Half E types spread across the football pitch behind Jaguar's factory that has been used as a background for numerous publicity shots over the years. Above left: a fixed-head coupé; below left: a roadster with its hardtop in place; above right: a Two Plus Two; below right, a topless roadster.

You see very few tatty Jaguars in the States. The people who bought them initially are the same type that buy a Ferrari or a Rolls-Royce in Britain. The people who buy them after that are the enthusiasts. Sales are chiefly grouped around New York, Los Angeles and San Francisco. You are lucky to see an E type elsewhere in America. As it happens, salt is not popular on the roads in the West Coast, so corrosion is no real problem there, although the E type owners in New York have to be especially careful because their roads are subject to even more salt than those in Britain. But the mechanical side is a terrible problem to all American E type owners with no exchange units being readily available there. It is becoming quite fashionable to take a European vacation and to buy up as many spare parts as possible; imagine the American's surprise when he finds that the British often have just as big a problem with spares!

Americans have to look out for bonnets and front seats, too. Most of the E types stolen in the States quickly lose these parts. The bonnets are easily wrecked by American parking techniques and like leather seats, they cost a fortune by the time they have crossed the Atlantic. There is also the extreme delay in getting spares, so there is a considerable incentive for thieves. The only other part that disappears with any regularity is the back axle. It is one of the few independent suspension systems readily adaptable for specials that can absorb the power of a huge V8 engine.

Nobody was more eloquent about the virtues of an E type than the road testers and magazine scribes in the early 1960s. *Car and Driver* opined in 1965 that there were not very many two-seater sports or GT cars around below $6,000. In fact there were three: the Corvette, the Sunbeam Tiger and the XKE.

'No Jaguar was ever perfect,' said *Car and Driver*, 'and yet no other make has ever fired the enthusiasts imagination to the same degree, or over such a sustained period of years. The XK120 overheated regularly but it electrified the keen-types of the late Forties and earliest Fifties. The XK120M was too fast for its brakes, but nobody cared: it was beautiful and it made the most purely sexual noise ever emitted by an automobile. The XK140 and XK150 were fat, over-decorated versions of the lithe, taut XK120, but they were Jaguars, by God, and that was enough for the men who bought them.

'Then came the XKE. It had been predicted by the "experts" ever since the waning days of the XK120 series. Everybody knew that Jaguar was going to produce a street machine based on the fabulous D type racing car. And finally after more than one false start, it came. Who cared if it still had the old Moss transmission? Who cared if there wasn't any room inside and the seats weren't comfortable? Who cared if it didn't have proper fresh air ventilation? Nobody, that's who.

'It was a new Jaguar! . . .

'A man six-foot could wedge himself into the driver's seat, acknowledge the fact that he could not possibly drive the car, and still want one worse than he'd ever wanted anything in his life. An old hand, an ex-Jaguar owner, could say that he had had bad luck with his previous Jaguar and that he'd never own another one, only to rush pell mell to the Jaguar showroom the first time an XKE droned past.

'There's something sensual, so elemental in the appeal of that car that few men can resist its siren song. It's like that woman you used to love, the one you'd never waste another minute on. You can avoid her for months, but one night she calls and you'd crawl naked across three hundred yards of flaming gasoline and broken bottles to get her. Obviously, a car that can excite such primitive urges is bigger than a non-synchro first gear or bad oil consumption.'

Bob Miller was an American who was bitten by the Jaguar bug when driving an Austin Healey. Bob's income was only in the new Austin Healey bracket, so he had to have a second-hand E type. Six years after his 1963 model left the factory and three years after he bought it, he wrote to *Road and Track*, telling them of his experiences. Bob's urge to own a Jaguar had started with the XK120 and was strongly reinforced when the E type was introduced in 1961. A two-year-old E type retailed at about the same price as a new Austin Healey 3000, and Bob worked out that the maintenance, depreciation and running expenses would average out at about the same amount for each car. So he went for the E type: a 15,000-mile model that had been owned by a racing driver who had not used it for competition work. Bob and his wife loved the oodles of power even though his wife took three months to learn not to crunch the Moss box!

He had no problems with the car going out of tune, he told *Road and Track*, but had plenty of trouble with the brakes. On one occasion the fluid got a bit sticky and seized the rear brakes, which made Bob glad that the car had independent braking systems front and rear; this was designed into the car even before American regulations demanded it. That meant, of course, that he could drive home with front brakes only after the back brakes had cooled down and freed themselves. More braking trouble at a later date convinced him that it was wise to change the brake fluid fairly frequently and to cover the fluid reservoirs with aluminium foil to help insulate them from the heat under the bonnet.

He had trouble too with a rust-peppered header tank, although he managed to get it soldered up in New Orleans, having failed to find a replacement south of the Mason-Dixon line. He eventually got a new one from England.

In more than 40,000 miles over three years, Bob had no engine, transmission or drivetrain trouble, he got 24 mpg at a steady 70 mph and discovered that the depreciation was much less than that on a new Healey and that the maintenance costs were comparable.

'Would I buy another used Jag?' asked Bob. 'Well, the major faults on my car were improved on the 1965 models and later models with redesigned brakes, a larger cooling system, alternator and four-speed synchro transmission. In fact, I've been thinking if I could afford a low-mileage 1969 roadster. . .'

Jaguar clubs are booming in the States now with the E type as one of the favourite models. There are more than thirty clubs registered in America and two in Canada, with around 4,500 members. This figure is climbing fast, such is the soaring appeal of the E type in the States. The organisation is similar to that of the British Jaguar Drivers' Club, whose activities are detailed in the penultimate chapter of this book: they differ in that the concours events are the main competitions of the year, not the

Plate 6 Above: Arch enthusiast Ed Harrell took his Series One Two Plus Two all the way from England to California and back, covering 186,000 miles in ten years. *Picture courtesy Carter Alexander.*

Plate 7 What a contrast! the mighty E type, all muscle under its bonnet, and its super-slim ancestor, the XK 120, pictured together at the Jaguar Drivers' Club Beaulieu meeting in 1972.

Plate 8 The grand old war horse believed to be Dick Protheroe's first racing E type. It certainly looks as he left it.

Plate 9 Below: Inside a Series Three coupé, emphasising how little the interior of an E type has changed over the years.

A New York E type prepares for circuit racing in 1962.

club racing as in Britain. Every club in North America runs a concours, and each one counts towards the National Championship of North America. Owners have to enter their immaculate cars for three events in a year; this entails driving about 1,500 miles or more to the widely-scattered events. The entrants' three best scores are added up and divided by three, with the resultant best average qualifying for the championship. In Canada, Jaguar enthusiasts suffer from similar problems to those of British drivers, because of the extensive use of salt on the roads. They also suffer from the North American syndrome of lack of readily-available spare parts, such as fan belts, so they have to be really keen to keep an E type going in such conditions. Roy Hills, a member of the Ontario Jaguar Owners' Association, is typical of the Canadian E type owners. He had owned a Jaguar for several years before deciding to buy an E type.

'Purchase of an E type had been planned for 1968 or 1969,' [said Roy], 'but when the, to us, incredible news of the merging of Jaguar with Leyland was made known, we started shopping at once—who was to know what would happen? As it turns out, things were not so bad as many of us imagined they would be, but I still believe it was a blunder.

'Having owned a 3.4-litre saloon for about six years, we were sorry to part with it; it had covered 65,000 miles with little trouble—a split heater hose, a problem with the steering idler arm bearing (repair shop induced), Panhard rod bushings breaking up—were about the only problems in those years of ownership. In fact, you always wonder if you are doing the right thing, selling such a good car. And three days after selling it I tried to buy it back, but somebody had snapped it up already.

'Driving the new E type home was not all pleasure. I had driven others before, but they did not have a new engine to be run in; it was dusk and everybody following seemed to be in a great hurry—the E type seems to have a weird effect on other drivers. Many of them, it seems, cannot resist driving as close as possible when following one. If you as much as touch the brakes, they would be unable to avoid hitting you and this is still true with my car nine years later. The other habit is following close, then overtaking, and then pulling in front and immediately slowing to about 10 mph less than when they were seemingly frantically attempting to overtake. It only happens with the E type, not other cars.

'With about 1,000 miles on the clock, it was back to the selling dealer for my car's first service. The only fault was an extremely high differential gear noise at 40 mph to 55 mph, which sounded very much like a Viscount aircraft passing low overhead on its landing path. The first service took most of the morning as the dealer's premises were about thirty miles from my home. So I roamed the town for a couple of hours and went back for the car. They were adjusting the mixture and an hour later they were still doing it before they seemed satisfied. There was nothing wrong with the car's tune when it went in, but it was hardly driveable on the way home. It idled fine when hot but over 1,000 rpm, it was terrible. After getting it home I corrected the settings to specification, and in the next 40,000 miles it has been set up only once more—yet people are always speaking of the so-called tune-ups needed every two or three months. Incidentally, during this thirty-mile drive home, nearly all the enamel vanished off the exhaust manifolds.

'Perhaps I have been fairly lucky, but I believe only four items have given mechanical trouble over the nine years of ownership. The heater core started to weep coolant at about 1,000 miles and soon after the fuel gauge sensor unit in the fuel tank leaked and was giving incorrect readings. I was not able to get a float by itself, so I repaired it in much the same way as I repaired the numerous motor cycle carburetter floats I have handled in the past. Then, after about 30,000 miles, the brake master cylinder failed due to moisture in the fluid corroding the cylinder bore. A change to silicone fluid was made at this time to avoid this problem of corrosion in high-humidity climates. At the 42,000 mile level, the ignition coil failed in a convenient place—my garage.

'Over the years, of course, many parts have been replaced as precautionary

Plate 10 It may look sweet and serene, but JDU 877E had a hard life as a Jaguar test car.

measures: the brake lines, the contact breaker points, the high tension cables, drive belts, exhaust system and battery—but they are routine items for any vehicle here.

'The rear end noise was a worry in the early days until I wrote to the factory. They explained what was making the noise, saying that it would go away after about 5,000 miles, and so it did to a large extent. But at about 25,000 miles I really got tired of the 3.54 to 1 axle ratio, especially on the long runs for which the car was mainly used—it felt as if the car was in third gear the whole time. I have never understood the fitting of this ratio to North American E types. Perhaps it is to limit the performance to a maximum of 120 mph, which is more than most people can handle anyway. But for relaxed touring, it is no good. My old 3.4-litre saloon was able to easily handle 26 mph per 1,000 rpm in overdrive, so I thought that the E type, weighing 600 lb less and having 50 bhp more, would have no problem with a 2.88 to 1 rear end ratio. And so that is the way it is now. Moving off from being stationary is perhaps not always so smooth as before. Perhaps this is because my car is one of the last fitted with a close ratio gearbox in which the first gear is fairly high. But the conversion transformed the car for me—the magic carpet effect makes long-distance trips enjoyable and restful, whether it is a nine-hour, 600 mile overnight trip to visit relations in Cape Cod for a weekend, or even longer trips, one is always in fairly good condition at journey's end.

'For my part, the brakes are the poorest part of the E type. In fact, I have not driven one with good brakes. On wet roads, I find them grim—at least mine are—and the delay in any retarding effect after applying them seems an age. The only time they work well is when they are really hot, such as driving in a twisty, mountainous district, or running in a slalom event. But you cannot keep them warm on most North American highways as it is sometimes one or two hundred miles between any required braking.'

Chris Colebrook, vice president of the Ontario Jaguar Owners' Association, shares Roy's enthusiasm for the E type, having owned two, a 1966 coupé and a 1972 Series Three roadster.

'All cars are compromises,' [says Chris], 'but Jaguar's Es are surely a landmark for value for money, fun, performance and so on. A finer set of compromises could not be found. Jaguar's motto used to be Grace, Space and Pace. Only the latter is a trifle lacking in the E type, but surely nothing is lacking in the first two elements of the motto. But there are things to be wary about with an E type.

'I regularly carry an extra fuel pump, fan belt in the case of the '66 car, and two quarts of engine oil, plus a collection of bits of wire, tape, jump leads, tow rope and fire extinguisher, and of course, a good set of tools. I had to replace a fan belt once in the middle of the prairies in Saskatchewan, and carrying the spare certainly saved a lot of time and money. In rural North America, sometimes even American-built cars have parts problems, but for Jaguars this can be even more so. That's about all so far as trials and tribulations of a North American E type owner are concerned. Just the spares—as if that isn't enough I hear people

The late, great Mark Donaghue paces the field in a SCCA production car race, with a Series Three E type.

saying Otherwise it is many miles of driving enjoyment in a car that was a classic before Coventry even stopped making it.'

Then there were the other people who bought E types in North America, the people who never joined clubs and the old men who had Jaguars for other reasons. To quote one former roadster owner, a girl from New York: 'I just loved that lovely long bonnet. And the way that car didn't get away from me when it came to getting away from all those MEN in their Mustangs at the traffic lights. That car had everything. It was chic for a chick. It was like a Gucci handbag. It was like a Cartier lighter. Every time you touched it, it went. And it was so elegant and your hands didn't get greasy like they did in an MG or an Austin Healey. When mine got old I couldn't sell it to a dealer. I gave it away to a boy who loved it.'

Then there was the other people who bought the roadster. A cutting from the *San Francisco Chronicle* in 1968 revealed: 'Still the jauntiest 9 am sight on the Old Broadway: Ed Gauer, Roos/Atkins board chairman, riding to work in his two-seater Jaguar XKE, top down, his uniformed chauffeur at the wheel. . .'

Ed Harrell, Roy Hills, Chris Colebrook, the thousands of members of the Jaguar Clubs of North America, the girl from New York and Ed Gauer were the people who bought E types across the Atlantic.

X

E Types Around the World

ONLY 20,000 E types were left after America and Canada had had their share, and of those 20,000 cars, only 12,000 were sold on the home market. Where did the other E types go? To seventy-three different countries, from Zambia to Mexico, with Australia and New Zealand taking the lion's share. It is estimated that there are about 1,500 E types in Australia and New Zealand, where they appear to be having a rather hectic and unconventional life. In one survey in an Australian state, eighty per cent of the older cars listed had been in a major crash at one time or another. Perhaps this, plus the high cost of spare parts, helps to explain why it costs so much to insure an E type in this part of the world. This is the case in many other parts of the world, too, of course.

Sales of E types in Australia are quite phenomenal with some cars having had dozens of owners. Again, the high cost of insurance and spare parts, plus Australia's frustrating 60 mph blanket speed limit, are probably a factor here. All this sounds rather bad for the E type, but there is a good side to the Australian scene. Australians seem to be extraordinarily good at preserving and restoring their cars. It is here, of course, that the world-famous engineering firm, Repco, are a great help. They seem to be capable of making virtually any major spare part. They even made Jack Brabham's first world championship Grand Prix engine from bits and pieces before anybody else had time to develop a reliable unit.

The experiences of Harvey Hingston, of the Huirangi School, near New Plymouth, are in many ways typical of E type owners in New Zealand. For a start, he had a lot of trouble finding the model, he wanted, a Series One. When he did find it he did not have much trouble persuading the owner to sell it, but he had to pay a rather high price and meet the owner's other terms. Then Harvey did a wonderful restoration job on the car before veering away from the more usual pattern of his fellow E type owners in Australia and New Zealand. He could not bear to part with his 4.2-litre coupé.

Harvey was not always like that. He had several sports cars in the 1950s and 1960s buying and selling them as quickly as anybody else. This applied even to the three XK Jaguars that he owned at one time or another and the new Mark Two saloon he bought later. In fact, at the time he caught the E type bug, he was down to a Vauxhall Viva for everyday transport, after returning from a two-year teaching spell in Canada.

'After a few months with only the Viva, I got the urge,' says Harvey. 'The urge to buy another Jaguar. I thought . . . it must be an E type, as my wife, Jill, and I had a "sensible" car and the E type could be used solely as a fun car. Finding an E type in good condition was the start of the problem. I fancied a 3.8-litre model, but none of those that I saw was in good enough condition for me to consider. I had a few dollars left in overseas funds, so I advertised for one in the British motoring magazines, in the *Jaguar Driver*, and contacted Henlys in London

'I also wrote to a friend we had made when we visited the Jaguar factory in 1969. Although I had about five replies, my good friend and adviser, David Young, who seems to know more about E types than almost anybody else in New Zealand, told me to be very careful with British cars because of salt corrosion underneath. I took his advice, and started an intensive search within New Zealand, aided by Moller Motors and their dealer network

'A response came almost immediately from Archibalds in Christchurch, who expected to be trading in a choice 3.8-litre in original condition. I had made arrangements to fly down with Dave to view the car, when Archibalds sent me a telegram saying: "Regret to advise that E type now withdrawn from sale." So it was back to base one, and by this time I was feeling pretty frustrated. I then heard of another for sale at Palmerston, but this car had just had a complete restoration, and that is just what I wanted to do with the one I bought, so that was not the answer. At this stage I gave up, and decided that I would look around for an Australian muscle machine. This was just after Christmas 1972, and Jill said she would like to look round Wellington for a couple of days. So, we gave the Viva a quick check up, and set off. We saw Sybil Lupp about an E type, and she did not know of any currently available, except for one being rebuilt after an accident.

'However, although Sybil did not realise it, she did us a great big favour by recommending us to stay at a new motel called the Town House overlooking Oriental Parade. We had a fifth floor suite, and the view was tremendous from the balcony. One evening, around 7pm, Jill was leaning over the balcony when she called to me and said: "Harv! What's that parked down there outside the yacht club?" One quick glance from me established that it was a light blue metallic E type which looked (from that height at least) to be in pretty good shape. The elevator to the ground floor was too slow, so we shot down the stairs five at a time to see this car at ground level. The owner was not there, although a pair of shoes and socks were carefully parked in the E type's luggage area. On close inspection, the car appeared very tidy except for the usual beating around the front from stones. The owner still had not arrived half an hour later, and during this time, I had been thoroughly under and over the car, and couldn't find anything amiss. There was a dairy opposite, so I asked the staff if they knew who the car belonged to. One member did, so I left our phone number in the hope that he would make contact. He did, and it didn't take long to establish the fact that he was in love with the car as well. I kept upping the price until he had to sell it to me—he had no intention of selling it at the start of the conversation. Luckily, I had caught him at a good moment, as he was in the process of buying a half share in an ocean-going yacht. He agreed to sell the car for the price offered, but I had to let him go for his annual holidays in it first.

'I wasn't too happy about this, but he seemed a careful driver, and seemed to have respect for fine machinery, so I agreed. I had to, if he hadn't been able to go on his holidays in it first he would not have sold the car. However, we drew up an agreement to say that if he damaged the car in any way, the deal was off. We then motored to Wanganui to tell Dave what we had done. He stared at the ground, asked a few questions to which all the answers were "Yes", and then told us to drop the car into him as soon as we had taken delivery. This we did, and Dave spent a good hour putting our purchase under the microscope. The worst thing he found was a leaking rear diff seal, which he agreed to put right as soon as he had finished with jet boating for the season.

'This suited me fine, as I would get stuck into the sprucing-up programme in the interim. The first thing I did was to trade in the Michelin X A S tyres for a set of Aquajets with the v speed rating. The Michelins were a fine handling and steering tyre, but the noise they made at low speeds was too much for me. The Aquajets completely eliminated this noise. Before I put the wheels back on to the car, I gave one each to four of my mechanically-minded pupils, and told them that the one who could shine their wheel the best would be taken to the pictures. I supplied small brushes, kerosene and dusters. They really got stuck in, and with their small fingers gave each spoke preferential treatment. Under the grime the chrome was in real good condition, and the wheels were soon sparkling

New Zealander Harvey Hingston: proud owner of a Series One E type.

under the concentrated efforts of the boys. After two lunch hours, the boys admitted that they could not get them any cleaner, so I was then faced with the problem of judging the best. This was impossible, so I took them all to see *The Poseidon Adventure*. Dave then had the car for a couple of weeks, and I had his Borgward in my garage. During this time, all the chromework was redone, and the cam covers and carbs polished. I gave Dave a free hand to do what he needed and when I took delivery, it felt much more responsive, and completely vibration and rattle free. The next step was a repaint in the original colour, so I went to see many painters on the subject. My brief was to make the car equal to new—I would strip the car and rebuild it—they only had to paint it. I finally found an elderly gentleman in Stratford who agreed to paint the car better than original —to quote him: "I will spend three weeks on your car, Jaguar spent only half a day on it when they painted it—but . . . it will cost you plenty if you want my best work.""Hhhhhow mmmmmuch?" I asked. "Gosh, that's plenty all right," I said, "but go ahead." His reply was that it would have to be done before any snow got onto Mount Egmont . . . apparently weather conditions are critical when seeking perfection. So it was down to Wanganui again to do the stripping. We unscrewed everything that was unscrewable. Door trims came off, all weather stripping came off, even the windscreen came out, and a new one was fitted with less pitting from stones. Then it was back to Stratford in decidedly uncomfortable conditions—amazing how noisy a car is (and draughty) without its trim. Three weeks later, it was back to Wanganui to rebuild the bits removed, and this took a lot longer than taking them off. It took two full days to put the Meccano set together, and those fiddly light covers . . . ugh! I was thrilled with the result, and anxious to push it outside into the sunlight. Yes! The painter had kept his promise—the finish was better than the original. Even Dave said so!

'Since the painting there has been little to do. I had the steering wheel redone by a retired cabinet maker, and the back of the seats redone in original wool moquette—the moths had eaten patterns in the original. The gearlever had only a rubber gaiter at the base, which was too much like a Volkswagen, so I sent to the factory for a Series Two base which has a leather gaiter and a chrome ferrule— much sexier. The air freight on this was the same cost as the goods.

'I then turned my attention to the exhaust system. Dave said that those chrome mufflers at the back could be removed without detracting from the performance, and with not much noise differential, so off they came. My brother-in-law, who is a very talented engineer, took the problem out of my hands, and made twin pipes about four feet long out of heavy gauge stainless steel tubing, made in three parts to get the angles right, welded together, and polished. I hate crinkle bends. He even put a bell mouth at the end. The fit is so precise where it joins the main pipes underneath the car that no clamps are necessary. "Just belt 'em on with a piece of wood," he said. When the car was on display with the Taranaki Jaguar Drivers' Club at Hawera to support the Rotary Club, one spectator said: "What a funny place to have your carb cold air intakes!" Was he on the level? Maybe the club will organise a sprint some time on the flat roads south of Wanganui. With the 50 mph limit probably here to stay, there's no chance of winding it out on the roads around here.

'One of the reasons, I guess, that I had so much trouble finding my car was that I really wanted a 4.2-litre model, as I consider that this car, with the slim-line bumpers, the small grille opening and the enclosed headlights is the most desirable model, as well as the fastest. I have had no reason to regret my purchase, as I am constantly getting offers for it four years after I bought it, probably because it is one of the truly immaculate and original cars left in this country. There is absolutely no trace of rust anywhere.

'My only regret when showing potential buyers is afterwards, when I find it necessary to wipe the saliva marks off the paintwork. We built a new home a year ago, and I thought that the E type would have to go in order to help with the finances. Jill strongly objected, her words being: "You could never replace it." so I have it still, and I'm sure it enjoys its retirement in the surroundings provided. I have had the usual Jag troubles—the clutch plate and leaking diff seals—but the engine at 60,000 miles is very sweet, and apart from a bit of valve lapping a year ago and the sump being cleaned out, nothing else has been necessary.

'My brother-in-law has made me something else for the car, too, a pair of stainless steel trumpet air intakes identical to the steel ones available from the factory competition department, except that they are made in a heavier gauge and polished like his exhaust pipes. With a set of competition carburetter needles that I managed to get hold of, and the stroppy noise from the exhaust that is music to my ears, these modifications suit the engine admirably. I even leave the side windows permanently hinged open to suck in the sound. And in a recent club sprint, the car hit 124 mph and braked to a stop in just under three quarters of a mile.

'I would not like to use the E type for everyday motoring, as they are so vulnerable to clumsy parkers, and the usual vandals that seem to be a feature now of most of the world's towns. Recently, in a small provincial town forty-five miles south of here, an E type whose owners was staying in a nearby hotel, had every panel dented, and it was obvious that some drunken louts had given it a good "stomping". We never leave our E type unattended, and do the majority of the routine servicing ourselves.

'We have an honest Jaguar dealer in New Plymouth, ten miles from the school, and the New Zealand distributors for Jaguar spares are also very handy. I was permitted to see through their warehouse, and E type parts, including body panels, were in abundance.

'The cost of spares here in New Zealand is high—I would imagine about three times higher than what you would pay in the United Kingdom. Car running costs are high also, $1.27 a gallon for fuel, with correspondingly high costs for registration, insurance and the twice-yearly warranty of fitness.

'The open-road speed limit is rigidly enforced by radar, and as you know, 50 mph is attainable in first gear in an E type. On the credit side, the New Zealand climate is kind to cars, with no snow to speak of and no corrosion-causing chemicals are ever used on the roads. Cars built in the early 1930s are in everyday use and are not an uncommon sight.

'We give our E type a good hard run once a month of thirty miles, which includes a climb from sea level to 3,300 ft. We are fortunate in having an 8,260 ft mountain on our doorstep and the road that leads to one of the resorts nearby is pure joy in the E type. The road is well graded and sealed—there are very few dirt roads in our Taranaki province. It is flanked on either side by tall native trees of the sub-temperate zone, and the exhaust noise bounces off this curtain of trees in a crescendo of pure power as 5,000 rpm is used in second and third gears. We usually plan to have a short stop at the end of the road where there is a look out tower which spreads the province out like a map. I always check the exhaust colour here, and after this run, I am always rewarded by the light grey dusting which is an indication that all is well in the induction and combustion areas.

'At the end of this run, I squirt raw upper cylinder lubricant down the caburetter intakes until the engine starts choking on it, and then I switch off. This is to ensure that after standing for a month, the cold start will not be on a dry bore. The car is then very lightly hosed below window level and leathered off before covering with a dust sheet.

'We have a heart-and-soul relationship with our E type—it is more than a car, it is a beautifully tooled instrument of power. When will I sell it? Only when I am too arthritic to climb in and out! The more I see of the latest crop of cars, products of the elephantine sausage making machine, the happier I am to think we are lucky enough to own one of England's greatest sports cars of all time.'

The way Harvey looks after his E type is typical of the modern enthusiast in Australia or New Zealand, but the way he enjoys it and intends to go on using it are unusual. Many of the Australian E type owners seem to buy them chiefly as an investment or just for prestige. They certainly look after their cars well, with the help of Repco and firms like Terry Moore's spare parts centre (Terry has just opened a branch in Australia) but they do not appear to enjoy driving them so much as Harvey. In fact, their chief pleasure appears to be selling their E types at a profit, with second-hand models fetching up to 12,000 Australian dollars. They have five really good clubs, too, but only a small number of the E type owners join a Jaguar club, let alone help with the organisation of functions and so on. This was discovered by Tony Prins, of the Jaguar Club of Tasmania, when he attempted a survey of all the E types on the Apple Island.

'It should have been a simple one-night project,' [says Tony]. 'But like so many other small jobs on the classic sports machine, it turned into a two-month nightmare with phone calls and trips to all parts of Tasmania. I had thought that about a dozen E types would fill the bill, but, alas, to date I have discovered twenty-eight of the beasts, with owners ranging from doctors to university students. Of the twenty-eight, four are 3.8-litre cars—the best, of course—nine are 4.2-litre Series One machines, ten are Series Two models, and there are five Series Threes. Only three of the twenty-eight are soft top models—something to do with the weather, I guess. The most prominent colour is red, followed by white, primrose, grey, maroon, green and sable.'

Facing page, above: Foot hard down: H. Steunetrink storms the Col de Braus in his rally E type.

Facing page, below: The Works E type that raced to fourth place in Le Mans 1962 in the hands of Roy Salvadori and Briggs Cunningham. Its fuel injection engine for that race was number XK4960; the chassis number is 860630.

The E type is number one for this German competitor in British Club racing.

Tony owns the earliest E type in Tasmania, a 1961 fixed-head coupé, chassis number 860134, which was first registered in England in 1962. The car was shipped to Tasmania in 1968 and despite having had eight owners, it is still in excellent condition, with a very low mileage on the clock. Although the history of every one of the twenty-eight Tasmanian E types was not readily available, Tony discovered that about one third of the cars were bought new in Tasmania with the rest being shipped in from Britain or Australia.

'Of the earliest ten, only two had not been involved in a series prang, which probably explains the high insurance rating and the difficulty in obtaining adequate cover at a reasonable cost,' [says Tony]. 'Eleven of the cars which I surveyed are on the market or have been traded over the past six months. From my point of view, it suggests that the real enthusiasts are still in the minority and the true value of the E type has still to be recognised in this state. Prices asked

recently range from $3,200 for a 1962 car in poor condition to $11,950 for a 1973, which I consider to be overpriced.'

I doubt whether anything could persuade draughtsman Dave Caro, of Claremont, Tasmania, to part with his 1969 E type fixed-head coupé, though. He had to put a great deal of effort into restoring the car, which he bought in 1970. It was only two feet high then, following a tremendous crash. Everything was shattered, with the roof, doors and tailgate torn to shreds. The six-foot long bonnet was unrecognisable and every piece of glass was smashed.

Dave's restoration really was a great work. It consisted of re-shaping the battered body, building new sub-frames and re-forming the roof (called the turret in Australia), doors and so on, which is easier said than done. In fact the work took hundreds of hours and Dave says he would never again attempt such a project, but he shows no sign of selling the car. When you look at it, you can see why; the car is immaculate.

It is surprising that more Jaguar owners in Australia and New Zealand do not belong to the clubs there with their excellent range of activities and magazines. Apart from the Tasmanian club, there are the Jaguar Car Club of Victoria, which meets in South Melbourne; the Jaguar Drivers' Club of Australia, based at Leichhardt, New South Wales; the Classic Jaguar Club of Western Australia at Thornlie; the Jaguar Drivers' Club of Southern Australia, which meets in Adelaide, and the Jaguar Drivers' Club of Canberra. They run club races as part of the long Australian season, together with concours events, rallies, parties, picnics and film shows. They also produce good club magazines and a national publication called the *Jaguar Journal*. This deals with all aspects of club life and gives racing a good coverage, which is fine for the E type because most Australian racing is confined to production car events. Two of the most famous E type racing cars in Australia are the lightweight purchased new from the factory by Bob Jane (who has resisted all attempts by other enthusiasts to buy it), and the 4.2-litre factory-prepared racing coupé owned by the Australian Jaguar distributors, Brysons. They have branches in Sydney, Melbourne and Adelaide, and by all accounts, do an excellent job in keeping Australian Jaguar enthusiasts happy, even though their prices for spares are, necessarily high. This expense is made easier to bear, however, by the service provided. It takes Tony Prins only twenty-four hours on average to get his spare parts from Melbourne, much quicker than many parts can be bought in the United Kingdom!

The owners of E types in other parts of the world are truly dedicated to their cars and are reluctant to part with them. They have almost invariably had to go to a lot of trouble to buy their E types in the first place, sometimes having waited up to two years for delivery of new cars. The Scandinavians seem to go in for restoration in the biggest way, paying vast sums to Britons selling their E types or spare parts. The Germans and Italians are rather in the same mould. But the French have different ideas. They are more prone to sending their cars back to Britain for restoration than doing it themselves. One of their greatest enthusiasts is Dr Phillipe Renault, who has no less than five E types in his Jaguar collection in Paris.

Number one is a 1963 lightweight with a 3.8-litre wide-angle aluminium block engine, fuel injection and ZF five-speed gearbox. Number two will be the lightweight crashed at Montlehéry in 1964. Its crumpled remains—the car was shorter than a Mini after the crash—were impounded at the track in Paris for twelve years until Dr Renault spirited it away and back to England for John Harper and Forward Engineering to rebuild. Dr Renault's other E types are a beloved Two Plus Two that he finds perfect for grand turismo, an early roadster and a 4.2-litre coupé that used to belong to world champion racing driver Jack Brabham. 'My only regret is that I cannot buy a new E type,' says Dr Renault. 'For me, the perfect car would have been a new short wheelbase fixed-head coupé with fuel injection, synchromesh and the wide wheels of the Series Three E type.' The owners of E types all over the world feel that way. It *is* such a pity that you cannot buy a new one any more.

IX

The Men Behind the E type

IT WAS essentially three men who made the E type: Sir William Lyons, Bill Heynes and Malcolm Sayer, supported by back room boys such as Claude Baily, Harry Munday, Wally Hassan, Harry Weslake, Phil Weaver and Peter Taylor at various times between its first appearance on a drawing board in 1955 and the last car being sold somewhere in America in the summer of 1975. 'It was a derivative of the original C type Jaguar, which we produced to compete at Le Mans,' Sir William told a Press conference when the last car had been sold.

'We had not really had a car which was competitive before we produced the C type—and having been to Le Mans at the time when Leslie Johnson drove the XK120 in 1950 and did so well that he got up to third position with an almost standard car until the clutch went—this put something into my mind. Bill Heynes was with me at the time and we thought it was a race that we could win, and we went back home determined to produce something that could win.

We felt that it could be more competitive than the XK— after all most of the cars competing at Le Mans were prototype models, whereas the XK was a production model—so we felt that we had sufficient licence to produce a car very much lighter, and with much more power—and we would be able to take certain steps with the engine which were not standard. Therefore we went to Le Mans the next year, and as you know, we won it at a record speed. That was, of course, the start of the whole picture and we felt that we could do even better. Three years later we produced the D type, which was extremely successful, and it did, of course, establish us and did a lot for the Jaguar name.'

But Sir William, ever the hard-headed businessman, knew that motor racing was expensive and that all available resources must be concentrated on producing a new car to capitalize on the D type's success at Le Mans. So in 1955, Malcolm Sayer, an aerodynamicist who once worked for the Bristol Aircraft Corporation, drew up the first E type in consultation with engineering director Bill Heynes, and with Sir William looking over their shoulders.

The first E type appeared in metal in 1958, soon after the D types had quit top-line racing. It was rather like a scaled-down D type, powered by a 2.4-litre XK engine, and was used chiefly to evaluate the main features of the great sports car to come,

The men who made the E type: from the left, back row: Claude Baily, Harry Munday, Sir William Lyons, Wally Hassan, Malcolm Sayer. From the left, front row: Bill Heynes, Phil Weaver, Harry Weslake. The car is an E type prototype number two. *Artwork, courtesy Tim Holder.*

notably its brand new independent rear suspension. Then, in 1959, came the next prototype E type, a steel car bearing a close resemblance to the actual production models that were to appear two years later. It is this car which is the subject of the Tim Holder drawing, with Sir William and the designers and developers as they might have gathered around it. Both these cars have long since been banished to the scrapyard, but the third E type, the prototype which raced at Le Mans in 1960 is still with us. Unfortunately, Sayer is dead, but his car lives on as a lasting memorial to his genius. His first Jaguar work was seen on the 1948 XK, on which he smoothed out the body lines among other contributions. But the C types and D types were largely his work, and extremely effective at that. Their functional shape was distinctive and beautiful. They always looked as fast as they were, characteristics that became evident in the E type. As with all Jaguar sports cars, great attention was paid to streamlining, which was Sayer's department.

The bodies were very carefully developed, using one-tenth scale models in wind tunnels. A reduction in drag was not the over-riding consideration though, as the effects of side winds and the alteration of the car's attitude through wind pressure were investigated, too. As Bill Heynes said later of the work that Sayer and Sir William did: 'It is surprising how close the results obtained in the wind tunnel are carried out on the road. In fact, we find it possible to predict, within three or four per cent, the speed a sports car will achieve before it is built.' It is worth remembering that Heynes said this in 1960 when, by the appearance of many cars rolling off the production lines, such considerations were far from the minds of many manufacturers. Computers were not being used much then either.

Sayer was responsible for most of the exterior changes on the D type, such as its occasional long nose, but like the E type, his first shape was so good that even the technical personnel at the Royal Aircraft Establishment at Farnborough, Hampshire, who collaborated on the design, could find little to improve.

Vivid evidence of Sayer's work was seen on the racing E types. Dick Protheroe's second racer, the low-drag coupé, was a development of the normal E type shape used on most lightweights. With its slim top, low-raked screen and long nose, it had an even more favourable drag factor than normal E types. But this search for a lower drag co-efficient meant sacrifices. They were acceptable on the track—and indeed preferable from the performance point of view, where it was questionable if the lightweight's alloy engines and five-speed gearboxes were worth the trouble—but in effect the more advanced Sayer changes highlighted the quality of the first E type shape.

On road cars, it is not practical to cut down further on interior space or make the nose longer as on Protheroe's low-drag car. A longer nose alone would mean over-heating in traffic jams—a condition not unfamiliar to E type drivers of normal-nosed cars, let alone long ones—and even more damage by parking and generally sloppy driving. Also, nobody but a midget had any illusions about reducing the room inside an E type. It will remain a matter for speculation, too, as to who made Protheroe's low-drag coupé look rather like the current opposition, the Ferrari G TO, in some respects.

Sayer never appeared to be a plagiarist—you only had to look at his racing cars—but Sir William certainly did not mind benefiting from other people's ideas. In fact, it is even rumoured that he 'borrowed' his original firm's name, SS, from the great motor cycle manufacturer, George Brough.

Protheroe had a lot of success with his low-drag coupé, so Sayer gave some drawings to Peter Lumsden and Peter Sargent, who with two other Peters, Lindner and Nocker, raced two of the fastest lightweight E types. They used the Sayer blue-prints to good effect, producing cars rather like that of Protheroe. It is interesting to note that their cars showed no tendency to lift at about 170 mph as did similar-shaped racing E types of the same weight and power. Perhaps, under Sir William's watchful eye, Sayer could have developed the E type shape further to its advantage, but he was already working on its projected successor, the X J 1 3. Unfortunately, the X J 1 3's chassis development turned out to be a potentially too expensive venture in terms of manpower so it was dropped.

All the Sayer-Lyons sports cars have strong family likenesses, and none was more apparent to the man on the showroom floor than the similarity between the D type and the E type; they were closely parallel in shape and in aircraft-style construc-

Above: Side view of Dick Protheroe's low-drag coupé, showing Sayer's long nose and slim tail to advantage. Not for the first time in its life, the car is beset with cooling trouble; note the steam pouring from the half-open bonnet.

Plate 11 Opposite page: Every man's dream of a car . . . the Series One E type roadster.

tion. As Sir William said of his relationship with Sayer: 'We decided from the very first that aerodynamics were the prime concern, and I exerted my influence in a consultative capacity with Malcolm. Occasionally I saw a feature I did not agree with and we would discuss it. I took my influence as far as I could without interfering with his basic aerodynamic requirements and he and I worked on the first styling models together.'

Then there was Heynes. To everybody in the European motor industry, the name of William Heynes is inseparable from that of Jaguar, they are so closely linked. For thirty-four years, he directed the engineering fortunes of the company which achieved a meteoric rise to fame not least by reason of the advanced design and widespread appeal of its products. Add to this a reputation as one of the most successful sports racing car designers in the world and you have some indication of the calibre and versatility of the man.

W. M. Heynes C.B.E.—Bill to his many friends—spent his whole life in the motor industry, passing from school via an apprenticeship with Humbers, before joining SS Cars in 1935 as chief engineer.

For its success, Jaguar had always relied on a combination of advanced engineering and individualistic styling, coupled with a high standard of quality and the very competitive selling price, which could only be achieved by long production runs of the sort associated with the E type. Such parameters give an engineering team a very wide sphere of operation and it is obvious, even to the least technically-minded, that Heynes and his staff have always taken full advantage of the opportunities so presented. From the very outset, the result has been a steady stream of outstanding models, each of which has set the standards by which competitors have been judged. The E type's first real ancestor was the SS100 two seater, one of only a handful of sports cars which, pre-war, were capable of exceeding a genuine 100 mph, yet it was sold at less than one third of the price of its nearest rival. The E type's next real

ancestor was the XK120: a car which has passed into history as one of the most successful sports cars of all time and which, on its introduction, rendered utterly obsolete all previous concepts of sports car design and performance, and whetted the appetite of Americans or motoring in the European manner. Heynes' C type and D type sports racing cars vanquished the finest cars and drivers that manufacturers in Europe and America could produce. Add to these the series of saloons—the Mark VII VIII, IX and Ten; the Mark One and Two, the S types and 420s, to say nothing of the sports cars, the XK120, XK140, XK150, and the ultimate, the E type—all of which, without exception, enjoyed tremendous commercial success, and you begin to appreciate not only the versatility, but also the industry of Heynes and his team.

To his colleagues, Heynes has a further claim to fame as one of the few engineers capable of original thought on long-standing problems and thereby able to provide new solutions for them. The use of ball-type kingpin joints to locate and control wheel movement in independent front suspension systems was evolved and developed by him and is now universally adopted as standard practice, and is of course, used on the E type.

But it is in the fields of braking and tyre development that his pioneering work is perhaps best known. In conjunction with the Dunlop Rubber Company, he initiated, as far back as 1950, a major design and development programme on the disc brake which resulted first in the string of Le Mans wins and then in a Jaguar car being the first volume production car to feature this equipment. It has since become standard equipment, not only on all Jaguar products, but also on an ever-increasing number of other makes.

The same desire to find a completely original solution to tyre problems resulted in new concepts of tyre design and construction from which, in turn, were evolved the high-speed type of tyre, now in general use. These tyres offer safety at maximum speeds without the necessity of having to use extreme pressures, and without them there would have been no E type.

The list of Heynes' achievements seems endless. The XK engine with its twin overhead camshafts, is without a doubt the most versatile and successful power unit ever produced. It has been used in everything from Centurion tanks to the E type. It owes its design concept and development to Heynes, who initiated it with Sir William and Claude Baily nearly forty years ago, when such a design was thought to be too advanced for use in production cars and incapable of volume production.

The exploitation of monocoque construction, first in the D type and subsequently in the E type, and the development of the unique design of independent rear suspension, first in the E type and then in all other Jaguar cars, merely serve to underline the fertility of ideas and far-ranging interests of Jaguar's engineering director.

In the post-war years, Heynes built up the company's engineering division into one of the most successful units of its kind and one which, irrespective of the increasing severity of competition, is fully capable of keeping Jaguar to the forefront in the world of automobile engineering.

Heynes was recommended to Sir William by motor industry contacts, but another man responsible for the great success of Jaguar sports cars must be Harry Weslake, the cylinder head genius who runs his own engineering firm at Rye in Sussex. He was introduced to Sir William by a customer who wanted his new SS to go a bit faster and it was Weslake who was later·responsible for much of the development work on the twin-cam head that is the key to all X K-engined cars. He also developed the V 12 engine with Heynes, Hassan and Baily, and in fact, right to the time Heynes retired in 1969, the engineering director kept up his visits to Rye to work with Weslake.

Two men took over from Heynes: Wally Hassan and Bob Knight. Knight was responsible, with numerous racing and test drivers, for developing and improving everything from the C type to the E type, plus many other less sporting Jaguars. First Phil Weaver, and then Peter Taylor, were among the better-known development engineers, and there can be hardly any motoring enthusiasts who have not heard of Hassan. He spent ten of the most glorious years with the Bentleys when they were winning everything in the 1920s, he went on to join Raymond Mays and Peter Berthon at E R A, worked with John Cobb on his world land speed record-breaking Railton Mobil Special, and finally he joined Sir William for the first time in 1938.

Series Three E types on the production line at Jaguar's factory in Browns Lane, Coventry.

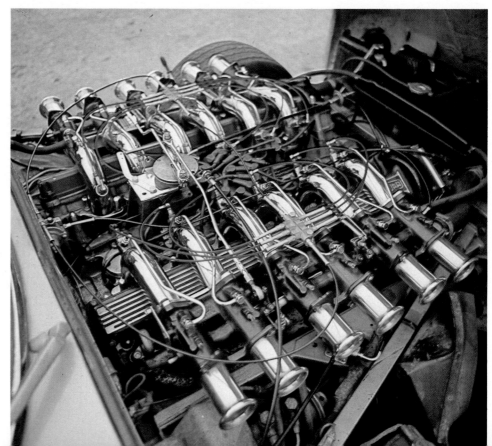

Plate 12 Above: E type in action: one of the ex-Briggs Cunningham dynamic duo of lightweight racers on its way to mopping up yet another historic race.

Plate 13 Right: The mind boggles to think of the complexity of tuning a fuel injection twelve-cylinder E type. But the power output of Guy Beddington's racer is mind boggling, too.

Plate 15 Opposite page, below: What it looked like to start with: much simpler and more practical.

Plate 14 Above: Portrait of a man who really loves his E type: prolific concours winner Alan Hames with his wife Angela and AVV I, their Series Three roadster.

After a brief wartime spell with Bristol he returned to Jaguar as experimental engineer, working on the XK engine. Having helped design that wonderful unit, he left for Coventry Climax, where as chief engineer, his engines gained four world championships for British Grand Prix cars at a time when everybody had given up. With the acquisition of Coventry Climax by Jaguar in 1963, Hassan was brought back into the fold again and a year later became chief power unit engineer, with the V12 engine as the result.

There are many other personalities who helped make the E type, of course, including Lofty England, who as service manager, helped make a practical car after his racing experiences with the D types at Le Mans, and who still drives a V12 E type in his retirement in Austria.

The racing drivers also played a small part in the development of the cars; they quickly found out any faults in their E types. As Graham Hill said of his experiences in the first E type to win a race, the ex-Tommy Sopwith Equipe Endeavour car (now in the Danny collection)

'It was a bit of a pig to start with, because we were racing straight off the production line. You know, you need to sort a car to protect it from the type of stresses we subject cars to under racing conditions, but we got it into shape and it became a very, very fine car to drive.

'Roy Salvadori was a great rival at the time in Jaguar saloon cars. Sopwith and Coombs were great rivals as entrants in saloons too, so we were having a very good race in both camps. I remember the E type on that day. We came out in practice and we were having a lot of trouble with the brakes and we couldn't get the thing stopped. The brakes were overheating and boiling the fluid and we were having to pump the brakes a tremendous amount to get the thing stopped.

'The other problem was a question of fuel surge. Obviously the car was not built for racing, and we were getting fuel all in one side of the tank and it was sucking in air and not picking up. Coombs solved this problem and rather sportingly told us what to do. I promptly went out and beat his car. I was having a very good race with Roy until he eventually faded away with some sort of trouble—brakes I believe it was! At any rate John Coombs was really brassed off about it—but we had a very good race and, of course, I was delighted to win in an E type in its very first outing on a racetrack.

Thanks to men like these, the E type was a winner from the start. Such was the excellence of their product and the cheapness of their price that only twice in the future did production ever overtake orders. The first occasion was when XK150 production ended in January 1961 and it took until the summer months of that year to sell the cars in stock after the E type was announced in the spring. The second time was when the E type production ended in autumn 1974 and it took until the summer of the next year to sell all the remaining cars. It was not that the XK150 and the E type were unpopular, it was just that the many potential XK buyers held off when the E type was announced and E type production was stepped up dramatically in 1974 to utilise an excess of V12 engines before the production of XJ12 saloons and XJS coupés was fully integrated.

XII
The Interchangeability of Parts

IT IS obvious from just looking at an E type that many of its basic components are common to other Jaguars, making the replacement of spare parts a much easier business than with most classic cars. But it is knowing just what components you can swop with parts from other Jaguars which is the perplexing business for most enthusiasts. In fact the parent company, British Leyland, have still not worked out anything like the full range of variations! One or two parts dealers, particularly Terry Moore and G. H. Nolans of South London, are really knowledgeable, but because they rely on this information, accumulated over many years, for a living, they guard their secrets closely.

There is also the problem of availability of spare parts. We all know how difficult it is to get all the pieces we need at any one time from a dealer. There is always something out of stock, which you are sure is available somewhere else, if only you knew where. As E types grow older and the stock of spares dwindles, this problem will get worse. One firm who have done a lot to solve the problem are Ipswich Computer Services. They operate a computer stock control for more than sixty Leyland distributors, many of whom hold Jaguar franchises. As a part of the ICS's stock control system, subscribers are provided with a composite list of all Jaguar parts held on file. In addition, ICS produce a redundant parts list, and constantly update their index sheet. The best way for an enthusiast to benefit from this system is to try to persuade his local dealer to link up with it or contact Ipswich Computer Services at The Thoroughfare, Woodbridge, Suffolk, for the name of the nearest appropriate subscriber.

Once contact is made with a dealer subscribing to the service, the enthusiast searching for spares can, in effect, have the stocks of all other subscribers throughout Britain searched for the part he needs, and have it despatched to his local outlet. Otherwise, it is a question of contacting the specialists, such as Terry Moore, whose addresses are available through the Jaguar Drivers' Club. It would be pointless to publish all the names and addresses in this book because they will change from time to time.

But what about all this knowledge that the specialists are keeping secret? It is based on the fact that the main units of an E type are often interchangeable with those of saloons produced in the same year. There are some notable exceptions, of course, in this catalogue of interchangeability, which only tends to deepen the mystery. And

Plate 16 The ultimate lightweight racing E type: the ex-Lumsden/Sargent low-drag coupé pictured at Woodcote Corner, Silverstone.

things get really complicated when you try to swop around parts from Jaguars prod-uced in different years. Jaguar not only constantly changed parts in detail as they produced their cars, but also as they changed their models. The golden rules to observe when searching for new parts is first to check if the part number is the same as that listed in the official spares catalogue and then to compare the new bit with the old if the parts number is different. Many parts numbers were updated over the years, so that identical components often have different parts numbers and yet another set if the same spare was used in a car of a different make. The essential rules to watch while searching for second-hand spares in scrapyards and the like are to find out exactly which car they were taken from or even still fitted to, and then to compare the parts, visually if possible. Otherwise use a tape measure, a gauge or anything to check before parting with your money.

Generally speaking, though, all six-cylinder XK engines, except the 2.8 litre, can be fitted to an E type, although small modifications are sometimes necessary and it is hardly worth fitting the units from the 2.4-litre and 3.4-litre saloons. Basically, the same 3.8-litre unit was fitted to 3.8-litre XK150 cars and to Mark IX and Mark Ten saloons, 3.8-litre Mark Two saloons and 3.8-litre S type saloons; the same 4.2-litre unit was fitted to the 420 series cars and the XJ6 saloons. But beware: you have to change the sump pan for that of the original E type engine. It is possible to swop the 4.2-litre for a 3.8-litre engine; my own 4.2-litre Series One chassis is fitted with a 3.8-litre engine from a 1961 E type that I used to own. But when this change is made it is essential to keep the distributor for each engine. You cannot swop a 3.8-litre's

Even a great car like an E type can be improved. The stainless steel header tank on this car looks virtually the same as the standard unit, but it does not rust away.

distributor for that of a 4.2-litre engine. There are other small differences too, such as the lack of a rear mounting bracket for the 4.2 litre's alternator on the 3.8-litre block. But luckily the alternator—which incidentally fits any of the post-1965 Jaguars—will run perfectly well without a rear bracket mounting. Basically, all the triple carburetter set-ups for 3.8-litre and 4.2-litre cars are interchangeable, although emission equipment should stay on emission-controlled cars. It is also a false economy to fit twin carburetters to a triple carb engine. You save nothing on fuel consumption and risk engine trouble.

It is a great help that 3.8-litre and 4.2-litre cylinder heads are interchangeable and early series oil filter assemblies can be exchanged for those fitted to XJ6 units. Obviously, minor components such as hoses are peculiar to an E type, and 4.2-litre inlet manifolds and header tanks on Series One cars are different from those on 3.8-litre cars because of the water heating arrangements. They can be changed however if the subsidiary units go with them. The same goes for the Series Two cooling system. It can be fitted to an earlier car, but you have to take a lot with it. Apart from ancilliaries then, it is an easy task to swop XK units around. The same goes for the V12 unit with those fitted to the XJ12 saloon and the XJS coupé, although dropping a twelve-cylinder engine into a six-cylinder chassis is beyond the capabilities of all but the most resourceful enthusiasts. Almost everything, including the front sub-frame, suspension and steering has to be changed. And you cannot have unpowered steering on a Series Three car: it is too heavy too allow you to turn the steering wheel.

Gearboxes and clutches from almost every Jaguar made from around 1952 can be swopped around with alacrity, although a careful note must be taken of the comparative gearbox ratios, and I have never heard of anybody who actually fancied fitting one of the earlier Moss boxes to an all-synchromesh car. Many people have fitted later series boxes to Moss-equipped cars, though, for obvious reasons. One problem that can crop up when swopping gearboxes for ones of a different series is the propshaft length. This should be checked before any major work is contemplated. Starter motors are not interchangeable though.

Unfortunately, the complete rear suspension unit on an E type is not interchangeable as a unit with that of the other independently suspended Jaguars. The track widths are different for a start and the E type has an anti-roll bar. At the best the wishbones and half shafts always have to be changed to give the replacement unit E type measurements. But the differential units are interchangeable with those of the Mark Ten saloon, an S type saloon, 420 series saloon or XJ, but like the gearbox, the ratios must be checked. It is best to stick to high ratios for an E type. This is because, with the extremely low ratios, such as the 4.55 fitted to 2.8-litre overdrive XJ6s, there is a tendency to chew everything up when they are subject to the extra power of an E type engine. Road E types feel and run better on higher ratios, too, with the 3.07 and 3.31 being the favourites. It is possible, of course, to convert a late automatic E type to a manual or vice versa, but the changes are extensive and almost certainly mean fitting a 2.88 rear axle ratio. The cost of the parts alone probably make this sort of change prohibitive.

Some parts from the front suspension can be swopped for those of other Jaguars, particularly the stub axles on an E type, which come from a Mark Two saloon. And

Plate 17 Left: Better than a show-room shot: an American specification Series Two roadster stands at ease in front of an Englishman's castle.

Plate 18 Below: Wouldn't anybody be on top of the world with a brand-new Series Three roadster?

almost all the brakes are interchangeable, although it is best from the stopping point of view to opt for the latest-possible braking system. Generally speaking, 3.8-litre E types benefit from having the entire braking system of a 4.2 litre fitted, preferably from the Series Two version of this car. Likewise, the Series One 4.2 litre is better with Series Two brakes and even better with those of a Series Three, but fitting Series Three braking parts to any of the earlier series cars involves changing many components and is, as a result, very expensive. Enterprising specialists market conversion kits for updating Series One cars at minimum cost.

One useful and relatively cheap change for an early E type is to fit the front brakes from a Mark IX or Ten saloon, which are less susceptible to fade than the original E type discs, because they were intended to stop a far heavier vehicle. But which ever brakes you fit to an E type, be sure to keep the correct E type pads; this is of vital importance.

The handbrake on the E type is a notorious Achilles heel. After a relatively short time it loses its efficiency, particularly with the non-self adjusting version fitted to early models. It will be of some consolation to E type enthusiasts to learn that the handbrake assembly on independent rear suspension saloons fits an E type.

In keeping with the brake changes, master cylinders and clutch, the slave cylinder can be swopped around, and those from earlier saloons, such as the Mark IX, can be adapted for E types. Generally speaking, instruments can be exchanged for those from other Jaguars and certainly the switchgear can be exchanged if the year of manufacture is roughly the same. The centre panel of four instruments, with its attendant wiring, on a Series One E type is exactly the same as that of the Mark Two

Six Weber carburetters in place of the normal emission-control units dramatically improve the performance of a V12 E type.

saloon. All the rev counters driven by their own generators from the back of one of the camshafts are the same too. Just make sure that the clock in the rev counter is of the appropriate earthing: Jaguars changed from positive earth to negative earth with the 4.2 litre's introduction in 1964. The instruments from XKs and their equivalent saloons can be used in E types too, with some modification, but the magnificent 160 mph speedomenter is pure E type.

Most of the interior is pure E type, too, although the interior of a 3.8-litre E type and that of a 4.2-litre Series One car are interchangeable except for the parts peculiar to the roadster, the fixed-head coupé and the Two Plus Two variants. The Series Two and Series Three interiors are virtually identical. Minor fitments, such as door and window handles, which can be so difficult to obtain from dealers, are common to those fitted to the Mark Two and many earlier saloons and even those fragile door arm rests on the early 4.2-litre cars are easy to get—providing you know that they were the same as fitted to many other BMC models of the same years—including Austin's three-ton truck! All sorts of odd parts are interchangeable, such as the gear lever boots and so on (it is best to compare parts before purchase). The permutations are endless.

The ultimate in E type conversions is to change the whole monocoque and build yourself a replica D type.

The actual light units—not the surrounds—are common on almost all Jaguar cars and many other BMC vehicles. For instance the headlights were the same throughout as those fitted to the Mini, a fact that has caused considerable comment from E type owners whose speed has been restricted by lack of light. Where the lighting systems do vary considerably, of course, is in those fitted to conform with the laws of individual countries, which means that E type owners outside Britain have to exercise the same care when obtaining lighting spares as they do with some of their other parts which might have been fitted only to cars exported to their countries.

Fuel pumps are interchangeable, too, and it is worth updating the early 3.8-litre models by simply fitting the standard SU pump in its 4.2 litre position in the right-hand rear wing, leaving the submersible unit in place, but disconnected. The later series pump is the same as fitted to many BMC cars (including the Mini again!). Another common problem with early E types is damage to the exhaust manifold flanges at the hands of strong arm mechanics wrenching away at the bolts holding rotten exhaust pipes. It can save a lot of money to know that these expensive items can be swopped for those of virtually any other Jaguar XK-engined car, provided the rake for the downpipes is the same. Be warned: the rake on the exhaust manifolds of a 2.8-litre XJ6 is different, for instance. Exhaust manifolds seem to lose their enamel paint pretty quickly and rarely look good, which can be to the advantage of the enthusiast scouring scrapyards. There are few dealers who realise how much it costs to buy a new version of one of their rusty old manifolds, which can soon be cleaned up and fitted to an E type.

Batteries and fan motors for any twelve-volt car can be swopped around with alacrity, provided the physical size is the same. And so can wheels and tyres, providing the arches are flared if earlier series cars are fitted with wheels and tyres from a Series Three. Wire wheels and solid wheels are interchangeable, too, providing the hubs are swopped at the same time.

Body panels are a real problem on an E type, of course. Skilled metal surgeons can adapt almost anything to fit anything else, except perhaps the front wings of an E type. There were no less than four types of wing made for the E type, according to headlight position, and it is almost impossible to adapt wings if they are not the correct part. This is because of curvature and the frequent attacks of corrosion in vital areas. Front wings should not be a problem to obtain though as it is possible to get all E type body parts now from the specialists plus the components in alloy from RS Panels, Classic Autos and Terry Moore.

As a matter of course, it is possible to swop the bonnets between any series of E type, providing provision is made for the wide tyres if you are fitting the better-looking earlier-style bonnet to a Series Three. Doors can be swopped about between short wheelbase models of the same body style and they can be changed between long wheelbase models if they are not mixed; the Two Plus Two doors are much longer of course. The rear end of the bodywork is the same or adaptable for all E types, depending on whether they are open models, fixed-head coupés or Two Plus Twos, and the bootlids are the same. This criteria applies to the glass, too, with the exception of the windscreens, which varied from model to model and even year to year in the mid-1960s. Hardtops and hoods are standard on all Series One and Two models, but are

Plate 19 Opposite page: One of the prettiest E types in circulation: the immaculate Series One roadster of David Morris. Note the lovely registration number 38 XKE.

longer on the Series Three. The clips that hold them down at the windscreen, and which sometimes snap, are the same whether fitted to hood or hardtop.

All this information may sound dreadfully complicated, but this is the sort of knowledge that E type owners and the people repairing them are going to have to know intimately as the years go on and the availability of spares shrinks and the price rises. It should never be forgotten that there is no substitute, in the form of either time or money, for actually removing the parts that need replacement from a car—provided that they are fitted in the first place—and comparing these parts with the spares available. It is virtually impossible to list all the options, even on a particular series or year of E type. Not even Jaguars have been able to do it, such has been the apparent flexibility of their assembly lines.

XIII

Improvements for the E type

THE GREATNESS of the E type's design is no more apparent than when the fanatics who own them try to improve them. They soon discover that there are very few points of the car that it is possible to change radically without spoiling it for road use. But there are a few things that can be done, which, in the light of fifteen years' development are a definite improvement, and they centre chiefly around the suspension and tyres.

The first thing to do to your E type is to fit Dunlop SP Sport tyres or if you are very rich, Michelin XWXs and forget about increasing the rim width. Anything above the standard width upsets the balance of the car and is bad for roadholding. SP Sports really are the best compromise between roadholding, durability and price, and it is not just me talking. This is the opinion of all the specialists. In more than 200,000 miles of E type motoring and probably half as much in the basically very similar XJ6 saloons, I have found no better tyre than the Dunlop SP Sport. It will last up to 25,000 miles of hard driving and maybe 40,000 miles of gentler use, although it must be accepted that the rear tyres will never last as long as those on the front. Such is the price of power. Throughout their legal life, their roadholding characteristics hardly change and they are exceptionally predictable in wet or dry. Goodyear G800s last longer on average, but their rubber compound seems harder and much more prone to let the car go; anybody who has ever driven an E type on a twisting road will know the ease with which the rear end can be unstuck.

It is reassuring to have a tyre that does not allow this too soon. Michelin XWXs are very good in my opinion, much better in fact than any other Michelin on an E type, but they are dreadfully expensive when wear rates are taken into consideration, although Jaguar development engineer Peter Taylor swears by them for racing. American drivers, especially those with wide wheels, seem to favour Firestones, particularly when wear rates are of paramount importance. Around the middle of the Sixties a majority of E types were fitted with Pirelli Cinturatos, and it can only be said that Pirelli have improved their rubber compound since then. In those days they could become totally unmanageable in the wet. The original Dunlop cross-ply tyres were acceptable in their time, but almost all the later tyres have been an improvement. Dunlop SP41s, fitted by the factory as standard equipment for years, were very good, before they were overtaken by the SP Sport.

The next most dramatic improvement to an E type is any sort of solid wheel, but only from the point of view of handling, because the wire wheels are ideal for appearance and pretty good for brake cooling. Chrome wires are the ultimate wheel for appearance if they can be kept really clean, but, especially in the case of the spokes fitted with the old style 'curly' hubs, they are prone to breakage. The post-1968 easy-clean hubs did a lot to clear up this problem, although I have found that stove-enamelled spokes are less brittle in any case.

This is because of the process the spokes have to go through to be chromed. All carbon steels are affected by chroming in direct proportion to their carbon content and the degree of processing necessary for plating. As wire spokes are, or should be, in the high carbon category they are affected by the retention of hydrogen, commonly known as hydrogen embrittlement. The tensile strength of alloy steels can be reduced by as much as eighty per cent by neglect of this procedure. The problem can be overcome by sustained heating to a point short of the steel temper, or damage to the plating already carried out. In the case of the latter, the relieving should be done as soon as possible after the plating process, particularly if the spokes have been acid-pickled before processing.

It is generally accepted though that the best wheels for E types are the Magna made by J. A. Pearce, the Minilite and the Wolfrace in that order. Magna knock-ons with their three-eared hub nuts are probably the best in appearance, with Wolfrace a close second. Fitting Wolfrace wheels means changing the hubs though if you have wire wheels, because these alloy wheels are available only in bolt-on form. Minilites can be supplied in knock-on or bolt-on form and limited supplies of replica D type wheels are available in the fifteen-inch diameter needed for an E type. All solid wheels improve the roadholding and general feeling of tautness of an E type, although wire wheels still have the edge on brake cooling.

The next most apparent improvements can be made in the suspension. First make sure that all the rubbers, including the Metalastik mountings at the rear, are in first-class condition, because anything less than 100 per cent here will be felt in the general controllability of the car. This applies also to the anti-roll bar rubbers, which take much of the axle-swinging power of the mighty engine. Deterioration—and this can start after only a year of normal road use—can be felt also in the front suspension rubbers and those mounting the rack. It is possible to mount the rack solidly, but this needs the utmost precision in assembly and lots of maintenance, so it is practical only for track cars, which often dispense with much of the other rubber too. On one car, the road E type used by journalist Denis Jenkinson of *Motor Sport*, the tow bar is rigidly mounted not only to the bottom of the luggage boot, but to the rear sub-frame too, which shows that the more solid the connection with the body the better, except perhaps for the sound insulation. The solid way the rear sub-frame on Jenkinson's car is connected to the body has certainly had no adverse effect on the roadholding.

Shock absorbers are the next most important item in conjunction with the springs. Standard Girling units are fine providing they are in first-class condition, but they have a tendency to wear out fairly quickly, particularly at the back end. This, and weak rubbers, caused much of the bottoming and weaving that was so evident on hard-driven early E types. Four rates of springs are available for the back suspension, although they are sometimes hard to get. My choice is the hard-riding super-stiff variety marked with a splash of purple paint. They can be stiffened still further by using the double thickness collets from a lightweight E type underneath them if you can obtain these parts, and fitting them around Spax or Koni shock absorbers. Spax have the advantage of being adjustable while still on the car. You have to remove Koni dampers to adjust them, although top suspension tuning experts recommend using the first setting only in any case. Girling are non-adjustable and Konis are reputed to last the longest, although it must be remembered that they are the most expensive.

Experiments can be made with the castor angle on an E type with varying results, but roadholding is always improved by the application of negative camber. Up to $1\frac{1}{2}$ degrees is practical, but it must be remembered that tyre wear increases with camber adjustment.

Most of the modifications of this racing E type are also applicable to road cars, notably the six-branch exhaust manifold and lightweight bonnet shown here.

Substitution of rear wishbones from a Series One E type can help stiffen up the rear end of a later E type. This is because the bearing area on the inside pivot of Series One bones is larger. A certain degree of adjustment of the torsion bars to give a nosedown attitude can help the throttle-hard-down cornering techniques of some drivers too, but these improvements are getting into the finicky area.

The best standard gearbox is that from the 4.2-litre roadster of late 1964, 1965, 1966 or early 1967 and the fixed-head coupé of the same era up to early 1966; it had the closest ratios, although the old Moss box has been made to work well with luck and careful assembly. Four-point-two clutches are a great improvement and so are Series Two brakes, although the cost of fitting the later brakes to earlier models is considerable. Terry Moore's Phoenix Engineering market a conversion kit which includes a replacement for the Kelsey-Hayes servo on the first cars. It is possible to

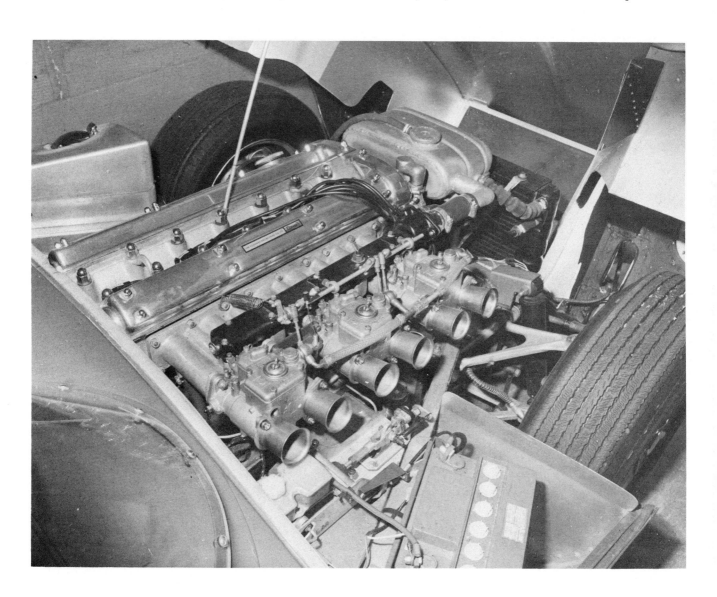

fit the braking system from a Series Three E type to any E type, but it is hardly worth the expense on the earlier cars because of the number of parts that need to be changed.

A certain amount can be done to the engine of any six-cylinder E type and indeed the twelve cylinder, but it is to be recommended that the engine is rebuilt at the same time, although startling results have been obtained in the case of the twelve cylinder simply by throwing away the emission gear and bolting on six big Weber carburetters. A good idea is to buy a 3.8-litre engine from a scrapyard for as little as £15 and start from there. You do not need a 3.8 from an E type of course; any of the straight port head designs will do. You just have to change the sump in some cases to that of the E type engine already fitted to your car, plus the odd ancillary. Old Mark Ten units come in handy this way. There is a lot, however, that can be done to the 4.2 litre and V12, although the ultimate road conversions on these are a good deal more expensive than those available for the 3.8 litre.

Ron Beaty of Forward Engineering at Kenilworth, near Coventry, is probably the best man to tackle any Jaguar engine job, from a straightforward overhaul to the most complicated tuning. Ron started Forward Engineering in 1967 after spending thirteen years with Jaguar as one of their top development engineers. From the start, his company specialised in the development, assembly, testing and installation of Jaguar engines in high-performance vehicles and boats. And his cars have won countless races all over the world. In the United Kingdom alone, drivers using his engines have won the Jaguar Driver of the Year competition for three consecutive years, the British Empire Trophy, the Over Three Litre Thoroughbred Championship and the JCB Championship.

As a result of his years of practical work, which started in 1954, Ron can offer an astonishing variety of Jaguar engine conversions and components, which can give from around 200 bhp for a 2.4-litre engine to more than 500 bhp from a single overhead camshaft V12. He also does almost everything needed to make a Jaguar go faster or better, although the engines are the real speciality.

In his catalogue, he lists valves of several different sizes, steel tappets, numerous valve springs, oversize tappet shims, at least six camshafts, various cylinder heads, nine different pistons with three different compression ratios, competition crankshafts, bearings and clutches, shot-peened con-rods, Weber and SU carburetter kits, three different types of flywheel, special exhaust systems, oil and water pumps, plus modified distributors, oil coolers and timing chains.

Ron's cylinder heads are all gas-flowed with a choice of standard valves or larger inlet valves of 1.820 ins or 1.875 ins on the sixes. His V12 heads have reprofiled standard valves, with oversize valves to special order. Two different camshafts are available for the V12—road or competition—and four different cams for the sixes: full race, high torque race, competition and road. He supplies oversize tappet shims for reprofiled camshafts and lightened steel bucket tappets for high-revving engines. His carburetter kits are chiefly Weber conversions, although he can supply SU kits to replace emission equipment. The Weber kits for the V12 E type are made up of six 44 mm LDF carburetters with special manifold, balance pipe, petrol pipes and linkages, which, with an engine rebuild, will churn out about 345 bhp with no more modification, or 330 bhp using six 40 mm Webers. It was one of these conversions, simply bolted on to a Guyson V12 E type, that brought it up to Ferrari Daytona performance, although, as Ron says: 'The actual engine had seen a good deal of use by then and was not in very good condition.' Remember, nobody has made a production car faster than the Daytona, which was in the £15,000 bracket when the E type was retailing at £3,300 plus the cost of Ron's conversion which amounted to a few hundred pounds.

Similarly, Ron supplies a Weber conversion kit for six-cylinder engines, comprising three 45 DCOE twin-choke carbs with special manifolds and so on. It must be noted though that these conversions can be used on straight port heads only although E types with other heads are very rare indeed. His triple SU pack to replace U.S. Federal emission equipment applies to the straight port head only, of course.

Forward Engineering exhaust systems are designed to give improved fuel economy and, or, performance, and consist of intermediate pipes, silencer box and twin tailpipes. These give the best results when combined with the appropriate six- or twelve-branch manifolds, and in the case of racing engines, an extra 30 bhp can be extracted by the use of critically-tuned pipe lengths.

There are a whole variety of pistons available for the V12 and XK engines. Forged pistons with special crowns to give an 11.5 to 1 compression ratio are listed for the V12 and similarly made pistons give a 10 to 1 compression ratio for 3.8-based racing engines, which end up as four-litre jobs. Solid skirt pistons with special crowns are listed for Ron's speciality, the one and only 4.5-litre road or track engine. These incredible units are based on a re-linered 4.2-litre block and in racing form a 4.5-litre was the first XK engine to beat the one-minute barrier on Silverstone's club circuit. In road form, it not only gives tremendous power, depending on other modifications such as carburetters but extra torque. Other pistons are available for practically every application, with 20, 40, and 60 thou oversize measurements for all units except the 4.5 litre.

Ron recommends specially-treated crankshafts as one of the most important components in any Jaguar engine, with fully-balanced Tuftrided units available for all engines, plus his other great must, shot-peened connecting rods for extra strength. Bearings are available in undersizes of 10, 20 and 30 thou and there are a variety of lightweight flywheels. You must remember, of course, that the resultant improvement in acceleration is at the expense of smoothness.

Heavy duty competition clutches with solid centre plates are available for all six-cylinder engines, and are to be recommended, as the standard clutch has a hard time absorbing the heat that can be generated by violent use. Special sumps for the V12, and competition breather kits to reduce the threat of oil loss, also help to keep things cool.

Forward Engineering's V12 and six-cylinder racing engines are probably the ultimate in their classes. The V12 competition unit has improved sump baffling, fully balanced clutch, flywheel and crank assembly, shot-peened rods, forged pistons with special crowns, gas-flowed cylinder heads, hot camshafts, 1.820 in inlet valves with special springs, six Weber carburetters with Mangoletsi manifolds, and all bearing surfaces microfinished. After fifteen hours' test-bed running it is guaranteed to give

This real bunch-of-bananas exhaust system on Anthony Hutton's racing E type is typical of the Forward Engineering products.

more than 485 bhp at 7,500 rpm. This is without generator or starter motor, of course.

Six-cylinder engines are built in much the same way with 1.875 in inlet valves and triple Webers. Their minimum guaranteed power output is 300 bhp for the 3.8-litre at 6,000 rpm; 310 bhp at 5,800 for the 4.2-litre and 320 bhp at 5,000 rpm for the 4.5-litre.

How is all this achieved? 'Chiefly by meticulous assembly and odd little safety first modifications such as the use of spring washers instead of tabs,' says Ron. 'It is amazing what damage a tiny piece of dirt can do to an engine and it is equally surprising to some people how much difference little things like carefully setting up the piston ring gaps can make.

'Basically, we try to keep everything simple. Our cars do not use oil coolers on ten-lap races, for instance. Much of the trouble with racing engines originated from lubrication and there is more to go wrong when an oil cooler is fitted, although they are vital for longer races, of course.

'We would not win any races for time spent in assembling an engine, but it is worth spending a lot of time here if the engine is going to last the life of the car, as it should with Jaguar units. It takes us about forty-five hours to rebuild a six-cylinder unit and about ten hours longer for a twelve.'

This is the real way to improve your E type power, of course, providing you consider it worth the expense. Send it to a specialist like Ron Beaty whose garage does everything else besides engines, or Terry Moore, or Albert Betts in Clapham, South London, or alternatively, send the parts to various specialists such as Harry Weslake in Rye, Sussex, for cylinder heads, Oldham and Crowther in Peterborough for bodywork and so on. Otherwise, do it yourself.

More mundane improvements centre chiefly around rust-proofing and are easy to do yourself, although commercial firms make a good job of this. The body apart, the number one corrosion spot is in the header-tank on the Series One cars. It seems obvious that the metal in this unit is bent or crimped at too acute an angle during manufacture with the result that they rot through at the corners at an alarming rate. It is always wise to keep a spare header tank for an E type Series One, although Phoenix Engineering and Grand Prix Metalcraft can supply stainless steel or alloy units. Several specialist firms in the US have made brass and copper header tanks, too, and it must be remembered that the very first E types were fitted with alloy tanks as standard. It is a great pity that Jaguar changed to the cheaper steel although the later Series Two and Three cars have not suffered from this problem to this extent, it seems. Petrol tanks on all models go much the same way as the Series One header tanks, although careful painting can help alleviate this problem. The petrol tank fits so closely in the car's tail that it almost forms a second skin and condensation and moisture in the boot rots it away at the corners from the outside of the tank.

Almost every part of an E type below the top of the sills rots away in a damp country like Britain with its salt-laden winter roads, and apart from the anti-rust treatments detailed in chapter seven, there is little that can be done about it apart from metal surgery. If panels have to be replaced however, they are best bought from specialist concerns such as Phoenix Engineering, who can supply thicker-than-standard galvanised panels, or Classic Autos or R S Panels who make components from alloy. There are also the specialist fibreglass panel makers, such as Guys, at Alcester in Worcestershire, whose panels are lighter, but they are sometimes difficult to fit. Phoenix also specialise in marketing the body parts which are no longer available from Jaguars, as do Oldham and Crowther, but, to my knowledge, Phoenix are the only firm who can lend the jigs needed for replacing the floors of E types and give free stage-by-stage fitting advice for the enthusiast or garageman working in his own premises.

The E type's massive bonnet is rust prone, as I have said earlier, and the best way to improve the car and get rid of this problem is to buy a new bonnet from R S Panels or Classic Autos in aluminium or get a Guy bonnet in fibreglass until you can afford the alloy job.

Other improvements are detail ones only, such as fitting late type S U fuel pumps and alternators with suitable adjustments for the change of polarity to 3.8-litre cars and almost any type of spotlight that does not detract from the car's appearance for

Ventilation and extraction of air have always been open to improvement on the E type; this lightweight shows a neat solution to the extraction problems.

night driving. Lagging the heater pipes can reduce the cockpit temperature as can the more expensive air extracting vents on the lightweights. On models with power steering it is possible to reduce the pressure at the steering wheel by having the rack rebuilt using an Aston Martin torsion bar in place of the Jaguar part.

All these ways of improving your E type may sound formidable, but they are very few compared to those on most cars; it must be realised that, rust apart, the E type is a very good car as it stands.

XIV

The Concours Men

PUBLICAN Mike Cooper is a concours man. He runs a smart little pub, the Brick-layers' Arms, in Burnham, Buckinghamshire, and runs an even smarter Series Two E type. There is never a speck of dirt on 428 KO nor a chip off its paint. The engine sparkles and you can see your face in the chrome wire wheels. The exhaust pipes are spotlessly chromed and even the suspension is painted. Yet Mike drives his beloved E type 20,000 miles a year and has even won races with it as far away as Italy.

How does he keep such a well-used car so immaculate? 'By bloody hard work,' says Mike. He polishes it twice a week and keeps it under cover in a garage when it is not being used on the road. Every time it gets wet it is rubbed down with a chamois leather and it has been resprayed once in its six-year life. The 1970 E type cost Mike £2,000 when he bought it in 1973, to replace his Jaguar 420, and it has cost him £2,000 in running expenses since then. Most of that went on a new engine and that respray, plus, of course, all those cleaning materials he must have used. The rest went on all the other bits and pieces you need to keep a car looking better than when it left the factory.

What is even more extraordinary about the immaculate appearance of 428 KO ('428 is my phone number and the car's a knock-out') is that Mike hardly ever has the hood up, just like another E type fanatic, Denis Jenkinson. Like Denis, Mike likes the fresh air—'I won't work in the pub at lunchtimes'—and he spends as much time cleaning the interior of the car as he does the exterior. The fantastic gleaming wheels are the result of a near-daily washing on the car, and frequent removal so that the inside of the rims may be scrubbed and the car's suspension may be polished.

Why does he do it, apart from liking to line up enough cups to fill the space behind the bar of his pub? 'To me, the E type is the greatest car in the world and I want mine to look it,' says Mike. 'I don't despise the people whose cars are far from immaculate, like yours and Denis Jenkinson's, Chris. So long as they go like the owners want them to go, that's all that really matters. I was offered £6,000 for my car in Italy, but I wouldn't part with it then, although I'm thinking about getting a V12 next.'

Mike vividly recalls one of his three trips to Italian Jaguar Day, written up in the *Jaguar Driver* magazine.

It's bonnets up and doors open as the E types parade for inspection at a concours.

'We left Burnham at 5.15 am on April 29, 1975, to board the 8.30 am Hovercraft to Calais. After passing through the French customs, we were on our way to St Omer by 9.20 am. I followed the route mapped out for me by the A A through Arras, Rheims and Biscanon to Lausanne, then round Lake Geneva to Mastingey and Brig, where we arrived about 12.15 am on April 30. After an overnight stop, we were away at 7.30 am to Stressa and the Italian Autostrada, passing through Milan, Bologna and Firenze, down to Rome, which we reached about 6.0 pm. After considerable trouble, we managed to find the Via Condotta, which is more or less the Bond Street of Rome, only to find that the organiser of the event was not at his office, but at the venue, which was two hours back up the road to Firenze at a town called Pelugia.

'However, next day we met the organiser, Dr Roberto Causo, who turned out to be a very charming man who really could not do enough to make us welcome. We were accorded excellent hospitality and we were guests of the club for the day.

'They do things very differently over there in as much as they have organised races between cars of different classes, and all makes of car are welcome other than just Jaguars. I managed to win the race that had all the Jaguars entered including XK120s, XK140s, 3.8-litre S types, and I also claimed the award for the car that had travelled the longest distance to the event, and won the concours.

'I have two superb cups sitting on the bar as a reminder of the trip, and also a very decorative plaque on the dashboard of my car, which must be unique as I am the only member in Great Britain to possess one.

'What exactly happened at the event? Well, we arrived at the Autodrome Magione, about twenty minutes' drive from Pelugia, at 9.30 am for the issue of plaques and details of races and classes. Cars then practised and those in attendance were three XK120s, two XK140 dropheads, two 3.8-litre S types, one Mark VII saloon and my E type. Other cars included several Lancias, two Ferraris, two OSCAs, several specials and three MG TDs. After lunch from 1.00 pm to 3.00 pm, the first of four races started, followed by prizegiving at 5.00 pm. The circuit is exactly one mile round and it is a properly laid out circuit rather like those in this country, with pit facilities and full Tannoy system; it is owned by the Italian Jaguar Club and all their racing is properly organised. After the day's events and prize giving, we went back to the Royal Bruffani Palace Hotel in Pelugia, where we stayed for a celebration dinner.

'Next morning, we were off to an early, if befuddled, start, back up the Autostrada to Milan and thence to Turin and Aosta, which we reached about 7.30 pm. After a break, we went through the Great Bernadino Pass to stop the night at a lovely little hotel just the other side of Bourg St Pierre.

'Next morning, we made another early start—not quite so bleary this time —passing through Mastingey and Geneva to Dijon and thence to Paris, which we reached at 8.0 pm. We stayed at the Hotel Splendid (if you ever go there remember to take your own soap. I couldn't find any and had to go out to buy some).

'Next morning I tried to get three francs taken off the bill on account of the soap, but didn't succeed, so again we were off to an early start and away up the autoroute to Dunkirk and Calais, where we arrived at about 2.30 pm, just in time to catch the boat to Dover.

'Away from Dover £6 lighter, due to the attention of the Customs, and after several road-up delays we arrived back at Burnham at 8.30 pm, tired but happy with our well-earned loot.

'I clocked 2,650 miles and with the price of petrol abroad, I was skint. But the car went like the proverbial bird, never missed a beat and I wasn't passed all the way there or back. A tremendous drive, most of the way with the hood down, the weather being glorious.

'I am now quite bald, having spread my few locks all over three countries. You know . . . the rugged hair-in-the-wind E types.'

There are other concours competitors like Mike, but most do not use their cars anything like as much. Some even take their cars to the competitions in vans for fear

The lightweight E type that Roy Salvadori used to drive would be a worthy entrant in any concours: it looks as good as the day it left the factory.

of getting them soiled before the great show. But when judges like Terry Moore are around, he deducts points for that and will give full marks only if a car has covered at least 7,000 miles per year of its life, and he does not rely on speedometer readings only.

One man who gets consistently good marks at concours events in Britain is Alan Hames from Northampton, but like Mike Cooper, he does not just spend his time polishing his E type. He has patiently analysed all the faults—such as they are—of his Series Three car bought new in October 1972 and then tried to cure them.

One of the most puzzling faults with his E type, registered AVV 1, was caused by the sparking plugs. The standard plugs were Champion N-10Y, which worked perfectly for 500 miles, then developed a particularly bad mis-fire when the engine was under full load. Alan found that the cure for this was to fit NGK plugs, number BP5ES. Other E type owners with similar problems on six-cylinder engines have

Portrait of a happy man: Mike
Cooper in his E type, 428 ко.

Road-going E types stand just as good a chance of winning a concours as the more exotic racers, as this happy entrant shows at Shelsey Walsh in 1972.

found that Champion UN 12Y plugs work well, particularly when their old Champion N 5s start to soot up.

Alan's next puzzle was the rotor arm. He says that some of the earlier V 12 models were fitted with rotor arms from a batch which were porous, and over a period the rotors absorbed moisture. Then the ignition's high tension current tracked to earth and this proved to be a difficult fault to locate, because the rotor arm looked perfect on inspection. He had covered 7,050 miles before he sorted out that problem, and judging from the other sources from which I have heard this story, there must have been quite a number of these porous rotor arms about.

Then there was trouble with the air cleaner elements on Alan's car. 'These should be fitted very carefully in order not to break the bands on the inside face of the elements,' says Alan. 'On checking mine, I discovered that they had been broken when fitted new. The corrugated paper had broken up and about one third of the cleaner has disappeared through the engine at 5,600 miles—but luckily no damage was done.'

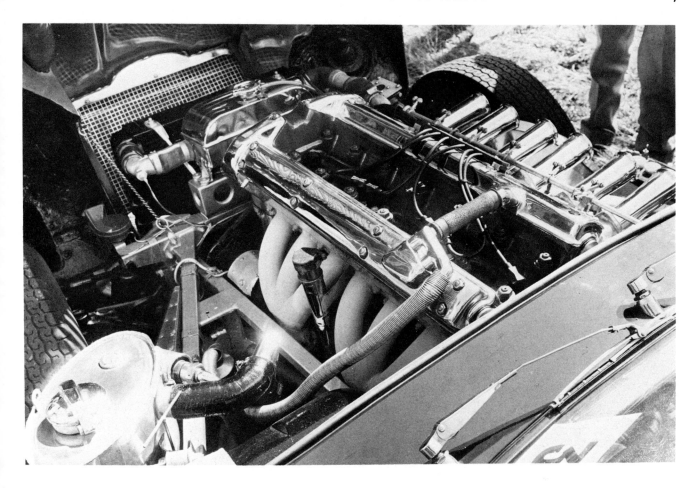

Still on the engine side, Alan has had continual problems with the large number of vacuum pipes. Their rubber ends have repeatedly split, causing erratic running.

Further back in the car, Alan says that the frequent differential leaks can often be traced to the gasket behind the differential rear access plate. He found this tedious to replace, having to remove the rear silencer box and the plate immediately under the differential housing at 8,850 miles to get at the offending part. Alan had trouble with leaking shock absorbers, too, at 10,600 miles, and, of course, the only cure was to replace them. While on the subject of the rear end, Alan has found that the four-branch tail pipe trims are rather rust prone. The corrosion appears to attack then from the inside, even if the interior is cleaned regularly. He has to buy at least one of these expensive units every year, and the only means he has found of improving their life is to spray the interior with Sperex VHT before use. He had much the same trouble with the rear silencer box at 11,900 miles.

The seat belts have given a lot of trouble too. Alan says: 'On all the later models of E type using the Kangol reflex belt, the push button on the central fixed portion of the belt has a tendency to break up, because the plastic does not appear to be strong enough. I am on my third central section of seat belt in four years.'

A beautiful under-bonnet view of 'Rosie', Brian Corser's lightweight E type, at the Shelsey concours in 1972.

On items of a more mechanical nature, the water valve on his car's heater has given trouble, with the result that he now carries a bypass hose to short-circuit the heater should the valve fail again when he is out on the road. This trouble reared its head at 14,250 miles, just 600 miles before the water pump had to be replaced when the seal around the pulley bearing failed and a fine spray of coolant appeared on the underside of the bonnet.

Two thousand miles later the back of AVV 1 started to rumble, which turned out to be rear hub bearing trouble. Alan says:

'Locating which side has failed can be a problem, but if the car is cornered hard on a left- and a right-hand bend, so that each hub is loaded in turn, it becomes obvious which is the faulty side. Generally the failure will be due to the hub being inadequately packed with grease when new. I suggest that the cap located in the hub through which the hub is manually packed with grease—not an effective way of filling the hub cavity—should be fitted with a grease nipple. When filling the hub, in order not to overload the seals behind the bearings, the cap should be loosened so that when the hub is full, the cap and nipple will be ejected. It can then be replaced when the excess grease has been removed.'

Almost from the time Alan bought AVV 1, it has been winning concours awards all over Britain, and it must have been heartbreaking when, during high winds one January a seven-foot brick wall belonging to a neighbour fell on the car, causing £1,300 worth of damage and necessitating countless hours of matching up spare parts and so on. 'In some cases I had to reject three or four replacement parts, such as rear bumper sections, before I found a part which would fit perfectly,' says Alan. The car stood in a garage for a considerable time while it was being repaired, and the clutch seized.

'I tried releasing the clutch by rocking the car back and forth with first gear engaged, but this was ineffective and the only advice from the service manager of my local Jaguar distributors was to remove the engine and gearbox and dismantle the clutch, as either the plate was stuck to the flywheel or the driven plate was stuck on the splined centre shaft. I finally decided that I would have a last try at releasing the clutch.

'This involved warming up the engine with the gearlever in neutral, then with the engine switched off I put the gearlever in second and with two people pushing, I started the engine. The car then travelled along in gear whether or not the clutch was depressed. To free the clutch, I then accelerated and decelerated while stamping the clutch pedal up and down and also applied further loads to the transmission by operating the footbrake. This was successful before I had covered fifty metres and may well save another E type owner from major expense.'

All this happened at 20,450 miles, 1,000 miles before the next bit of bother, this time much smaller. The inner rubber seal and the outer vinyl boot of the gearlever both gave up. 'The only remedy for the inner seal is regular replacement, but if the outer boot is remade in thin black leather, it appears exactly the same as original, but does not split.' Alan had trouble with his windscreen, too, when moisture found its way into the bottom corners of the screen and got between the laminations. The first sign of this happening was the appearance of a clouded area on the screen.

'Even from new, faults are to be found with the bodywork, from paintwork blemished to minor dents. But be wary of causing damage to the car when closing the boot lid. This can be very easily dented on the roadster if it is slammed carelessly. Under no circumstances should it be slammed while pressing the centre of the lid below the V12 badge. If the lid is closed with a hand on each bottom rear corner, then no damage will ensue.

'Further bonnet damage is a possibility from the dipstick if it is not pushed home fully. On a number of cars it touches the bonnet even when fully depressed. To avoid damage, the whole dipstick tube can be bent to give a minimal clearance.

'You may think from my catalogue of faults that I am dissatisfied with my car, but I am still an E type fanatic and believe that most cars experience this number of problems, but most owners do not keep a thorough record of them as I have always tried to do. I have tried, where possible, to improve my car without altering its appearance and consider that it would be a good idea if some of this type of work could be recognised in concours events rather than frowned upon with the possible loss of points. For instance, I have replaced parts of the mudsplash panels on the front wings of my car with replica parts made from stainless steel. When they are painted, they appear no different from the standard parts and have the advantage of not rusting. It's a good idea, too, on the Series Three car, to turn the spare wheel upside down in the boot so that the well in the inside of the wheel can be used for storage space. All you have to do with the locating screw is to tap out the swivel pin and cut the screw down to the appropriate length, then drill a new hole and remount the swivel pin. And remember to fit a piece of rubber on the boot floor where the centre of the hub rests to prevent damage.

'Then there's the battery tray. The standard fitting on the Series Three car is made from steel, with no water outlet. This means that it corrodes quickly. I suggest that it can be replaced with a Series Two E type battery tray, which is made from plastic with a water outlet. A tube can be fixed to this outlet and led through a convenient hole in the undershield, so discharging water that might be contaminated with acid well clear of the car.

'The underside of the bumpers, both front and rear, can develop a great deal of rust. These can be protected after the rust has been removed by first applying rust killer then a coat of underseal. One of my handiest modifications has been the fitting of a Series Two E type expansion tank to the radiator overflow. This cures the loss of coolant on hot days when as much as a gallon can be ejected by the engine while the car is at a standstill in traffic and the airflow through the radiator is restricted. I had a bit of trouble with the car's rear jacking points, too. If these are used repeatedly for regular maintenance, they can collapse. The steel pressing which supports the side jack locating lug is hollow and the lug simply disappears into the pressing with repeated use. This can be repaired by cutting off the old jacking points and, before welding on new ones, filling them with shaped pieces of steel welded into place. This particular fault developed at 14,000 miles on my car.'

Alan Hames really is a mine of information when he is talking about his E type, he has devoted so much time to it. There are many equally devoted owners in America, whose only competitive appearances are in concours events; some of the things they do in America to win a concours are quite extraordinary.

Barry Eckhaus was not satisfied with the factory paint job when he bought his Series Three roadster new in 1974. Within a month of delivery, he had it resprayed before starting to show the car. In 1975, he tied for third place in his national class was within just over a point of being the best car in the country. One of the organisers, Karen Miller, from Hawthorne New York, spotted the possible reason his car was not the best. She said: 'My husband was doing some of the judging this year, and I heard him mention to Barry that he saw some overspray on the door rubber mouldings. So Barry went home and had both doors off immediately to fit new rubbers!' It is that sort of attention to detail that is needed in American concours events, and it is not only confined to the pieces of rubber you can see. When the judges in one event could not decide between two cars, they removed the petrol filler caps from both, prised back the rubber seals and adjudged which was the cleaner underneath!

You only have to listen to some of the American concours winners talking to realise how much their cars mean to them. Robert R. White of Overland Park, Kansas, won his class in a Jaguar concours for cars made before 1968 and said later:

'My winning car is a 1967 X K E Two Plus Two and I am the original owner. It is Olde English White with a black interior. The car is completely original and has only 14,000 miles on the odometer. My wife Esther and I showed it at Jaguar car shows in 1975 at Kansas, Wichita, Chicago and Tulsa. We are very proud of the car as it still looks as new as the day we purchased it.'

With only 14,000 miles in nine years, Mr White must have spent more time polishing it than driving it, but it just goes to show how much he loves his E type.

Joe Gander of Allentown, Pennsylvania, feels much the same way about his 1969 roadster, which won its concours class despite having trouble with the weather clerk. Joe reported in the US *Jaguar Journal*:

'The 1975 concours season was full of many obstacles and frustrations. In contrast to the '74 season, when we competed in six shows, winning first in class each time out and one best in show, we were able to make only three shows in '75 to qualify for the nationals. We didn't plan it that way, it just worked out like that.

'Having had a good '74 season, we decided to do a little work over the winter to put us in a more favourable position. We wanted to go to more shows, but the early spring shows were a long way from home and heavy rains and foul weekends kept us garaged. This put us in a position of "all cleaned up and no place to go" until August. Thus we decided to have a go at challenging the Big Cats at Lime Rock, where we proceeded to capture third place in the men's novice speed trials and gymkhana. A friend, Kathy Eckert, was placed third in the women's novice spring race. The car, however, was not impressed. Never before was she asked to do so much in just two days, and she looked it. Stone chips, dulled brightwork in the engine compartment, dust, oil and dirt in and on everything; plus a cracked head gasket to boot. And the remaining events of the concours season were only a few weeks away. But thanks to Ed Miller for putting the engine back together again and Kathy for finding the chrome again on the wheels. Many tubes of Simachrome later, we were back in shape for our first show at New Hope, and then on to Empire. However, after Empire I caught pneumonia and while the car was in good shape, I was not going anywhere for the rest of the season, and figured that the national championships were out of reach. However, it turned out to be a nice warm October day and Delaware Valley was having the last concours of the season. The car was clean, I was feeling better, we went, we showed, we qualified and we conquered.'

It just goes to show what can happen when a concours man is bitten by the speed bug in mid-season.

Stormy weather played havoc with the concours preparations of Tom DeWitt, from Tulsa, too, but his 1971 V12 coupé twice won highest marks in his championship year. He says: 'My wife Phyllis and I have driven our Jaguar to each of the out-of-town shows, but unfortunately they were all plagued by rain and generally disagreeable, nasty weather. Countless hours of meticulous attention to components such as wire wheels, suspension parts and brightwork were wiped out in one fell swoop and all the effort at preparation had to be duplicated overnight.'

The men and women who compete in concours events are like that. They spend months preparing their cars to the most incredible degree, then see it all wiped out overnight, whether by a storm in Oklahoma or a gale in Northampton. But they always fight back with hours more work, restoring their cars to their former glory—looking better than when they left the factory—and believing that *their* car is the best in the world.

XV
From the Beautiful to the Bizarre

SEVERAL top designers have tried to better the E type's lovely lines with special-bodied versions, mostly in the first few years of the car's production run; and they all failed, which says so much for Malcolm Sayer, Sir William Lyons and company. One of the best attempts was one of the earliest; the Michelotti creation of 1963 that bore a distinct resemblance to that most beautiful of Ferraris, the 250 GT Lusso. But Lusso lines did not look so lithe on an E type, and the body had much the same bulky appearance of the Trident Clipper that appeared in small quantities almost a decade later.

Perhaps one of the most practical special E types was that by Frua for Jaguar dealer John Coombs of Guildford in 1965. Frua's E type looked very much like the Maserati Mistrale and Alfa Romeo Duetto from the front and rather like a Series Three E type from behind, with pure Series One E type in the middle. And surprisingly for a special-bodied car, it makes a very practical road car. The prototype was built on a 1965 fixed-head chassis number 1E21041, engine number 7E6388–9, and was eventually sold to a Roy MacCulloch in 1966. Six years later he reported in the *Jaguar Driver* magazine that the car, registered KPH 4C, was still running well, although some of the welding at the front was about to come apart.

The Frua E type, which Coombs had hoped to market, did not look too bad, although nobody claimed that it looked better than the original; just different. But one man with a yearning for an extra special E type, Raymond Loewy, really went to town. He was convinced that his French-modified E type fixed-head coupé with Ferrari 166-like nose was much better than the Sayer classic. In fact, the gaping nose was ten inches shorter, which was just great for parking as Mr Loewy pointed out, and the gigantic grille was just right for cooling, even if it did knock many miles per hour off the top speed and make the front of the car look like an advertisement in the fish fryer's gazette. Loewy turned the distinctive E type bonnet centre bulge into an air scoop too and he shortened the rear end of the 1966 model's bodywork for good (or bad?) measure. In all, his modifications brought down the E type's overall length to around thirteen feet, which, in his opinion, made it the ideal city car. City, maybe, but not pretty. The back looked a sight too, with an oversize window for extra visibility and Chevrolet Corvair rearlights for the same purpose. The side windows behind the doors were swept up as on the Reliant Scimitar GTE and four quartz iodine headlights were incorporated in the nose. Just for good measure the wheel arches were scooped out rather like those of an Aston Martin DB3S racing car, to let out all the air that had been scooped in by the monstrous mouth. It seems hardly likely that the engine ever warmed up.

The next year, however, saw a much different E type, the Bertone-bodied Two Plus Two built for the *Daily Telegraph Magazine*. To many motorists, the Pirana, as it was called, was a dream car. The chassis was basically that of a Two Plus Two with widened track and Dunlop racing tyres. The body, which looked remarkably like the G T Ferraris to come, was built in less than five months by the Italian master coach-builder, Nuccio Bertone, at his Turin factory and incorporated such mouth-watering luxuries as a special air-conditioning system by Smiths Industries, revised instruments and tape recorder and radio system, with marvellously curved glass by Triplex. Joe Lucas supplied special new lights, Connolly Brothers a new leather for the interior, called Anela, and Britax came up with some super new seat belts. Everything possible was electric, such as the windows, radio antenna and other fittings, and the air conditioning was arranged so that warm air rose from the floor and cold air swirled

The front of the Frua E type, showing clear signs of the inspiration that led to the Alfa Romeo spider of 1967, but that did little for the E type's appearance.

around the roof. An automatic speed control warned it when the chosen speed was exceeded, which could be as much as 145 mph with its better aerodynamics. No doubt the price would have been upped by more than a few thousand pounds if the car had gone into production, as it was, the car was sold at a New York auction for £6,000 in the next year.

Hill climb champion Jim Thompson had a much more practical idea years later when he crashed his Series Three E type near Wetherby in Yorkshire one wild and slippery night. As managing director of Guyson International, who make much of the shot-blasting equipment used in the car industry, he commissioned former Aston Martin designer William Towns to turn out the most incredible—and some say the most beautiful—special-bodied E type ever. Nothing has ever looked quite like the creation that Towns completed two years later in 1974. The smooth, dart-like body attracted eye-goggling interest, as the *Yorkshire Post* reported when the first of Mr Guyson's cars hit town. They told how our Jim had found a man from British Leyland 'drooling over the car' at a motorway halt and saying: 'Why don't our people

Facing page, above: Four big-bore exhaust pipes and a special light cluster adorn the back of the Frua E type built for Coombs in 1965.

Facing page, below: Pirana, the Bertone Jaguar, pictured in 1967. Its long sweeping lines show it to be a clear ancestor of the Lamborghini Espada. Below: The interior of the Pirana, although far more like that of a standard E Type, has a touch of the Lambos too.

give the Jaguar a body like this?' The man from Coventry was, apparently, astonished to find that there was an E type lurking beneath the fibreglass.

Towns, who later converted his own V12 E type to Guyson specification, changed the shape of the E type by stripping off the bonnet—Jim had wrecked that anyway—the bootlid and wheels, then plastering the car with clay. This was moulded by hand to the intended body shape and glassfibre moulds were taken directly from the resultant mass. The clay was then stripped off and glassfibre body sections made from the moulds. These were fitted directly on to the E type's panelling with screws and resin. None of the stressed panelling was affected otherwise, and the car was increased in width by only half an inch or so. Various modifications were made to the mechanical side of the vehicle and it promptly beat a Ferrari Daytona in a test by *The Motor* magazine. The mechanical modifications were, of course, those by Ron Beaty detailed in chapter thirteen. It was planned to market the whole conversion for around £2,000, but unfortunately the E type went out of production soon after the first two prototypes were completed.

Mr Thompson says:

'The concept of the Guyson V12 Jaguar was to change the shape of the Jaguar by the addition of cosmetic panels in glass fibre so that the vehicle could be quickly converted by the removal of the bonnet and substitution of the new shape bonnet, plus cladding of the existing body from the bulkhead backwards. This would ensure that should the owner wish to convert the vehicle back to standard it would be necessary only to remove the glassfibre external panels and refit the bonnet and bootlid. At present there are only two Guyson E12s, in existence, the one owned by my company, which is painted yellow, and one owned by Mr Towns, which has a standard engine and is painted blue.'

Fast Car magazine's pulse rate rose when they saw the Guyson E12. 'When a product becomes established in one particular form, it's almost inevitable that before long a green light will flash and signal all those brave pioneers to move in with their alternative ideas on styling,' they noted. Then *Fast Car* really waxed lyrical.

'Kits and custom packages are launched on us in all shapes and sizes, but it's probably a good thing to know that some individuals are not prepared to lie back apathetically and accept ideas (often boring), meted out by car manufacturers today. But perhaps this is due to the desire an individual has to be different, to be an individual in every sense of the word. Or maybe he requires just a little more for his money. Whatever the reason, it goes without saying that variety is the spice of life and with any theme, you'll find a Rachmaninov with pen poised, ready to write an appreciation.'

Some appreciation and some conversion for the price.

The Guyson E12 was no joke, but the car in *Road and Track* in 1971 was. *Road and Track* have always liked to play jokes, and they really excelled themselves with their trick photography just before the Series Three E type was introduced. One of their writers solemnly reported that he had tested 'the most incredible straight twelve-cylinder E type', with a bonnet more than three feet longer than normal, surely one of the most bizarre E types ever. With all due respect, he said that Jaguars had cast two engines together in line, stretched the bodywork and made it all work, even if the turning circle was a bit on the large side at fifty-one feet.

The XKEE, as the writer christened it, was absolutely fantastic with its 8.4-litre 480 bhp engine running on no less than thirteen main bearings and breathing through four huge carburetters and bellowing out of a twelve-branch exhaust. His suitably astounded readers really should have smelled a rat when he quoted the listed extras: hardtop, stereo, tinted glass, and 'for the first time on a production passenger car' closed circuit television, a system using a small camera mounted on the front bumper, sending signals to a compact screen on the dashboard, so that the driver could see what was menacing him when he was trying to emerge from a side street into a road full of fast-moving traffic. This system would prove rather expensive, said *Road and Track*, but would be an essential extra, in their opinion.

While the XKEE is not perhaps as radical a departure as was the XKE when it appeared, it is certainly radical enough and a most significant development in the

One of the only two wedge-shaped E types in the world: the Guyson E12 before its giant Weber carburetters were fitted. These were so big that they protruded through a hole in the bonnet, breaking the clean lines.

field of two-seater sports and GT cars and promised to keep the name of Jaguar well out in front for years to come, wrote the *Road and Track* joker, who took the opportunity to scotch any rumours of a V12 E type to come. Surprisingly enough, many people believed the magazine. But it is hardly surprising that nobody has made a commercial success of a special-bodied E type. Just a pity in the case of Bertone and Guyson.

XVI
A Comparison
with Contemporary Rivals

THE E TYPE had no real rival when it was launched in 1961. Only the most exotic cars such as Ferrari, Aston Martin and the Mercedes 300SL could match its performance, and they could not match its price and in many respects its reliability. Only the Chevrolet Corvette could match its price abroad and in part its performance, but that car suffered more than a little when it was required to do anything other than take part in a traffic light grand prix. Ask a Sting Ray to go round a corner quickly or descend an Alp and you were asking the impossible. It was not until the late 1960s that Chevrolet got anywhere near like sorting out these basic defects. And few people would dispute that the E type was the most beautiful of the lot. It certainly caught more crumpet than any other sports car known.

Perhaps the Ferrari 250 GT was the closest rival to the E type on merit in March 1961. It was in the same league on the race track, but the more mundane—what a word for a Ferrari—road versions were capable of only about 125 mph, although they could reach sixty miles per hour from rest in around seven seconds. These Italian classics did only 13 mpg and cost nearly three times as much as an E type. It is significant that in many of their road tests, excuses such as slipping clutch, or back axle trouble were made after performance figures were taken. There was also some difficulty with spares, but the Ferrari, a rather square sort of a car in those days, was the nearest thing to an E type fixed-head coupé in terms of speed, comfort and road-holding. The only real advantage that they had over the E type was that they were very rare; not always a very happy quality.

The giant French Facel Vega with its huge V8 engine—'it had more steam than the Robert E Lee' wrote *Road and Track*—certainly beat the E type on comfort and would actually build up to 140 mph, but it was left behind on everything else, especially roadholding and price. What a price, too! The best of the Facel Vegas, the Facel 11, cost £5,000 on the road complete with its £300 fitted luggage, which was even more than a Maserati. But its combination of a giant American engine— the Chrysler—with European luxury coachwork started a trend that was eventually to pose a threat to the E type a decade later. The current Maserati 350GT—by reputation the most reliable Maser ever—was like all its breed, very expensive and more of a promise than a practicality. In any case could it only manage around 125 mph, with a 0 to 60 time of 7.5 seconds, and that was provided you had a team

Over: An E type catches up with a whole host of rivals: from the left an MGB, a Lotus Elan, a Ferrari 250GT, a Porsche 365, a Porsche 911, a Lola, a Porsche and an Alpine.

of good mechanics. The great British rival in this sphere was the Aston Martin, which did pretty well at 140 mph, 0 to 60 in 7.5 seconds and (keep it quiet) 13 mpg, but, despite the undoubted superiority of its accommodation, the company could not manage to make enough to meet the demand in the States. Aston Martins have always been dreadfully expensive to run, as well.

The Lancia Zagato was a bit slow at 118 mph, 0 to 60 in 13 seconds and something like 16 mpg; but it was considered a futuristic design and might have sold better. The current classic car in the States, the Lotus Elite, was certainly as good as the E type, if not better, when it came to handling, and it was cosy, comfortable and quick at 111 mph, 0 to 60 in 12 seconds and more than 30 mpg, but like the Maserati, you needed a bunch of spanner benders to keep it going, and there was that 40 mph difference in top speed. Lotus could not make enough Elites either, rather like Astons. The people who could make enough sports cars, made so many that they cost half the price of the E type, but as a result fell far behind on speed and quality. The Triumph TR3, and later TRs, the MGA and then the MGB, plus the Sunbeam Alpine, sold well, but were left far behind with their 100 mph top speeds and 0 to 60 time of 13 seconds. For some reason, the Big Healey never sold well in the States, not as well as the E type that is. Perhaps it was a little too hairy and spartan, not the same wonderful blend between sports car and grand tourer.

The Mercedes 190SL was much more of a luxury tourer for the quasi-sporting, like all Mercedes coupés except the 300SL, which was something else. The little Mercedes did 106 mph, 0 to 60 in 13.5 seconds and would travel about sixteen miles on a gallon of petrol, giving considerable comfort to its fortunate occupants, and little of the excitement available in the E type. And like the 300SL, the 190SL cost a lot of money. There were also those traditional Mercedes swing axles to consider when attempting to corner quickly, which were even more evident in the 300SL at 134 mph, 0 to 60 in 7 seconds.

The Daimler SP250 was not so pretty and, as it turned out, not so very practical with even worse rust problems than an E type in the chassis department. It could do 127 mph with about 12 mpg and 0 to 60 in 9 seconds—if you could keep the doors shut—before Daimlers were bought up by Jaguars, which meant death for the SP250. One point where it made the E type look sick though, was in the capacity of the luggage boot, although that was probably a freak of design.

But on to more serious rivals. The Corvette of 1961 was considered by Americans at the time to be absolutely unmatched for performance per dollar at 128 mph, 0 to 60 in 6.6 seconds—think of the rubber left on the freeway—and around 12 mpg (few Americans cared much about the petrol flowing out of the wells and up into the atmosphere then). They soon changed their minds about sports cars though when they saw the E type hitting sixty in much the same time on its way to that legendary 150 mph. And it cannot do any harm anywhere to use less petrol at 17 mpg, even if it was considered to be only a small point in the States. It was a pity, though, that it took three months for the average person to learn to use the gearbox and Jaguars could not produce Big Cats at the same rate as Chevrolet churned out Sting Rays. All along the West Coast, too, the Porsche Super 90 was selling well with its wide doors for large Americans and 117 mph, 0 to 60 in 12 seconds and in excess of

20 mpg. It made moderate demands on maintenance too, even if the engine did wear out every 50,000 miles, as in the case of the 356-Series car run for 350,000 miles by British journalist Denis Jenkinson. Engine wear or not, Porsche became the E type's chief rival in its class in the States, with the home-brewed Corvette the best seller.

Gearbox and brakes apart, the E type did wonders until late 1964 when it was boosted by Merle Brennan's wonderful racing record and the arrival of the American-ised E types in the form of the 4.2-litre Series One. Porsche were quick to respond, of course, with the 911 series a year later and Chevrolet never stopped trying, with the 1963–7 Sting Rays considered to be the best of the long line made by General Motors although *Motor Sport* discovered in a 1964 road test that it took only a quarter of an inch too much throttle to spin a Sting Ray on a corner. Such was the race for sales between the two 'furriners', the E type and the Porsche, that the German firm wound up selling more cars in California than in Germany. Meanwhile, back in Blighty, the E type was miles ahead of every other competitor, without the Sting Ray and the Porsche to worry about. They were far too expensive to appreciably affect sales in Britain, and in any case they were inferior all-round cars at that time. In fact, the only cars that could match the E type were available in such small quantity in Britain that they did not matter much anyway.

The Triumph TR4A, at about half the price of the E type, was considered to be fairly old fashioned everywhere despite attempts to refine it, and much the same applied to the MGB and Sunbeam Alpine, although there was a brief flurry of competitive activity when the Sunbeam Tiger came out. The Triumph did 107 mph, 0 to 60 in 10.5 seconds and 23 mpg, and the ancient rival, the Austin Healey 3000, a little better, albeit in a rather wilder manner and with a heavier fuel consumption. The Tiger, in its most potent 4.7-litre form, could manage 122 mph, 0 to 60 in 7.5 seconds and 18 mpg, but it seemed to be killed by politics when Chrysler took over its manufacturers, Rootes, and were embarrassed to find that they had no engine they could pop in to replace the Ford unit powering the Sunbeam.

Various Americans kept trying hard, notably Carol Shelby with his Cobras, and the Shelby Mustangs, which did 124 mph, 0 to 60 in 6.8 seconds, and 14 mpg. The AC Cobra could hit 153 mph in highly-tuned form with 0 to 60 in 5.3 seconds, but the Thames Ditton firm were more interested in making low-performance invalid carriages and the mighty Cobra was never made in great quantities. In any case, it was nothing like so civilised as the E type and one seven-litre version that I drove locked up its back axle and leapt from one side of the road to the other when I tried to blast it up to 60 mph in its published 4.2 seconds. Cobras were fine in perfect conditions on a billiard-table-like surface, but they had a tendency to bend in the middle if you went over a really big bump like a hump back bridge. Altogether they were cars which gave you a rather uncomfortable feeling if you rode in them, although they looked great in theory.

Old Ferraris and other exotica apart, the E type's only real rivals up to 1967 were the Aston Martins and Jensen CV8 on one side of the Atlantic and the Sting Ray and Ford Mustang on the other side. The E type beat them all on top speed, with the best of the rivals, the Aston Martin DB6, hitting 145 mph, and the Sting Ray in its most extreme versions, somewhere near that; the Jensen did 127 mph and

It's Le Mans 1962 and an E type roars away from an Aston Martin DB4GT Zagato, a Ferrari and an Austin Healey 3000, with another E type in close attendance.

Graham Hill's E type leads one of its closest rivals in everything except price, the Aston Martin DB4GT.

a standard Mustang a measly 115 mph unless Shelby had breathed on it. The Porsche 911s lagged at about 120 mph depending on which version you drove, and the Sting Ray and the CV8 were marginally faster up to 60 mph, thanks to their big V8s, but also thanks to their big V8s, they were far behind on petrol consumption. The Big Healey was beaten on all scores in a straight line at 120 mph, 16 mpg, and half as long again as the E type to hit 60 mph. The Two Plus Two E type was much closer to its competitors on performance, being broadly similar to the Aston Martin DB6, Ford Mustang specials, Oldsmobile Toronado and the like on acceleration. The Aston was faster in the end and they all used a lot more petrol than the E type.

As I said in earlier chapters, the decline of the E type started in 1967 from the purists' point of view, although, of course, its rivals suffered from the same anti-pollution and concrete crash-block mentality that framed the American safety regu-

lations. Many people, particularly Americans, were starting to get the seven-year itch about the E type, too, and were wondering when Jaguars were going to come out with something new. Eventually, too, more modern cars such as the Lotus Elan started to catch up with the E type at 112 mph, 0 to 60 in 9 seconds and 22 mpg in the case of the Elan. Those might not sound to be comparable performance figures, but you had only to see an Elan going round a corner to realise that it would be practically as fast as an E type from any one point to another now that motorways were being subject to speed restrictions. There were never enough Elans about though, partly because of limited production facilities and partly because of their reputation for breaking down. The Lotus Europa was a little faster than the Elan, but it was awfully ugly and initially had an unattractive Renault engine to suit Britain's Common Market aspirations. Triumph got slower with the TR6 and suffered from uncertain pumping arrangements for the fuel injection, and the MG went a bit quicker with the C type which did 118 mph, 0 to 60 in 8.5 seconds and 18 mpg, but handled rather like a barge with a leak, quite unlike previous MGs. and nothing like so wild and challenging as the Big Healey it must have been meant to replace. It would be five years before anything came along to replace that Healey and the same length of time before MG could produce their delightful V8 version of the MGB, inspired by the exploits of a suburban garage proprietor called Ken Costello. Morgan pepped themselves up a bit with the essentially American-engined Plus Eight, which did more than 120 mph, 0 to 60 in 8.5 seconds and 16 mpg in extreme discomfort, although it was excluded from the lucrative American market before it even got started, on safety grounds. Not that that worried Morgan, though; they were happy to tootle along calling the upholsterers in on a Saturday morning if they had a four-seater to produce that week in addition to their normal quota of three two seaters. And, of course, Morgan's chief selling point was that it was as old-fashioned as the E type's pre-war ancestor, the SS100 (come to think of it, the Morgan Plus Eight is very much like an SS100), and so could hardly be considered to be a rival of the E type, except in the second-hand market. Jensen, who had produced Volvo's saintly sports car and the Big Healey under contract received an injection of capital from San Francisco sports car dealer Kjell Qvale and came up with the Interceptor series which did 0 to 60 in 7.4 seconds, 136 mph and 12 mpg on their big American V8s. As the latter day, and rather cheaper, successor to the Facel Vega, they were more of a threat to the Thunderbirds, Toronados and Rivieras in the States though, and with their Maserati Mistrale-inspired goldfish bowl back window, somewhere between the luxury GT class and the big American cars in Europe. As it worked out, the firm hardest hit by the Interceptors were Aston Martin, although the bulky product from West Bromwich was hardly in the same class when it came to finesse on the road. I suppose the Jensen cost the E type a few sales, but not many.

Maserati, as ever, promised more than they produced and the exciting looking De Tomaso Pantera—Ford's own Italian job—was never properly developed, although it did manage 0 to 60 in 6.8 seconds, 129 mph and 13 mpg. Ferraris, as ever, were in a class of their own, especially price, much the same as the Lamborghini produced by Ferrari renegades, and by the time Jaguar decided to do something about their top end of the market with the V12 engine, their body was outdated, and

Dick Protheroe's first E type, CUT 7, keeps ahead of Trevor Taylor's Lotus Elite, one of the few cars in 1962 that handled as well as the E type.

their bottom end of the market was being eroded by the Datsun 240Z imitation E types which knocked out 0 to 60 in 10 seconds, 112 mph and 20 mpg and felt as safe (sic) as a Big Healey.

All through their life abroad, Jaguars suffered from the reputation of being a troublesome car. The excellent magazine, *Road and Track*, carried out a survey of 100 E type owners in 1969 and came to the conclusion that it was, by American standards, inclined to go wrong a long way from any of the well-scattered dealers. But eighty-three of the 100 owners told *Road and Track* that they would buy another Jaguar, about the average for similar surveys of other cars, and a point which speaks well for brand loyalty. Obviously, then, the US Jaguar owner—rather like his British counterpart—is a grin-and-bear-it type, putting up with all sorts of trouble for the enjoyment and satisfaction of using the car when everything is on song. Of the seventeen per cent who did not intend to buy another Big Cat, half said that it was about time that Jaguar came up with something new or they did not like the 1969 styling changes, and the other half said the car was plain unreliable.

What were the problems that afflicted these Americans? Chiefly instruments which did not register right, cooling systems which lost their cool, oil which kept dripping out, electrics which played up, clutches which lost their grip, and body parts which fell off and rain which leaked in. The best features, said *Road and Track*, were considered to be the handling, styling, performance, comfort, luxury and brakes (in the case of the owners of 4.2-litre cars), and the worst aspects of the car seemed to be maintenance and repair problems, lack of ventilation, overheating, lack of space for your belly and feet and arms and head and backside, poor heating and demisting.

You will remember, of course, that Jaguar had done something about the gearbox and brakes back in 1964, and that the accommodation problems with the Two Plus Two in 1966, chiefly because of complaints from across the Atlantic. This survey, in 1969, took in eight 1962 models, seven 1963, eighteen 1964, twelve 1965, fifteen 1966, twenty-four 1967 and sixteen 1968 models.

The Jaguar E types in the survey did not score very well on reliability compared with their obvious rivals, despite having one of the best records for engine durability. The number of problem areas reported by more than ten per cent of the owners questioned amounted to nine with the E type; six with the MGB and Porsche; four with Volvo owners and three for Triumph.

Road and Track did point out, however, that the 'overheating' that might have been upsetting some owners would simply be the water temperature gauge registering 90-odd degrees centigrade, which is not unusual and does not necessarily mean that the car is about to boil over. Later Jaguars adopted the American practice of having only cold, normal and hot marked on their water temperature gauges, but somehow managed to have the needle set to register normal nearer the hot marking than the cold!

Water hoses and radiators sprang a lot of leaks with a lot of owners, but gradually the material for these components was improved so that this type of trouble decreased. It was interesting to note, too, that the survey revealed most clutch trouble on 1966 and 1967 cars, a period which coincided with the use of Laycock units. Perhaps that is why Jaguar went back to Borg and Beck clutches in 1968.

Soon after, that doyen of E type drivers, Denis Jenkinson, went for a spin in a lightweight E type in the course of his duties on the British *Motor Sport* magazine. Round and round the roads of County Durham he went and found that his own nearly new roadster was smooth, effortless and silent compared to the lightweight, which was harsh to say the least. But with the lightweight, the controllability and performance were vastly superior, even if the ZF gearbox was 'rather horrid' to use. It is easy to understand why Jaguars built their own synchromesh gearbox in the end, said Jenkinson. However, he found that the lightweight's engine was most impressive, very smooth and lively. 'At 5,000 rpm with the production engine, you were conscious of a great lump of machinery whirling around in front of you, but at the same figure the lightweight's engine was smooth and effortless for another 1,000 rpm.' Comparing the two E types with a D type owned by the same lucky man, Neil Corner, the grand old racing car was decidely twitchy with its antique back suspension.

A little earlier, Jenkinson had compared his previous 1965 E type with a 911E Porsche and a Mazda 100S which corresponded roughly to a Japanese Lotus Elan. Jenkinson, who had driven so many thousands of miles in a Porsche before he changed to an E type in 1965 was glad that he had. Despite having more than 70,000 miles on the clock, his E type easily left the test Porsche; admittedly a Sportomatic model and the rather expensive Mazda. The E type just lolloped away from them, said Jenkinson, who once partnered Stirling Moss in winning the Mille Miglia road race, confessing in the next breath that he could not really drive the E type at its 143 mph limit. 'Where do you go from an E type?', asked Jenkinson. And after analysing the three cars, he decided to stick to E types and forgot his dream of owning and driving a Ford GT40, which were just coming into their sadly limited production run then. And now, seven years later, as Jenkinson admits that his second E type, a 1970 roadster is long overdue for replacement, he is still searching for something practical.

It is significant that *Road and Track*—which is every bit as much of a bible across the Atlantic as *Motor Sport* is in Britain—chose the Sting Ray of the day, a Porsche 911T and a Mercedes 280SL for a comparative test with the current Jaguar E type in 1969. They might have been all in the same class to the Americans, but how they varied in basic configurations! One, the Chevrolet, had a V8 engine, the other three sixes, although one, that of the Porsche, was laid out flat. And of the two in-line sixes, one had a single overhead camshaft and the other, the E type, twin overhead cams. The Jaguar was becoming a bit of a eunuch, of course, with its second phase de-toxing gear. 'In engine size,' said *Road and Track*, 'the displacement ranges from just under two litres to almost six litres, and they aren't even located in the same end of the car and while three are water cooled, the fourth is air cooled.'

And so it went on, with *Road and Track* pointing out the vast differences between the construction of the four rivals, noting that the E type was the quickest through the quarter-mile-from-rest, had the most accurate speedometer, the narrowest seats, the smallest doors and the nicest smell inside. The Sting Ray came out fastest at 132 mph, with the Porsche second at 122 mph, the E type third at 119 mph and the Mercedes lagging at 114 mph. But the E type was way ahead on acceleration, doing its quarter mile in 15.7 seconds, against 16 dead for the 'Vette, 16.2 for the Sporto-

The Forward Engineering E type, good old 7 CXW, goes hunting a Big Healey and a Corvette Sting Ray at Castle Combe in 1972.

matic, and 17.1 for the Merc. The Porsche won hands down on fuel consumption at 21.3 miles per American gallon, with the E type next best on 16.2, the Mercedes third on 15.5 and the Corvette gobbling along at 14.3. You only have to listen to a Sting Ray to hear how they gobble. But overall the *Road and Track* testers rated the Porsche the best buy at $6,418 against the E type's $6,495, the Corvette's $6,392 and the Mercedes' $7,833. It was a sad outcome for the car that at the beginning of the decade had had no rival.

As recently as 1974, *Road and Track* included a Series Three E type in a comparative test between what they considered to be five exotic rivals, the Ferrari Dino 246GTS, a Porsche 911 Targa Sportomatic, a Mercedes 450SL and a Sting Ray—not the same model, there have been dozens of them—and a 1973 E type. Unfortunately the E type did not fare very well, *Road and Track* repeating their earlier road test opinion: 'What was such a magnificent engine doing in such an outdated body?' The Dino and the Porsche came out best on general performance, although, like the Mercedes, they could not catch the E type on all-out speed, despite the E type's

low-compression heads. *Road and Track* did, however, admit that there was a lot of olde-worlde charm about the E type and that it was certainly good value for money, being, like the Corvette, considerably cheaper than the other three. They were not too keen on the heavy clutch, but loved the mighty engine's torque. They noticed, too, that the E type was the only car to have an adjustable steering wheel—a good relic—and an easily-handled hood. Their overall conclusion was that the Dino and the Porsche were outstanding cars at an astronomical price, the Mercedes was an outstanding luxury tourer at an equally high price, the Chevvy was a good domestic, and the E type was an obsolete British job with an excellent engine.

There was a kick in the tail of the E type comparative tests, though. *The Motor* magazine tested the Guyson E 1 2 described in the preceding chapter. This wedge shaped Series Three had been somewhat modified by Ron Beaty, and the plastic wonder reached 60 mph from rest, faster than the world's current quickest-ever production car, the Ferrari Daytona. The engine conversion cost less than £500 and that would have made the E type still only one third of the price of the Maranello marvel.

The Salvadori/Cunningham E type hard on the heels of a Lola, driven by David Hobbs and Richard Attwood, at Le Mans in 1963.

XVII

Your E type Log Book

IT IS AMAZING how much individual cars change over the years. A car may leave the factory resplendent in pale blue paint or some such colour and, perhaps, dark blue upholstery and interior panels with matching trimming. Two or three years later the car changes hands through a dealer, who gives it a quick 'blow over' in pale blue of a similar hue, and some time later the car falls into the hands of an enthusiast who renovates some of the interior and fits new black racing-style seats. He changes many of the mechanical parts and resprays the car red. And so it goes on, the car changes with almost every owner in some cases and all the colours change with age and sometimes the mechanical parts, too, which is always a tremendous headache to the person who, years later, restores the car, and wants to make it look exactly as it left the factory. This quest for originality is evident everywhere, particularly in the United States. It is a fact that the really valuable E types are the ones that are original, unless the modifications have some historical significance and are period pieces in themselves.

The mechanical specifications of the E type have been dealt with in earlier chapters, but it would have been impractical to list all the colour options. They warrant a chapter in themselves, plus the basic original specifications, listed here. How well do you think you know your E type? Check it out against the data listed here.

E type 3.8-Litre Series One Open Two Seater

ENGINE
Cubic capacity 3,781 cc; **bore and stroke** 87 mm × 106 mm; **max. power** 265 bhp (gross) at 5,500 rpm; **max. torque** 260 lb ft at 4,000 rpm; **compression ratio** 9 : 1 (8 : 1 optional); **cylinder head** straight port; **carburetters** three 2 inch S U HD8

CHASSIS
Weight and front/rear distribution 24 cwt (51 per cent front, 49 per cent back); DIMENSIONS: **Wheelbase** 8 ft, **front track** 4 ft 2 ins, **rear track** 4 ft 2 ins, **length** 14 ft 7½ ins, **width** 5 ft 4¼ ins, **height** 3 ft 11 ins (with hood erect); **front suspension** ind. wishbone, torsion bars, anti-roll bar; **rear suspension** ind. lower wishbone

upper drive shaft link, radius arms, coil springs, anti-roll bar; **brakes** Dunlop discs, vacuum servo; **gearing** 1st–11.18 : 1, 2nd–6.16 : 1, 3rd–4.25 : 1, 4th–3.31 : 1 alternative final drive ratios: 4.09, 3.77, 3.07 and 3.27; **tyres and wheels** Dunlop 6.40 × 15 RS5 (racing tyres optional) on 15 inch × 5K wire wheels (rear 5½K wheels supplied with racing tyres)

E type 3.8-Litre Series One Fixed-head Coupé

ENGINE
Cubic capacity 3,781 cc; **bore and stroke** 87 mm × 107 mm; **max. power** 265 bhp (gross) at 5,500 rpm; **max. torque** 260 lb ft at 4,000 rpm; **compression ratio** 9 : 1 (8 : 1 optional); **cylinder head** straight port; **carburetters** three 2 inch SU HD8

CHASSIS
Weight and front/rear distribution 24.1 cwt (49.6 per cent front, 50.4 per cent back); DIMENSIONS: Wheelbase 8 ft, **front track** 4 ft 2 ins, **rear track** 4 ft 2 ins, **length** 14 ft 7.3 ins, **width** 5 ft 5.2 ins, **height** 4 ft; **front suspension** ind. wishbone, torsion bars, anti-roll bar; **rear suspension** ind. lower wishbone, upper driveshaft link, radius arms, coil springs, anti-roll bar; **brakes** Dunlop discs, vacuum servo; **gearing** 1st–11.18 : 1, 2nd–6.16 : 1, 3rd–4.25 : 1, 4th–3.31 : 1, alternative final drive ratios as for open two seater; **tyres and wheels** Dunlop 6.40 × 15 RS5 (racing tyres optional), wheels as for open two seater.

E type 4.2-Litre Series One

ENGINE
Cubic capacity 4,235 cc; **bore and stroke** 92.07 mm × 106 mm; **max. power** 265 bhp (gross) at 5,400 rpm; **max. torque** 283 lb ft at 4,000 rpm; **compression ratio** 9 : 1 (8 : 1 optional); **cylinder head** straight port; **carburetters** three 2 inch SU HD8

CHASSIS
Weight and front/rear distribution 25.1 cwt (49.5 per cent front, 50.5 per cent back); DIMENSIONS: Wheelbase 8 ft; **front track** 4 ft 2 ins, **rear track** 4 ft 2 ins, **length** 14 ft 7 ins, **width** 5 ft 6 ins, **height** 4 ft 0¼ ins; **front suspension** ind. wishbone, torsion bar, anti-roll bar; **rear suspension** ind. lower wishbone, upper driveshaft link, radius arms, coil springs, anti-roll bar; **brakes** Dunlop discs, vacuum servo; **gearing** 1st–8.23 : 1, 2nd–5.34 : 1, 3rd–3.90 : 1, 4th–3.07 : 1, alternative final drive ratios as for 3.8-litre car; **tyres and wheels** Dunlop 6.40 × 16 RS5; wheels as for 3.8-litre car.

E type 4.2-Litre Two Plus Two

ENGINE
Cubic capacity 4,235 cc; **bore and stroke** 92.07 mm × 106 mm; **max. power** 265 bhp (gross) at 5,400 rpm; **max. torque** 283 lb ft (gross) at 4,000 rpm; **com-**

pression ratio 9 : 1; **cylinder head** straight port; **carburetters** three 2 inch SU HD8

CHASSIS

Weight and front/rear distribution 27.7 cwt (50 per cent front, 50 per cent back); DIMENSIONS: **Wheelbase** 8 ft 9 ins, **front track** 4 ft 2¼ ins, **rear track** 4 ft 2¼ ins, **length** 15 ft 4½ ins, **width** 5 ft 4 ins, **height** 4 ft 2½ ins; **front suspension** ind. wishbone, torsion bars, anti-roll bar; **rear suspension** ind. lower wishbone, upper driveshaft link, radius arms, coil springs, anti-roll bar; **brakes** Dunlop discs with vacuum servo; **gearing** 1st–6.91 : 1, 2nd–4.20 : 1, 3rd–2.88 : 1; **tyres and wheels** SP41 185 - 15 inch; wheels as for 3.8-litre car.

E type Series Three V12

ENGINE

Cubic capacity 5,343 cc; **bore and stroke** 90 mm × 70 mm; **max. power** 272 bhp (net) at 5,850 rpm; **max. torque** 304 lb ft (net) at 3,600 rpm; **compression ratio** 9 : 1; **cylinder head** sohc, flat-head; **carburetters** 4 Zenith 175CDSE

CHASSIS

Weight and front/rear distribution 28.8 cwt (52 per cent front, 48 per cent back); DIMENSIONS: **Wheelbase** 8 ft 9 ins, **front track** 4 ft 6½ ins, **rear track** 4 ft 5 ins, **length** 15 ft 4 ins, **width** 4 ft 1 in, **height** 5 ft 6¼ ins; **front suspension** ind. wishbone, torsion bars, anti-roll bar; **rear suspension** ind. lower wishbone, upper driveshaft link, radius arms, coil springs, anti-roll bar; **brakes** Girling discs, vented front, servo assisted; **gearing** 1st–9.00 : 1, 2nd–5.86 : 1, 3rd–4.27 : 1, 4th–3.07 : 1 (3.31 optional); **tyres and wheels** Dunlop E70VR - 15 inch on 15 inch × 6K wire or solid wheels.

E type Series Three V12 Two Plus Two

ENGINE

Cubic capacity 5,343 cc; **bore and stroke** 90 mm × 70 mm; **max. power** 272 bhp (DIN) at 5,850 rpm; **max. torque** 304 lb ft (DIN) at 3,600 rpm; **compression ratio** 9 : 1; **cylinder head** sohc, flat-head; **carburetters** 4 Zenith Stromberg 175 CDSE

CHASSIS

Weight and front/rear distribution 29.5 cwt (50.9 per cent front, 49.1 per cent back); DIMENSIONS: **Wheelbase** 8 ft 9 ins, **front track** 4 ft 6½ ins, **rear track** 4 ft 5 ins, **length** 15 ft 4 ins, **width** 4 ft 1 in, **height** 4 ft 3 ins; **front suspension** ind. wishbone, torsion bars, anti-roll bar; **rear suspension** ind. lower wishbone, upper driveshaft link, radius arms, coil springs, anti-roll bar; **brakes** Girling discs, vented front, servo assisted; **gearing** 1st–9.00 : 1, 2nd–5.86 : 1, 3rd–4.27 : 1, 4th–3.07 : 1 (3.31 optional); **tyres and wheels** Dunlop E70VR - 15 in; wheels as for Series Three V12 roadster.

E type Series Three V12 Roadster: US Specification

ENGINE

Cubic capacity 5,343 cc; **bore and stroke** 90 mm × 70 mm; **max. power** 250 bhp at 6,000 rpm (1972 spec.), 241 bhp at 5,750 rpm (1974 spec.); **max. torque** 288 lb ft at 3,500 rpm (1972 spec.), 285 lb ft at 3,500 rpm (1974 spec.); **compression ratio** 9 : 1 (1972 spec.), 7.8 : 1 (1974 spec.); **cylinder head** sohc, flat head; **carburetters** 4 Zenith-Stromberg 175CD2SE

CHASSIS

Weight and front/rear distribution 30.1 cwt (53 per cent front, 47 per cent back); figures variable according to extras fitted; DIMENSIONS: **Wheelbase** 8 ft 9 ins, **front track** 4 ft 6½ ins, **rear track** 4 ft 5 ins, **length** 15 ft 4 ins, **width** 4 ft 1 in, **height** 4 ft 3 ins; **front suspension** ind. wishbone, torsion bar, anti-roll bar; **rear suspension** ind. lower wishbone, upper drive shaft link, radius arm, coil springs, anti-roll bar; **brakes** Girling discs, ventilated front, servo assisted; **gearing** 1st–10.37 : 1, 2nd–6.73 : 1, 3rd–4.92 : 1, 4th–3.54 : 1; **tyres and wheels** Dunlop E70 VR - 15; wheels as for GB Series Three V12 roadster.

Index of colour schemes

The following charts list the original colour schemes of E types as they left the factory. For instance, all cream cars had a black interior and all Warwick grey cars had red, light tan, or dark blue interiors. It must be remembered, though, that until 1973 a customer could order a car in any colour, in addition to the standard schemes. 'It has even been known for somebody to bring in a piece of underwear to have it matched up to his (or her!) car,' says Martyn Crawford, who did the research for this chapter. But underwear or not, here are the factory colours:

Reference number	Colour	Interior
1	Cream	Black
2	Warwick Grey	Red, light tan, dark blue
3	Sherwood Green	Suede green, light tan, tan
4	Dark Blue	Red, light blue, grey
5	Black	Red, grey, tan, light tan
6	Carmen Red	Black
7	Opalescent Silver Grey	Red, light blue, dark blue, grey
8	Opalescent Silver Blue	Grey, dark blue
9	Opalescent Dark Green	Suede green, beige, tan, light tan
10	Opalescent Maroon	Maroon, beige
11	Golden Sand	Red, light tan
12	Pale Primrose	Black, beige
13	Willow Green	Grey, suede green, tan, light tan
14	Beige	Red, suede green, tan, light tan
15	British Racing Green	Suede green, beige, tan, light tan
16	Ascot Fawn	Red, beige, cinnamon
17	Sable	Beige, grey, cinnamon

18	Light Blue	Dark blue, grey, light blue
19	Regency Red	Beige, grey
20	Old English White	Black, red, French blue, dark blue
21	Fern Grey	Moss green, olive, tan
22	Turquoise	Tan, terracotta, cinnamon
23	Green Sand	Tan, olive, cinnamon
24	Heather	Maroon, antelope, cerise
25	Lavender Blue	French blue, biscuit, dark blue
26	Signal Red	Black, biscuit, dark blue
27	Azure Blue	Dark blue, biscuit, cinnamon
28	Indigo	Red, light blue
29	Pearl	Dark blue, red
30	Opalescent Dark Blue	Dark blue, red
31	Opalescent Gunmetal	Dark blue, light blue, red, beige
32	Imperial Maroon	Tan
33	Cotswold Blue	Dark blue
34	Mist Grey	Red
35	Bronze	Beige, red, tan
36	Claret	Beige
37	Sand	Black, beige
38	Opalescent Maroon	Maroon, beige

These are the basic colour options over the years, but occasionally in any one year the interior choice differed from the indexed scheme. In these cases, the alternatives are in brackets next to the appropriate index number. The schemes available in any one year were:

1961: 28, 6 (Biscuit, red), 15, 29, 30, 31, 9, 7, 32, 1 (cream, red), 8, 3, 5, 33, 34, 35, 36

1962: Same as 1961

1963: 37, 6, 30, 8, 9, 1, 7, 35, 31, 38, 34, 12, 29, 33, 5, 15, 3

1964: Same as 1963

1965: 1, 2, 3, 4, 5, 6, 7, 8, 9, 10, 11, 12

1966: Same as 1965

1967 from September: 1, 2, 4, 5, 6, (Red, beige, black), 7, 8, 10, 11, 12, 13 (Suede green, beige, grey, light tan), 14, 15

1968 until July: Same as 1967 from September

1968 from August: 1, 2 (Red, dark blue, cinnamon), 4, 5 (Red, grey, cinnamon), 12, 13 (Suede green, beige, grey, cinnamon), 15 (Suede green, beige, cinnamon), 16, 17, 18, 19, 26 (Red, beige, black)

1969: Same as 1968 from August

1970: 20 (Black only), 2 (Red, dark blue, cinnamon), 16, 13 (Suede green, beige, grey, cinnamon), 4, 5 (Red, grey, cinnamon), 17, 18, 19, 15 (Suede green, beige, cinnamon), 12

1971: from March: 20 (Red, light blue, dark blue, black), 2 (Red, dark blue, cinnamon), 16, 13 (Suede green, beige, grey, cinnamon), 4, 5 (Red, grey cinnamon),

17, 18, 19, 15 (Suede green, beige, cinnamon), 12, 26 (Red, beige, black)

1972 until October: Same as 1971 from March

1972 from October: 20, 21, 19 (Biscuit, cinnamon, russet red), 22, 4 (Red, French blue, russet red), 23, 17 (Biscuit, moss green, cinnamon), 24, 15 (Biscuit, moss green, cinnamon), 25, 26, 12 (Black, biscuit, red), 27

1973: Same as 1972 from October

1974: Same as 1972 from October

In addition, in later years, black and silver were added to the range of colours at special request, with a variety of interiors.

XVIII

The Jaguar Drivers' Club

JAGUARS have never been mass-produced cars in the true sense of the word, and far fewer have been made in any given year than, say, Mercedes or MG: but such is the character of the car, and the enthusiasm of a high proportion of the owners, that the Jaguar Drivers' Club of Great Britain is one of the largest one-make car clubs in this country; and there is a similar situation overseas, too.

The formation of the Jaguar Drivers' Club goes back to 1955, and surprisingly perhaps, the founders had difficulty in getting official recognition and help from the parent factory! This was due to an unfortunate incident just before the war when an official of the factory-sponsored S.S. Car Club ran off with the club funds after a large event; an episode which put paid to the S.S. Car Club and made the then Mr William Lyons extremely suspicious of any moves to launch a similar organisation. However, the Jaguar car chief was eventually talked round and an inaugural meeting of the new club was held in May 1955, with official RAC and Jaguar Cars Ltd recognition coming in November of the same year.

The founder members were mostly XK owners, but soon the club's handsome 'steering wheel' badge, with its bronze Jaguar head became a common sight on 2.4-litre saloons, Mark VIIs and—as they came into production—every model of Jaguar produced to this day. Paid-up membership now approaches 5,000, a figure which probably embraces almost twice that number of Jaguar and SS cars.

It is true to say that in the mid-1960s, with official Jaguar competition activities non-existent and the range of saloon cars becoming ever more 'executive,' that the Jaguar Drivers' Club suffered something of a decline. Happily this was halted, by the birth of the XK Register section in 1967–8 and it has grown steadily since.

This section soon climbed to 1,000 strong and injected new life into the club as a whole. Even more important, so far as the Jaguar Drivers' Club was concerned, was the E type Register which followed four years later. With every model of E type now gradually acquiring a more interested and knowledgeable type of owner, this still quite new branch of the club must have a huge potential. Certainly it is most impressive to see the hundreds of E types assembled at its national gatherings. Nearly 500 people are registered with the club at the moment.

Other Jaguar Drivers' Club registers cater for the Mark One and Two saloons, the Mark VII, VIII and IX range, S.S. Cars up to the Mark V, and the 'independent rear' saloons. All, including of course the E type Register, receive the club's professionally produced monthly magazine, the *Jaguar Driver*, while some publish their own newsletters too. Naturally the E type Register's newsletter endeavours to help E type owners by printing articles on maintenance, repair and restoration: it highlights spare part sources, and enables owners to advertise parts and cars. Like the rest of the club, membership is international, with owners being represented in most parts of the world.

There would never be enough room to mention in detail all the club's activities, but they include both local and national concours events and get-togethers, race, sprint and hill climb meetings, and monthly pub meetings in most parts of the country. While the E type Register's E type Day is highly popular, the club's premier event is still International XK Day, which in spite of its name includes every S.S. or Jaguar car and remains about the biggest gathering of Jaguars in the world. In 1967, E types outnumbered every other Jaguar at the event, including the XKs! XK Day usually takes place at the end of August or the beginning of September and literally thousands of Jaguar enthusiasts go to visit a unique assembly of Jaguars.

Because of its relatively large membership, it is not expensive to join the Jaguar Drivers' Club and its registers, and you can obtain further details from the club's full-time staff, who have their office at the Norfolk Hotel, Harrington Road, London SW7. Wherever you live, they will be pleased to hear from you and to post off the *Jaguar Driver* magazine and help with all sorts of queries, even where production of a Jaguar Drivers' Club card will get you a discount.

North America must be Jaguar's main export market, and it should receive the first mention under this heading; especially as one of the clubs based there can claim to be the first Jaguar club formed. This is the boast of the Jaguar Associate Group (JAG) of San Francisco, which was formed in January 1955.

Because the distances are much greater than in Britain, and the Jaguar owners are more widely scattered, the North American Jaguar clubs have a rather different pattern of existence to that of the Jaguar Drivers' Club in London. The country is covered by a large number of relatively small autonomous organisations, each being active on a mainly local basis, but recognised by the parent firm through British Leyland's New Jersey headquarters, which runs Jaguar Clubs of North America Incorporated. The JCNA publishes a quarterly magazine—the *Jaguar Journal*—which is distributed to the membership of all affiliated clubs, while nearly all the individual clubs issue their own newsletters, too.

It is good to be able to report that the position has never been healthier for the Jaguar clubs in North America. Nearly all report a climbing membership, and the Ontario Jaguar Owners' Association is no exception. Their club was formed in 1959 and at present has 102 members, although it has been as low as thirty. It meets once a month and the format follows British club meetings: minutes of the last meeting; business in hand; a few beers; and either a talk or a film show. New clubs are still being formed and at the present time some thirty-five are in operation; virtually all have strong E type sections among their membership, including the Eastern Jaguar Group (EJAG), of 1 Acton Road, Westford, Massachusetts 01886, which almost alone is not JCNA affiliated. Up to date information on JCNA activities can be

It's E type day at Donington Motor Museum in Leicestershire, with rank upon rank of E types. The E type now regularly outnumbers all other models at Jaguar Drivers' Club meetings.

obtained from Mr Fred Horner, JCNA, 600 Willow Tree Road, Leonia, New Jersey 07605. Apart from the Jaguar Associate Group, based at San Jose, California, other JCNA-affiliated clubs include: the Jaguar Automobile Club of San Diego, California; the Jaguar Owners' Club of California; the Jaguar Owners' Club of Oregon; the Jaguar Drivers' Club of Northwest America in Washington; the Classic Jaguar Club of Arizona; the Jaguar Club of Tulsa, Oklahoma; the Jaguar Club of Omaha, Nebraska; the Jaguar Association of Greater Chicago; the Jaguar Owners' Association of the Southwest, at Richardson, Texas; the Greater St Louis Jaguar Association at St Louis, Missouri; the Jaguar Affiliates Group of Michigan; the New England XK Association of Massachusetts; the Jaguar Club of Southern New England in Connecticut; the Empire Division Jaguar Club (New York City) in New Jersey; the Delaware Valley Club in Pennsylvania; the Jaguar Club of Pittsburgh in New Kensington, Pennsylvania; the Nation's Capital Jaguar Owners' Club in Virginia;

the Carolina Jaguar Club of North Carolina; the Nashville Jags of Tennessee; the Classic Jaguar Association of Washington; the Jaguar Club of Ohio; the Jaguar Association of Central Ohio at Bexley, Ohio; the Heart of America Jaguar Club in Kansas; the Great Plains Jaguar Owners' Association in Kansas; the Jaguar Club of Austin, Texas; and the Nova Scotia Jaguar Association and the Canadian XK Register at Vancouver in Canada, plus, of course, the Ontario Jaguar Owners' Association at 133, Goulding Avenue, Willowdale, Ontario M 2 M 1 L 5.

Leaving North America, the newest Jaguar club to be formed must be in Brazil, where the initial meeting raised forty members with the promise of many more to come. The club contact is William Halberstadt at Rua Haddock Lobo, 281–APT 122, Sao Paulo–SP–01414 Brazil. Australia has six clubs, New Zealand two and South Africa one. In Europe, the strongest club is probably the French Jaguar Drivers' Club, which is recognised even by some of those notorious French traffic policemen. I can well remember trailing along for what seemed hours behind a long line of juggernauts heading for Paris from Boulogne, when I was suddenly presented with the chance of overtaking the lot in one burst of E type acceleration. Sure enough, I hurtled past the lot at something over 100 mph, much to the admiration and obvious support of the trundling Volvo and Scania drivers, only to be stopped at a roadblock some three or four kilometres further along the road. As I pulled over onto the verge at the behest of a heavily armed French motor cycle policeman (stationary), I was asked to step out while he looked at the car. After he had examined every inch of it, another uniformed policemen got out of a large Peugeot van parked behind a hedge nearby. He invited me into the van, after admiring the E type, and informed me solemnly that I had been speeding and that he had fined the last speeder on that stretch some 100 francs. 'But first I must see all your documents,' he said sipping a glass of wine and fingering a picture of his family on the desk, bolted in the back of his van. I spread out my driving licence, log book, insurance and passport on his table, and he told me how his father had fought with the 'Tommies' in the First World War, how he had helped a Canadian airman while in the Resistance in the Second World War, and how he had watched Jaguar win at Le Mans, and, how he would have to fine me for speeding. But when he saw my Jaguar Drivers' Club card he really flipped. He told me how his wife's cousin's best friend knew somebody in the French club and he thought what nice people they were; he let me off with a caution! The secretary, incidentally, of the French Jaguar Drivers' Club is that great collector, Dr Phillipe Renault, based at 39 av. de Laumiere, 75019 Paris. The French Jaguar Drivers' Club is run close for enthusiasm by the Jaguar clubs formed by Italian and Swedish Jaguar owners. The addresses of these clubs, and those in other countries which may have been formed after this book was printed, can be obtained from the Jaguar Drivers' Club at the Norfolk Hotel, or from British Leyland's headquarters in the relevant country. It is not practical to print all their names and addresses here because they tend to change with the secretaries rather than to remain static at one headquarters.

To sum up, it is at club level that the greatest amount of Jaguar enthusiasm is to be found and if you have an E type—or any sort of Jaguar or fancy one you will find that your enjoyment of it will be greatly enhanced if you also belong to a club.

Wherever you go for motoring action, you will find E type, E type, E type, E type, E type, E type, E type. . . .

Not only will you be kept informed of Jaguar news and be able to take part in social or competitive events, but you will also benefit from the interchange of technical talk, advice and spare parts that is so much of the club scene today.

XIX

Why the E type had to go

WELL, why did the E type have to go? It was chiefly because the Americans killed it. No car with a monocoque and separate front sub-frame could withstand their projected crash tests. Safety to an American legislator is being able to almost demolish a concrete block. This block-busting mentality does not take in the finer points of a car which enable it to avoid hitting concrete blocks in the first place, given a driver of minimum ability.

It is my opinion that if somebody is sufficiently stupid or unlucky to hit a concrete block they are sufficiently stupid or unlucky to kill themselves no matter what car they are travelling in. It is infinitely better to have a car that is capable of avoiding concrete blocks than one that stands up to laboratory tests better. The E type's safety record is incredibly good. The car is really very strong and sure-footed, but as the Americans continued to ram their test cars harder and harder into concrete blocks and the sales of X J 6 saloons continued to soar, the future looked bleak for the E type. It also became apparent in 1973, just before the oil crisis, that there would be a good potential market for the X J 12. So the X J series took over the floor space that was vacated by the E type production line in Coventry and that was the end of the Big Cat. It was Jaguar's last true sports car; it was Jaguar's last open car; it was Jaguar's last link with the glorious racing years; it was Jaguar's last cheap car; it is Jaguar's last classic. Fortunately it is not Jaguar's last great car, but they will never make another car like the E type. The nearest thing they have to the E type is that long-legged luxury liner, the X J S.

Why is the E type Jaguar's last true sports car? Because there is neither the money nor the resources to make another out-and-out sports car, a fact of life that is common to every volume car manufacturer. They will still keep producing new models like the Ford Capri and Triumph T R 7, but they are not the sports cars of old, and they will still keep making cars like the big-engined Escorts, which are the sports cars of today. The man in the street can afford a fast Ford or the latest offering from British Leyland or General Motors, but he is not buying a sports car like the E type. It is true, that cars like the Escort R S series can out-perform almost everything except the few exotics that survive, but they have none of the character of the old sports cars, of which the E type was the very best. The E type was the king of sports cars, and touring cars, because it was so much better in every aspect than any

The E type as it might have been if only Jaguar had been able to build the XJ13 a few years earlier.

of its rivals. Its performance was in a different league (and still is); its roadholding matched the best (and still does); its ride and comfort was superior (and is still not inferior); and its price was in a different bracket.

Why was the E type Jaguar's last open car? Because the regulations that loomed in the United States in 1974 condemned open cars as a safety hazard. As it happened, something went wrong with the legislators' planning, but not in time to save the E type. It is a pity, because there is no pleasure or experience like that of riding in a real open car. The Porsche and Ferrari spiders of late are no more than tin-topped coupés with an extra large hole in the roof and a few more rattles. They are not real open cars and neither is that plastic wonder the Sting Ray, which is built on much the same lines. They can hardly ruffle your hair, let alone give you a blast of the raw

fresh stuff the Americans are fighting so hard to preserve.

Why is the E type the last link with Jaguar's racing glory? Because the classic age of motor racing ended at the time that Jaguar's gave up and nobody has since been able to recapture it. Witness the popularity of historic racing now, and nobody has been able to turn a racing car into a proper road car since those days. Racing cars have followed their own paths, becoming more and more like the models raced in slots by little boys. They are so far detached from reality on the road that there is little connection except in odds and ends of development that become useable on the road cars. The romance went out of racing when the wheels got wider and the driver sat lower. Soon cars will be designed for maximum advertising space and so on. Development costs have soared as racing has become more and more technical and as a potential road car, only the Ford GT40 looked to be a significant advance on the E type, but not even Ford could make the GT40 a practical production car. It took Sir William Lyons and company to turn a racing car into a road car and they were living in a different era.

Why was the E type Jaguar's last cheap car? Because Jaguar's have a different position in the motor industry now. They are part of a big corporation, and not completely their own masters. They have a different pricing policy as a result. If the XJS had been produced by the old firm of Jaguar, no doubt it would have been a car costing two-thirds of the £11,000 asked for that magnificent tourer. Just as many people asked why Jaguar's did not ask more for their cars ten and twenty years ago and wish they cost less nowadays. But British Leyland have to get their sums right or there will be no more Jaguars. It is just a pity they cannot do sums like Sir William Lyons. Their sums are not always expensive for the Jaguar enthusiast though: it was because of their policy that the E type was so cheap towards the end of its run. The Series Three E type became an incredible bargain in 1974 and 1975 because there was no change in its list price, although the price of its sister saloons kept rising. This apparent anomaly arose because the E type production line had closed down and orders for new cars were being met from stock. In fact, a number of warehouses, not to mention parking lots, were full of brand new E types. As these cars left the production line and were already costed out, then the price rises necessary on vehicles still being made were not added to the E type. This phenomenon—it was the first time there had actually been a surplus of new E types for sale—was partly due to Jaguars cutting down on their number of models, partly due to more cash being available from British Leyland for production line expansion, and partly because development to meet ever-changing American regulations was no longer necessary. More than £250,000 was spent on working out the best ways to build in emission equipment, rubber bumpers, recessed door handles and the like in the early 1970s. And because Jaguar had geared up to produce large quantities of twelve-cylinder engines and cars to go with them, the number of E types increased by more than one third in the last few months of production in 1974. The official end of the run did not come until February 1975, when nearly all those warehouses and parking lots were empty. So, over this period the car was the greatest bargain that Jaguars have ever offered—and that really is a fantastic bargain—which is reflected in second-hand prices only a year or so later. Already an unmarked E type can fetch double the old list price.

Was the E type Jaguar's last classic car? They certainly seem to think so, having painted all but one of the last fifty cars black. The odd car out was a green one sold to collector Robert Danny, who also had the first E type to win a race, the first fixed-head E type and Dick Protheroe's second racing E type, the experimental low-drag coupé. Jaguars have kept the very last E type for publicity purposes. In keeping with the E type sales pattern, most of the last fifty went abroad, all with dashboard plaques signed by Sir William Lyons.

The E type was the end of an era because nobody has shown the ability to make another car with so many qualities and so few faults. There probably is not the scope any more. None of the current open sports cars are in the same league so far as performance is concerned and none of them are directly descended from racing cars. None of them are cheap, and none of them are beautiful. That is why the E type is a classic and that is why Jaguars will never make another classic. They are committed to making lots of high quality cars for the large corporation of which they are a part. And large corporations cannot afford to be so philanthropic as to make classics anymore.

The ending of the E type has left people like Denis Jenkinson and myself with a terrible sense of loss. He admits that he should have changed his famous open roadster for a new car long ago, but can find nothing to replace it. He considered a Ferrari Dino Spider, but was put off by the cost and nagging doubts about reliability. His dreams of a GT40 never materialised and nothing else seems so good as an E type, let alone so reliable. Jenkinson now travels to many Continental motor races on a big motor cycle. Perhaps it is these blood and thunder machines that have taken over from the big sports cars. They are certainly one of the few machines that can compete with an E type for performance although they miss out on so many other advantages, of course.

But, after seeing the way prices of XKs soared away in the early Seventies, nobody has been caught napping by the E type (not that they ever were; no car was more certain to become a classic). Prices are rising steadily and their owners have stopped neglecting them. Specialist firms are producing replacement parts for E types even before all the factory parts have dried up. The Big Cat has become big business already. This and the love of enthusiasts all over the world mean that it will never die.

Index